Nationalizing a Borderland

JUDAIC STUDIES SERIES

Leon J. Weinberger

General Editor

Nationalizing a Borderland

War, Ethnicity, and Anti-Jewish Violence in East Galicia, 1914–1920

Alexander Victor Prusin

THE UNIVERSITY OF ALABAMA PRESS
Tuscaloosa

The University of Alabama Press
Tuscaloosa, Alabama 35487-0380
uapress.ua.edu

Hardcover edition published 2005.
Paperback edition published 2016.
eBook edition published 2016.

Typeface: ACaslon

Manufactured in the United States of America
Cover design: David Nees

∞

The paper on which this book is printed meets the minimum requirements of American National Standard for Information Science–Permanence of Paper for Printed Library Materials, ANSI Z39.48-1984.

Paperback ISBN: 978-0-8173-5888-4
eBook ISBN: 978-0-8173-9093-8

A previous edition of this book has been catalogued by the Library of Congress as follows:
Library of Congress Cataloging-in-Publicaton Data
Prusin, Alexander Victor.
Nationalizing a borderland : war, ethnicity, and anti-Jewish violence in east Galacia, 1914–1920 / Alexander Victor Prusin.
p. cm. — (Judaic studies series)
Includes bibliographical references and index.
ISBN 0-8173-1459-8 (cloth : alk. paper)
1. Jews—Persecutions—Russia—History—20th century. 2. Jews—Persecutions—Poland—History—20th century. 3. Jews—Persecutions—Galacia (Poland and Ukraine)—History—20th century. 4. Antisemitism—Russia—History—20th century. 5. Antisemitism—Poland—History—20th century. 6. Antisemitism—Galacia (Poland and Ukraine)—History—20th century. 7. Russia—Ethnic relations. 8. Poland—Ethnic relations. 9. Galacia (Poland and Ukraine)—Ethnic relations. I. Title. II. Series.
DS135.R92P78 2005
305.892'404386'09041—dc22
2004023849

To my parents

Contents

Preface

East Galicia ranks among the regions most devastated by World War I. From the summer of 1914 to the fall of 1917, this densely populated Austrian province became a fluid battlefield as Austro-Hungarian and Russian armies rolled back and forth, leaving behind a trail of blackened ruins. In early September of 1914, after a series of frontier engagements, Russian troops occupied the provincial capital, Lwów, and a month later subjugated the entire province. Claiming to liberate the "Slavic brethren" Ukrainians from the Austrian "yoke" and reunite Galicia—once a part of Kiev Rus'—with the empire, the military subjected the occupied areas to an intensive Russification campaign. Doubting the loyalty of the local population, Russian authorities arbitrarily arrested and detained potential opponents, requisitioned grain and livestock, forcibly converted whole villages to Orthodoxy, and deported thousands of individuals suspected of anti-state activities. One of the cruelest facets of Russian occupation was the persecution of Jews, who were accused of sabotage, economic subversion, and active collaboration with the Central Powers. Jewish settlements and city quarters were subjected to vicious pogroms, and when in the spring and summer of 1915 the Russian army retreated eastward, it brutalized and uprooted thousands of Jews.

The Russian retreat brought only a temporary respite for the battered Galician Jewry. Although popular and official anti-Semitism had been a mainstay of the Polish-Jewish discourse in the preceding century, it was the angst-ridden psychological atmosphere of World War I that gave anti-Jewish sentiments their fullest expression. Led by the intelligentsia, but supported by substantial peasant and urban elements, Polish nationalist groups based their vision of an independent Poland on common ethnic and religious identity. Consequently, they believed that Jews, "alien" by religion, culture, and language, could not and should not be assimilated to become loyal citizens. Jewish political activists, on the other hand, hoped that the victorious Central

Powers would grant Jews equal civil and political rights in postwar Poland and actively collaborated with German and Austro-Hungarian military authorities.

The collapse of the German and Austro-Hungarian empires in November 1918, however, shattered these hopes and brought the seething ethnic tensions into the open. Political turmoil and economic crises created a propitious climate for collective hysteria regarding the alleged "enemy within" as the nascent Polish state tried to reassert its dominance in the contested border regions. Allegations of Jewish conspiracies and sabotage resonated in a series of pogroms in which Polish troops played a leading part, and Jews suffered physical assaults, requisitions, and imprisonment as the Polish-Ukrainian and Polish-Soviet wars swept through the region. At the same time, Polish authorities conducted an *odżydzenie* (de-Judaization) campaign to try to force Jews out of regional trade and commerce.

This book examines the dynamics and mechanisms of the persecution of Jews in wartime East Galicia between 1914 and 1920. Archival records clearly indicate that two different polities—the Russian Empire and the Polish Republic—expressed similar concerns about the alleged intractability of the Jews. Consequently, personal attributes such as age, sex, and disposition of individual Jews to the state were beside the point because all Jews were considered potentially destructive. Russian and Polish responses to the putative Jewish peril were also strikingly similar—albeit different in magnitude—in that slanderous anti-Semitic propaganda campaigns were accompanied by harassment, violence, and efforts to limit Jewish participation in Galicia's economic and social life.[1]

Such analogous anxieties and reactions entail three crucial domains of inquiry. The first has to do with "social paranoia"—collective beliefs that Jews were responsible for military setbacks, economic crises, and social unrest. Some studies of anti-Semitism have focused on traditional "ancient" resentments toward Jews as driving forces of ethnic violence,[2] and others have suggested that power holders skillfully redirected their subjects' economic and social frustrations on Jews. For example, David Vital states that "[persecution] . . . drew on ancient, nourishing theological, social, and folkloric roots. It served admirably to shift the enduring question of public and political responsibility . . . well away from those who had actually wielded political power."[3] It is unquestionable that hatred of Jews stemmed from traditional negative images fostered, perpetuated, and shared by large segments of Russian and Polish societies. I would like, however, to expand our examination of ethnic conflict to demonstrate that the wartime climate infused traditional anti-Semitism with new elements, which made it especially ferocious. Obsession with potential saboteurs in the front zone generated an atmosphere of pervasive siege mentality among Russian and Polish troops, which invariably assaulted Jews as the ubiquitous secretive foe.

Just as consequential was the conjunction between ideological anti-Semitism spouted by the Russian military and the Polish nationalist leadership (the latter played an instrumental role in Poland's politics) and their attempts to nationalize East Galicia. The nationalizing campaigns aimed at protecting interests of the "titular" ethnic groups—Russians and Poles—and isolating and persecuting the "alien" ones—Jews.[4] To this effect, virulent anti-Semitic propaganda facilitated and justified reprisals against Jewish subversion, while numerous regulations restricted participation of Jews in cultural and socioeconomic spheres and severely curtailed their political and civil rights.

The second topic under consideration is the particular "stimulus quality"[5]—an intangible interaction of real and purported actions of Jews—that engendered Russian and Polish reactions. The situation of Jews between 1914 and 1920 in East Galicia (and, for that matter, in east and central Europe) highlighted two conflicting realities. On the one hand, it vividly demonstrated the intrinsic weakness and vulnerability of the Jews at times of political crises. On the other hand, Jewish relief, political, and diplomatic efforts strengthened popular convictions among Russians and Poles that Jews were a powerful and cunning foe with wide-ranging international connections. Consequently, such convictions, intertwined with the dictum that "who is not with us is against us," fortified the resolve to render Jews harmless.[6]

The bulk of this study focuses on anti-Jewish violence, which constitutes the third major theme of discussion. Violence was central to the nationalizing campaigns and evolved in two main modes: unauthorized or "wild" violence by troops and civilian mobs and "authorized" or institutional violence by the state. Driven by negative emotions such as fear or hate, and amplified by rumors and the atmosphere of uncertainty prevalent in the combat zone, unauthorized violence was carried out in the form of riots, pogroms, and looting. At the same time, consistent target choice indicates that the seemingly spontaneous character of unauthorized violence did not preclude a certain rationality in the acts of the assailants. Convinced of the necessity to punish Jews for alleged wrongdoings, the attackers believed that their actions had tacitly been approved by superiors and that looting and pillaging would thus trigger no adverse consequences for themselves. Concomitantly, the opportunity to rob and loot with relative impunity was often too powerful to resist, and the culprits timed their actions with inactivity or erosion of control agencies—government, military, and local administration.

On the other hand, "authorized" violence aimed to achieve a specific objective (as Hannah Arendt put it, "the end that must justify it [violence]"[7]): the redistribution of socioeconomic capital in an effort to diminish or eliminate

Jewish influence in Galicia. It manifested itself in restrictions, reprisals, expulsions, and deportations. Yet, frequently "authorized" violence degenerated into "wild" assaults, especially destructive during military setbacks, and represented the convergence of interests between state authorities and individual perpetrators who reaped economic and psychological rewards from pillage and robbery. Anti-Jewish violence in Galicia, therefore, served to satisfy the *expressive* and *instrumental* needs of the culprits—it released negative emotions and frustrations associated with war and simultaneously brought about immediate psychological, social, and economic benefits gained by looting, assaulting, or displacing Jews.[8]

~

A few words are necessary about sources, spelling, and terminology. The treatment of ethnic and religious minorities on the eastern front of World War I has only recently received due scholarly attention. The pioneering work of Daniel Graf in 1972 was followed by a series of studies in the 1990s that examined Russian wartime ethnic policies, mass deportations, and the problems created by the influx of refugees and deportees into the empire.[9] Similarly, in the last two decades several studies have been published about the post–World War I ethnic relations in Poland. Still, the bulk of scholarship on this topic has remained in Polish or German.[10] In comparison to the aforementioned works, this book has a narrower focus aimed at reconstructing local dynamics of ethnic conflict and placing them within a larger national and social context. Such an approach allows the examination of the interaction between national and regional variables that exacerbated ethnic animosities and triggered anti-Jewish violence.

Except for Russian periodicals and newspapers, all dates used here correspond to the Gregorian calendar, which ran thirteen days ahead of the Russian Julian calendar.[11] For the sake of consistency, East Galician localities appear in their contemporary Polish spelling, except those integrated into the English language (for example, Krakow rather than Kraków); Russian and Ukrainian names and places are transliterated in accordance with the Library of Congress system. The Austrian term "Ruthenians" ("Ruthenen" in German) was commonly used in official correspondence and literature of the time. This word derived from the latinized form of "Russian" and generally referred to the Ukrainian-speaking population of Galicia, Bukovina, and Transcarpathia. Although they spoke different dialects of Ukrainian, these people were the linguistic and ethnographic kinsmen of Ukrainians living under Russian rule. Therefore, for the convenience of the reader, the terms "Ukrainian" and "Ukrainians" are used in preference to "Ruthenian" and "Ruthenians."

The Austrian province of Galicia consisted of two parts. The eastern half, East Galicia, included the territory between the Zbrucz River in the east and the San River in the west. The city of Lwów was its administrative and cultural center, and Poles constituted its most numerous ethnic group, followed by Jews and Ukrainians. The western part of the province, West Galicia, with its capital at Krakow, bordered Austrian and German Silesia. In the north, Galicia faced the Polish Kingdom (Tsarstvo Pol'skoe)—the part of Poland integrated into the Russian Empire—and in the south the Carpathian Mountains separated it from the Kingdom of Hungary. In the Polish parlay after 1918 the so-called *Kresy Wschodnie* (Eastern Borderlands) included the Polish-Russian and Polish-Lithuanian contested territories of southeastern Lithuania with its principal city of Vil'nius, the western parts of Belorussia (White Russia), and the Volhynia region.

As used here, the term "persecution" refers to official restrictions and limitations in social, economic, and political spheres as well as reprisals, expulsions, and deportations. The Russian word "pogrom" denotes acts of collective physical assault, destruction, robbery, murder, and rape, and the term "excess" implies individual acts of violence and destruction of property. Finally, "anti-Semitism," "anti-Jewish sentiments," and "Judeophobia" are used interchangeably to denote hatred, resentment, and hostility toward Jews.

~

The first stages of this study go back to my dissertation research at the University of Toronto. It is with pleasure that I thank the members of the dissertation committee—Piotr Wróbel, Harvey Dyck, Derek Penslar, Susan Solomon, and Zvi Gitelman. The University of Toronto Department of History, School of Graduate Studies, and Center for Russian and Eastern European Studies supported my research. The Interlibrary Loan Department of the Joseph R. Skeen Library at the New Mexico Institute of Mining and Technology was extremely helpful in providing me with many books and articles.

I benefited from the advice of Eric Lohr, and my special thanks go to my friends Scott Zeman, John Staples, and Gabriel Finder for numerous suggestions and for correcting and improving my English. I also thank Kathy Swain for editing the manuscript and the two anonymous peer reviewers for their helpful comments. As ever I am grateful to my parents, Victor and Victoria, and my wife, Elena, for their financial and invaluable moral support during my research.

Map of East Galicia

Nationalizing a Borderland

Introduction

By the turn of the twentieth century, the majority of Galician Jews lived in close-knit communities and maintained a traditional socioeconomic and religious way of life under the relatively tolerant Habsburg rule. Their cultural, religious, and linguistic heritage made them a visible and distinct minority among their Polish and Ukrainian conationals. Jews predominated in certain occupations such as petty trade, innkeeping, and artisanship, and in urban areas they constituted a large group engaged in free professions.

The particular socioeconomic structure of the Galician Jewry was rooted in the history of the region. Between 1141 and 1340 Galicia was a part of the Galician-Volhynian principality of ancient Rus'; from 1340 until 1772 it was a province of the Polish-Lithuanian Rzeczpospolita (Commonwealth); and after the Polish partitions it was integrated into the Habsburg Empire (since 1867 Austro-Hungary) until it collapsed in 1918. During these three periods, Jewish cultural, social, and economic influence in the region was immense. Polish rulers granted their Jewish subjects religious freedom, internal autonomy, and protection from persecution in exchange for economic services, and the nobility welcomed Jewish traders as a steady source of income. In the countryside Jewish tax and customs collectors provided an important link between peasants and landlords and between villages and towns. After Galicia was incorporated into the Habsburg Empire, Austrian rulers continued the tradition of religious tolerance, although the state made several attempts to assimilate its Jewish subjects.

At the end of the nineteenth century the nascent industrialization in East Galicia sharpened an economic rivalry among Jews, Poles, and Ukrainians. In turn, economic developments gave rise to Polish nationalist groups who embraced anti-Semitism as a powerful ideology in the struggle against foreign domination. Socioeconomic and political interaction among the three ethnic groups would play an important role in shaping their mutual perceptions and attitudes after the outbreak of World War I.

Jewish Demography, Socioeconomic Structure, and Political Activities

"Jews everywhere . . . , and no matter where I look, I am in the kingdom of Jews. It seems that nothing runs here without them." So lamented a Russian traveler passing through East Galicia in the mid-nineteenth century.[1] Indeed, to any Russian accustomed to the sight of the Pale of Settlement—a specifically designated Jewish area of residence in the Russian Empire—the density of the Jewish population in Galician cities and towns, their participation in social life, and their predominance in the local economy presented quite an unusual phenomenon. Observers also did not fail to notice the flourishing religious and cultural life of the Jewish community and the distinct outlook and conduct of the Galician Jew, the *Galizianer.*[2]

The sheer number of Jews in the region partially accounted for the bewilderment of outsiders. On the eve of World War I, Jews constituted more than 12 percent of the total population, making them the third largest group after Ukrainians and Poles. In spite of substantial emigration in the late nineteenth and early twentieth centuries, the Jewish population continued to grow, increasing by 27.5 percent between 1880 and 1910. More than 64 percent of Jews lived in cities, towns, and small hamlets—the *shtetlach.* In urban areas they constituted the second largest group (after Poles) and predominated numerically in several important commercial and cultural centers, such as Brody, Buczacz, Dobromil, and Rawa Ruska. In more than fifty district centers Jews made up more than 37 percent of the total population, and in seventy-two towns they constituted between 17 percent and 25 percent. In the northern districts of the province, Jews were more evenly spread among Poles and Ukrainians, but in the south and southeast the Ukrainian population was much larger than that of Jews and Poles together. (See appendix for detailed population figures.)

Along with Bukovina, Galicia was the poorest province of the Austro-Hungarian Empire, and its backwardness was reflected in the ethnic profile of its socioeconomic life. More than 85 percent of Poles and Ukrainians were occupied in agriculture, and the rest found employment in a few industrial enterprises and in the backward railroad system. By comparison, 87 percent of Jews made their living by trade and artisanship, and their predominance in local commerce was unquestionable. The situation was similar in professions. Although the intelligentsia made up only 2.3 percent of the total Jewish population, 4,806 Jewish lawyers, artists, journalists, and doctors constituted 19 percent of all professionals in West and East Galicia. By 1910, out of 1,389 doctors, 411 were Jews. Among 384 lawyers in Lwów there were more than 80 Jews—22 percent of the total; in the countryside, out of 500 lawyers, 140 were of Jewish descent—28 percent. Altogether in West and East Galicia, Jewish lawyers constituted 58 percent, technicians 23 percent, architects 17.2 percent, and engineers 16.5 percent of the total. In addition, 10,295 Jews were employed in regional administration and educational institutions.[3] These numbers underscore the high rate of literacy among the Jews. By 1911 Jewish students made up one-third of the student body in German schools and up to 28 percent at Lwów University. Fewer Jews attended Polish and Ukrainian schools, but their numbers were also steadily increasing. Nevertheless, the number of Jewish teachers (especially females) in Polish and Ukrainian schools gradually declined because Jewish applicants were rarely accepted. On the other hand, there were too few Jewish schools to employ all Jewish teachers.[4]

Jewish commercial enterprises played a considerable role in the development of agricultural technology, cattle breeding, the grain and meat trades, and the alcohol industry. Five hundred and fifty-seven Jewish merchants and craftsmen in Brody were members of the powerful credit union (Kredit-Verein) that dominated local finances. From the 1850s the Galician oil industry was dominated by the families of the Natansohns, Kallirs, Horowitzes, and Koliszers, and some wealthy Jews even received noble status.[5]

Military service never attracted Jewish Galician youth, and self-inflicted wounds and bribery were common ways to shirk service. Nevertheless, a number of Jews served in the army, especially in the artillery and medical corps. Special army regulations allowed Jewish soldiers to perform religious practices and released them from duties on the Sabbath. Although the Austrian-Hungarian military was not immune to anti-Semitism, the presence of several generals of Jewish background in its ranks attests to its relative ethnic tolerance.[6]

As imposing as these statistics are, they convey only part of Galicia's reality, for despite the professional achievement and wealth of the few, the majority of Jews lived in abject poverty. In the last decades of the nineteenth century nascent industrialization portended a gradual decline of Jewish trade and commerce. Large foreign (especially German) warehouses and corporations took over trade with Austria, Italy, and Hungary and pushed out petty Jewish tradesmen. The growth of Polish and Ukrainian cooperatives and enterprises made the role of Jewish middlemen in the countryside obsolete and forced thousands of Jews to seek employment in urban centers. By 1910, 25 percent of Jews in towns and cities lived just above the poverty line, and in the entire region only 39 percent were employed in occupations otherwise than as house servants. Low income and crushing poverty forced large numbers of Jewish women to turn to prostitution, and in the first decade of the twentieth century almost one-third of prostitutes in Lwów were of Jewish extraction. Rapid pauperization of the Jews coincided with rapid demographic growth and overpopulation of the region, and thousands opted for immigration to Austria, the Czech lands, Germany, and the United States.[7]

Capitalist development in the region caused a radicalization of Jewish political life. Although the majority of Jews remained within the Orthodox mainstream, demands for social and economic improvement led to the formation of the first Jewish political groups, the Jewish Workers' Party and the Zionists. Adherents to different ideologies, the Orthodox, Zionists, Socialists, and Social Democrats, were at odds with one another and ferociously competed for seats in municipal government and the parliament. But whether striving for national rights, internal autonomy, or a Jewish state in Palestine, the majority of politically active Jews remained loyal to the crown. The same loyalty characterized the Jews who remained uninvolved in provincial politics. For them the majestic figure of the emperor symbolized the rule of law and order extended to all subjects regardless of their ethnicity, social status, or religion.[8]

Jews and Their Neighbors

Ethnic relations in East Galicia had been conditioned by fluctuating politics, a backward economy, and competition in the social sphere. The Poles were the most influential group in the province. From the mid-fourteenth century onward, Polish magnates and gentry held key positions in the regional economy and administration. The revolution of 1848–1849 and the subsequent military defeats in wars with France, Sardinia-Piedmont, and Prussia forced Vienna to seek a compromise with dominant national groups such as the Hungarians, Croats, and Poles. In Galicia, Polish became the official language (on par with German) in administration, secondary schools, and Lwów University. The Polish majority also dominated the Galician Sejm, the main provincial body empowered to legislate in cultural, educational, and social spheres. Poles, therefore, considered Galicia a crucial bastion of Polish culture and civilization within the empire.[9]

From the mid-nineteenth century on, Polish dominance was increasingly challenged by the Ukrainian national movement. Numerically superior to Poles and Jews, Ukrainians mostly lived in villages and constituted the backbone of the region's agriculture, and Austrian rulers skillfully used the incipient Ukrainian nationalism to check Polish irredentist aspirations. The enlightened Austrian monarchs, Maria Theresa and Joseph II, granted the Greek Catholic

Church equal status with its Roman Catholic counterpart and supported the introduction of Slaveno-Rusyn, a combination of the Church Slavonic and Ukrainian vernacular, in village schools. During the revolutionary years 1848–1849, the Austrian government supported the Ukrainian drive for political and cultural rights and emancipated the peasants in the spring of 1848. In the 1860s, Ukrainian political activists entered the parliament and became a factor to be reckoned with in regional politics. These activities were accompanied by the proliferation of Ukrainian cultural and educational institutions and the press. In sharp comparison to the plight of their kinsmen in tsarist Ukraine, who suffered from abusive Russification policies, Galician Ukrainians largely appreciated the Habsburg rule and considered Galicia their own "Piedmont"—the cradle of Ukrainian nationalism and national culture.[10]

Until the late nineteenth century, the majority of Jews confined their relations with Poles and Ukrainians to the economic and social spheres. Accordingly, anti-Jewish animosities arose largely from economic competition. The beginning of industrialization, however, witnessed the formation of Polish political groups that made anti-Semitism a political program aimed at consolidating the Polish people and fulfilling national aspirations. The 1880s witnessed the growth of industries, banking and credit institutions, and the market for bank employees, managers, and white collar and industrial workers. Because many of the Polish gentry, the *szlachta,* were impoverished by industrialization and trying to adjust to changing economic conditions, they turned to local commerce and industry already occupied by Jewish merchants, tradesmen, and manufacturers. Among the nascent Polish middle class this clash of economic interests produced strong anti-Jewish sentiments. At the same time, in spite of the slow progress of modernization, the life of peasants also began to change. Overpopulation and heavy taxation prompted large-scale migration of villagers to urban areas. For example, between 1880 and 1910 the population of industrial centers such as Brody, Buczacz, Stanisławów, Tarnopol, Drohobycz, Przemyśl, Kołomyja, and Lwów rose almost 10 percent. This demographic shift intensified economic competition among Poles, Ukrainians, and Jews. The Polish-dominated administration imposed severe veterinary limitations on the Jewish cattle trade and granted credit and a monopoly on salt, tobacco, and the sale of alcohol most exclusively to the Polish enterprises. During the first decade of the twentieth century, about forty thousand Jews employed in the alcohol industry lost their jobs. The proliferation of Polish and Ukrainian banks and cooperatives sharply narrowed the economic opportunities of Jewish merchants and artisans in the countryside. In 1893 the Catholic economic convention in Krakow called for the boycott of Jewish enterprises, and several layoffs in the oil industry rapidly reduced the number of

Jewish workers. This massive loss of jobs was particularly significant because Jews had constituted 20 percent of the labor force in oil production industries (Ukrainians made up 9.8 percent and Poles 70 percent).[11]

Socioeconomic rivalry between Jews and non-Jews alone, however, was not sufficient to produce an ideological anti-Semitic movement. In fact, from the mid-nineteenth century onward, Polish-Jewish cooperation in regional politics seemed to augur the decline of anti-Semitic attitudes. During the revolution of 1848–1849, Jews played an important part in raising money for revolutionary activities, formed units of the civil guard and civil committees, and sheltered Polish rebels. Such cooperation was instrumental in the struggle for Jewish emancipation, and in the 1860s Polish statesmen such as Count Władysław Badeni, Franciszek Smolka, and Galician governor Agenor Gołuchowski supported the demands of Jewish delegates in the parliament for civil and political equality.[12]

The rise of anti-Semitic political groups in Poland can be traced to the late period of "positivism," an intellectual movement that sprang up in the 1860s. After Russian troops crushed the last Polish uprising in 1864, Polish intellectuals and political activists became convinced of the futility of armed struggle. Grouped around a charismatic journalist, Aleksandr Świętochowski, they began promoting the necessity of so-called organic work, or "positivism," which encompassed economic and social reforms and peaceful political participation. In the long run these measures were envisioned as the only possible means to achieve national independence, and the main building stones of organic work were the fostering of a Polish national consciousness and national unity among peasants, burghers, and toilers.

Initially, the positivists envisioned cooperation between Poles and Jews as possible and desirable. Jewish-Polish joint actions in parliamentary elections in 1879 and 1885 seem to have confirmed such expectations because Jewish candidates joined the Polish faction in the parliament. As long as the terms "nationality" and "nation" were understood as meaning an all-inclusive and ethnically diverse community, and the slogan "For your freedom and ours" remained the main concept of Polish political activists, Jews were perceived as a useful ally in national struggle. As important was the fact that a number of leading members of the Jewish intelligentsia supported assimilation and promoted Polish national culture and language. In comparison to the French and German Jewries, however, the majority of Jews in partitioned Poland did not identify themselves with Polish society. Russian Jews, confined to the Pale of Settlement, limited their relations with Poles to economic contacts. Jews who resided in the German-held areas had largely integrated themselves into German society, whereas the loyalties of Galician Jews definitely rested with the government in Vienna; the Jewish-Galician intelligentsia also preferred German culture and education.[13]

In Polish western provinces, where Jews embraced Germanization, the leading Polish political group, the National Democratic Party—the Endeks—appeared as the epicenter of national resistance. To unify ethnic Poles in the anti-German struggle, the Endeks promoted national cohesion and ethnic exclusiveness of the Polish people, advocated the proliferation of Polish political and social organizations and businesses, and rejected the assimilation of Jews as German proxies with Polish culture. The exclusionary ideology of the National Democrats appealed to a growing Polish commercial and professional middle class, middle gentry, and large segments of the clergy in the kingdom and Galicia. The Endeks also skillfully utilized the pro-German and pro-Austrian tendencies of Jews by defining anti-Semitism as a symbolic realm epitomizing economic and political components of the struggle for national liberation. Indeed, as Brian Porter aptly observed, the Endeks first defined Jews as the enemy and then accentuated their specific socioeconomic profile.[14]

External factors added fuel to growing popular anti-Semitism. Pogroms in Russia in the 1880s generated an influx of Jewish refugees into the kingdom and Galicia, which corresponded with a wave of xenophobia in Austro-Hungary and Germany. Polish writers such as Jan Kominkowski and Teofil Merunowicz emulated German and Austrian anti-Semitic propaganda, emphasizing the "harmful" Jewish influence on Polish society and warning of the proliferation of secret Jewish societies thriving on the Polish soil.[15] Polish anti-Semitism also had a strong clerical coloring, and the Catholic press launched a blend of political, religious, and racial diatribes against the Jews, revitalizing the myth of the Jewish ritual murder. Jewish influence in local industries and commerce provided anti-Semitic propaganda with the forum to rave against industrialization and socialism, labeling Jews as its main promoters, and the Endeks called for *odżydzenie* of Poland's social and economic spheres. Increasingly, numerous pamphlets and books accentuated the notion that Jewish biological traits and religious beliefs effectively precluded their assimilation; thus, assimilation was not only impossible but highly undesirable. The total socioeconomic segregation of Jews from Poles was the only viable solution to the Jewish question.[16]

At the same time, the Union of the Polish Peasant Party, led by Father Stanisław Stojałowski, directed peasant economic frustrations against Jews. Anti-Semitic propaganda reached its peak in 1898, when violent attacks on the Jews took place in western Galician localities such as Wieliczka, Kalwaria, Jasło, Nowy and Stary Sącz, Sanok, and Gorlice. The majority of the Polish parties condemned the excesses, but anti-Jewish violence again erupted in

1903. In East Galicia, the Polish-Ukrainian political rivalry mitigated the violence because the Endeks hoped to win Jewish support in the local and provincial elections and abstained from provoking anti-Jewish riots. Nevertheless, as large numbers of Poles and Ukrainians migrated to the cities and as competition for jobs sharpened, attacks on Jews intensified. In June 1902, anti-Semitic propaganda, combined with workers' economic grievances, exploded into a riot in Lwów when Polish strikers attacked Jews on the streets.[17]

The expectations of the Endeks that Jews could be used as a counterbalance to Ukrainians were dashed in 1907 and 1911 when Jewish voters cast their ballots in favor of Jewish and Ukrainian candidates. Similarly, in 1912, during the municipal elections in Warsaw, Jews voted against the leading National Democrat, Roman Dmowski. From his point of view, Jews had unequivocally demonstrated their hostility to the Polish cause, and the Endeks responded with an escalation of anti-Semitic propaganda and organized the economic boycott of Jewish shops.[18]

Industrialization contributed to the rise of anti-Semitism among the Ukrainian peasantry as well. In comparison to the kingdom, a large number of Galician Jews lived in the countryside, where they owned land parcels. Although in East Galicia the majority of the landowning Jews owned small parcels of between one hundred to five hundred hectares, they were still one grade above the Polish and Ukrainian peasants, who on average owned between one hundred and two hundred hectares. The 561 most affluent Jewish landowners owned about 22 percent of large land estates in both halves of Galicia. In addition, Jews constituted about 50 percent of all land renters and 30 percent of estate stewards. Tavern keeping, trade, and moneylending were predominantly Jewish vocations, and for Ukrainian peasants usury and Jews became one inseparable image. In the 1880s, the growth of a money economy in Galicia caused a sharp economic decline among Ukrainian villagers, who abhorred Jewish land leasing and perceived the Jews as the main driving force behind industrialization. Jewish membership in municipal governments in small towns and villages was also a cause of friction, and a prominent Ukrainian activist, Julian Romanchuk, asserted in 1903 that the worst enemies of the peasants were landlords, tax inspectors, and the "cunning Jew."[19]

Resentment toward Jews, state officials, and Polish landlords sporadically flared up in physical assaults, especially when peasants came to market to sell their products. Warmed by vodka and rallying cries of "Death to Jews and Poles!" they looted Jewish shops and beat Jewish traders and bystanders. Physical assaults were recorded in Zabłotów (Śniatyń district) in September 1903 and in Karów (Rawa Ruska district) and Śniatyń in 1911, where several Jews were wounded.[20]

The Ukrainian intelligentsia voiced peasant grievances against Jews, stressing their alleged damaging role in the rural economy. At the same time, however, Ukrainian intellectuals recognized the Jews as a legitimate community of Galicia and promoted more liberal approach to the Jewish question. Writers Ivan Franko and Les' Martovych realistically described the miserable economic conditions of the Jewish poor. Ukrainian members of the parliament supported Jews in their struggle for national autonomy and the recognition of Yiddish as an official language. In 1907, Ukrainian deputies protested against Polish pressure on Jews during municipal elections in Galicia. Similar instances opened the possibility for closer cooperation in the future.[21]

The socioeconomic and demographic structure of East Galician Jews played a crucial role in their relations with Poles and Ukrainians. Traditionally Jews made their living by artisanship and petty commerce. From the 1880s onward, however, these occupations became the area of fierce contest among the three ethnic groups. Common perceptions that Jewish tradesmen and merchants were more successful than their non-Jewish counterparts also fueled envy and anti-Jewish resentment.

Industrialization of the region coincided with the rise of modern nationalism among Poles and Ukrainians. In the late nineteenth century, Polish nationalists promoted the idea of national unity by accentuating that the definition of "Polishness" applied only to ethnic and nationally conscious Poles. This exclusionary ideology rejected Jews as members of Polish society. The main objective of the nationalists—national independence—coalesced with the struggle against "harmful" Jewish influences. Political rivalry between Poles and Jews in regional politics was another crucial factor in fueling anti-Semitism. At the same time, Ukrainian grievances against the Jews, primarily confined to the socioeconomic sphere, also gained momentum. Both Poles and Ukrainians viewed Jews as harmful elements—the first seeing them as the ally of the government, the second seeing them as the fraudulent profiteers and the hirelings of Polish landlords.

Yet, in comparison to the situation across the Russian border, where Jews were treated as second-class citizens, the Galician Jewry considered economic crises, squalid living conditions in the *shtetlach,* and anti-Jewish excesses as unpleasant but bearable in day-to-day existence. Although before World War I anti-Semitic groups attracted diverse social layers of Polish society, they were unable to generate mass political mobilization of their followers. As long as the Austrian government maintained law and order, radical anti-Semitism was confined to propaganda and random outbursts of violence. Only the collapse of state institutions would propel it to the foreground of Galicia's political life and drastically radicalize ethnic biases.

I
Russian Rule in Galicia

1 / Russia Goes to War

"If we count the rewards we can expect from this war—there is no doubt it is mere madness. What should we expect to gain? Territorial accretion? But aren't the lands of His Imperial Majesty large enough? . . . Galicia? But it is full of Jews!" So on September 10, 1914, Count Sergei Witte, the prominent Russian statesman, grumbled to the French ambassador, Maurice Paleologue, about the senselessness of Russia's participation in the war.[1]

Although in Witte's opinion Galicia was merely a land infested by Jews, many Russian government and military officials had long held an entirely opposite view. Situated in the foothills of the Carpathians, Galicia provided an accessible route through Silesia to Austria proper and via Krakow through the mountain ranges to the Hungarian plains. Not surprisingly, St. Petersburg considered Galicia the second most "sensitive" strategic spot in eastern Europe (the Balkans being the first). Russian military planners also worried that in the event of war with Germany and Austro-Hungary (and in the first decade of the twentieth century this possibility was looming more prominently with each passing year), the enemy would be able to launch a pincerlike offensive from East Prussia and East Galicia and cut off the Russian army in the kingdom. In 1900 the Russian minister of war, General Aleksei Kuropatkin, reported to the tsar that Galicia had to be given close strategic consideration and that certain "rectifications" of the border were highly desirable.[2]

Russian strategic objectives in Galicia were augmented by ideological ones, which required as much attention as military preparation. The two dominant ethnic groups in the region, Poles and Ukrainians, whose ethnographic borders spread far beyond the Austro-Hungarian state frontiers, had always been a subject of Russia's close attention. The Russian government had long regarded Galicia as a part of the "primordial Russian lands" (specifically the Lwów, Tarnopol, and Czernowitz provinces in their entirety and a part of the Przemyśl province) destined one day to return to the bosom of Russia.

Imperial intentions of bringing all eastern Slavs under a Russian protectorate were verbalized already during the first Russian occupation of the Tarnopol province in 1809, when Alexander I urged the Russian governor to undertake policies to win the local population to the Russian cause. Of much significance, shortly before World War I the chairman of the Council of Ministers, Ivan Goremykin, referred to Galicia as the "last diamond to the Tsar's crown."[3]

Beginning from the mid-nineteenth century, Russian Pan-Slavists established close contacts with Galician Russophiles, a group of intellectuals who argued that Galician Ukrainians were kin to Russians, supplied them with money, and emphasized the common roots of the two peoples.[4] Contacts with Russophiles accelerated especially after the Russian revolution of 1904–1905 and exacerbated Austro-Russian tensions. The Polish viceroy of Galicia, Michał Bobrzyński, reported to Vienna that Russian money was fueling pro-Russian tendencies among Russophile groups. A further headache for the Austrian government was caused by the activities of the "Russian-Galician committees" that had emerged under the patronage of Russian cultural and political circles. The leading figure behind these groups was Count Vladimir Bobrinskii, who never failed to emphasize the "Russian character" of Galicia. With the end of the Pan-Slav Congress in Prague in 1908 and Bobrinskii's subsequent visit to Galicia, the Austrian General Staff recorded the increased activities of 1,450 Russophile educational, cultural, and religious institutions supplied and financed by the Russians. Galician-Ukrainian circles echoed the charges proffered by the Austrian security services and accused the Russophiles of being the spearhead of Russian expansionism.[5]

On the other hand, from the early 1860s on, the Polish national movement in Galicia became a major concern for the Russian government. The influential Galician-Polish group in the Austrian parliament, *Koło Polskie,* often protested against the heavy-handed Russian rule in the kingdom. Polish protests, in turn, immediately provoked remonstrations by St. Petersburg to Vienna. Polish political and cultural dominance in Galicia provided a moral boost to Polish political activists elsewhere, and the Russian police were particularly alarmed by the activities of the Polish Socialist Party, the PPS, whose major aim was the restoration of Polish independence by revolutionary means.

After the Russian revolution of 1904–1905, Polish émigrés from the kingdom set up paramilitary organizations in Galicia under the auspices of Austrian authorities. These groups carried out espionage and anti-Russian propaganda. During the Bosnian crisis of 1908 the tensions between Austro-Hungary and Russia heated up, and Russian protests to Vienna sounded increasingly belligerent. In May 1909, the newspaper *Kievlianin* published an article, allegedly based on authentic documents, revealing the activities of Polish paramilitary groups in Galicia and the involvement of Austrian officials in training and financing Polish revolutionaries. The Austrians, naturally, vehemently denied these accusations. Secretly, however, the Austrian military was preparing to deploy Galician Ukrainians for sabotage activities in Ukraine in the event of military conflict. These plans received the full support of the Galician Greek Catholic Church and its charismatic leader, Metropolitan Andrei Sheptyts'kyi. The testing time for anti-Russian actions came during the Balkan wars, when Ukrainians from Galicia carried out acts of sabotage in Ukraine.[6]

The press war also gained momentum. In May and June of 1910, the Russian journal *Novoe vremia* published a series of articles about the Ukrainian question in Galicia, stressing the insidious role of Austrian authorities in inciting nationalist sentiments among Ukrainians. The Austrian press retaliated by charging Russia with interfering in Austro-Hungary's internal affairs. In October 1910, the Lwów police informed the Austro-Hungarian Ministry of the Interior that Bobrinskii planned to buy land near Kiev where a thousand Galician Russophiles would settle; after their thorough Russification they would return to Galicia as a Russian propagandist vanguard. The potential of Polish and Ukrainian issues for causing conflict between Russia and Austro-Hungary alarmed several prominent politicians on both sides. In July 1912, the Austrian foreign minister, Count Leopold von Berchtold, stated that Russian policies toward Galicia "not only hindered the rapprochement [between Austria and Russia], but also added fuel to the very combustible [political] atmosphere." In November of the same year, the Russian ambassador to Vienna, Nicholas Girs, emphasized that as long as Galician-Polish and Galician-Ukrainian questions were unresolved, friendly relations between the two states were not foreseeable.[7] Austro-Russian bickering over Galicia continued up to the outbreak of the First World War. During the first half of 1914, as a large trial of Russophiles took place in the Hungarian town of Marmaroŝ-Szeget and another in Lwów, the Austro-Hungarian press accused Russia of directing the subversive activities of the Russophile groups.[8]

Russia and Her Jews

It is generally taken for granted that before World War I Russia was the most anti-Semitic country in the world. Nowhere else was the government so persistent in promulgating drastic anti-Jewish laws and carrying out policies confining Jews to prescribed areas of residence and barring them from politics and institutions of higher learning. Prior to the last quarter of the eighteenth century, Russia had almost no Jews within her borders. This situation changed after the Polish partitions of 1772–1795, when Russia received much of Poland, including a Jewish population that constituted the largest Jewish Diaspora in the world. By the turn of the twentieth century, despite emigration, the Jews of Russia constituted about 9 percent of the total population. In western provinces, including the Pale of Settlement, Jews made up more than 23 percent of the total.[9]

The Jewish policies of the Russian government seldom displayed consistency and fluctuated according to the changing political, social, and economic situation in the country. Attempts to assimilate Jews at the beginning of the nineteenth century were followed by various restrictions and limitations during the reign of Nicholas I. The 1860s again began with reforms. Jews were permitted to buy property and live in urban areas in the kingdom, and affluent merchants, holders of academic degrees, and guild craftsmen were allowed to settle outside of the Pale. Inside the Pale, Jews enjoyed substantial autonomy in regulating their religious and cultural life, Jewish schools proliferated, and local communities were the centers of Jewish cultural and educational activities. Except for times of social and political crises, the relations between Jews and non-Jews were marked by relative tranquility and tolerance. Although specific quotas limited the number of Jewish students, a number of young Jews were able to enter and graduate from Russian colleges and universities. The assassination of Alexander II in 1881 marked a rapid shift in imperial ethnic policies, however. Anti-Jewish legislation, such as the prohibition for Jews to resettle in rural areas in the kingdom and the Pale, effectively nullified the reforms of the 1860s and were followed by further limitations in professional and educational spheres. In turn, these repressive policies made the Jewish intelligentsia especially susceptible to Marxist, socialist, and nationalist ideas, and the turn of the twentieth century witnessed the proliferation of such Jewish political parties as the Zionists, Poalei-Zion, and the Bund.[10]

Traditional anti-Semitism in Russia emanated from religious differences and economic competition between Jewish and Russian traders, merchants, and workers. Hateful rhetoric also found fertile ground in Russian villages, where Russian peasants believed Jews to be guilty of the ultimate crime, murdering Jesus Christ, and of trying to destroy traditional social order. Russian revolutionary groups such as the Narodnaia volia ("People's Will") also used anti-Jewish slogans as an expedient tool to win over Russian peasants. Even liberals who rejected anti-Semitism as a residue of the old, conservative Russia believed that Jews were "alien" to the Russian soil and potentially dangerous to illiterate workers and peasants.[11]

Nonetheless, the activities of Jewish political activists in the last two decades of the nineteenth century added new elements to traditional anti-Semitic sentiments. For Russian reactionaries, active participation of the Jewish intelligentsia in the revolutionary movement and the visible role of Jewish entrepreneurs in the Western economy and Russian industrial development heralded the emergence of a powerful international Jewish clique that aimed at world dominance. Such fears were reflected in the notorious *Protocols of the Elders of Zion,* which were doctored by the agents of the Okhrana—the imperial secret police. Consequently, Russian reactionaries used racist overtones to impute Russia's social problems and political turmoil to Jews. Anti-Jewish resentments flared in the outbreaks of social and political violence in the 1880s and during the revolution of 1904–1905.[12]

Still, anti-Semitism did not become a uniform policy of the Russian government. Some officials believed that a gradual emancipation of Jews would facilitate their integration into Russian society and ease ethnic tensions, and liberals and intellectuals such as Alexander Blok, Vladimir Nabokov, Paul Miliukov, Leonid Andreyev, and Vladimir Korolenko publicly supported and advocated equal civil and political rights of the Jews. In 1913, amid vehement anti-Semitic propaganda of right-wing groups, a jury in Kiev acquitted Mendel Beilis, a Jew charged with ritual murder.[13]

The Russian military's view on the "Jewish question" mirrored official and popular attitudes prevalent in Russian society. On one hand, with the introduction of the universal draft in 1827, the Russian military strove to incorporate Jewish recruits in the ranks on the par with other nationalities. On the other hand, it restricted promotions of the Jewish military personnel and blamed Jews for "seditious" activities. For example, in the 1860s, the army allowed Jews to enter military schools and become officers, simultaneously accusing them of draft evasion and contending that Jews were treacherous and unpatriotic and would use any opportunity to undermine Russia's war efforts.[14] During the Russo-Turkish war of 1877–1878, as the Russian army poured into Bulgaria on a mission to liberate "brother Slavs" from the Turkish yoke, traditional anti-Semitism, compounded by rumors that Jews were actively aiding the Turks, exploded into mass pillaging of Jewish communities, brutal pogroms, and the mass rape of Jewish women. Simultaneously, the army accused the Jews of reaping profit from Russia's victories and living off the "blood and sweat" of the Russian people.[15]

At the turn of the century, the stance of the military toward the "Jewish problem" remained unchanged. In spite of substantial shortages of personnel, the medical corps accepted only a small number of Jewish doctors because the latter, according to War Minister P. Vannovski, "adversely influenced" their Christian colleagues. The allegations of Judeo-Masonic clandestine societies had shaped the mentality of the Russian officer corps, and the imperial guards were among the first readers of the *Protocols;* its first publisher was a retired officer, G. W. Butmi.[16] Nevertheless, although the Russian officer corps protected its ranks from Jews, and the military emphasized that admission to military schools was contingent on ethnicity rather than religion, a number of Jewish converts were commissioned and achieved high rank in the army.[17]

During the period of 1907 to 1909, several military and civil committees requested that Jews be barred from the army as the most corruptive and unreliable element in time of peace and war. Suspicions toward the Jews were reflected in the dispersal of Jewish recruits around the empire, while Christian and Muslim draftees from the same regions were grouped together in closed units. At the same time, the War Ministry appreciated the professionalism and skill of Jewish artillerists and infantrymen and did not cave in to the pressure of the anti-Semitic factions, which demanded that the army rid itself of Jews. The press also treated the "Jewish question" in accordance with the political atmosphere of the period. In 1907 the journal *Russkii invalid* praised the valor of Jewish soldiers who fought in the Russo-Turkish and Russo-Japanese wars. In 1911, however, it accused Jews of draft evasion. The journals *Novoe vremia* and *Voennyi mir* echoed the charges and added that Jews were of an antisocial and "anti-state [nature]."[18] Several other periodicals suggested that the military reforms then taking place in the army be directed at creating a national army comprised only of ethnic Russians who were "healthy politically and physically." An exception to the rule would be other nationalities "who had organically integrated into the Russian state." Jews, as an "alien" element, were to be excluded. In December 1911, speaking from the Duma rostrum, renowned Russian nationalist N. E. Markov suggested that Jewish soldiers be sent to labor battalions deployed for drainage of the Pinsk marshes and for cleaning latrines.[19]

As the army geared up for war, radical elements within the military gradually prevailed over the moderates. Special blacklists were compiled in which the Jews were featured as potential spies and saboteurs. In December 1908, at a joint meeting of the members of the Ministry of the Interior and the general staffs of the army and the navy, the first Russian military counterintelligence office was set up to combat espionage and subversive activities against the army. The participants compiled a list of the "groups of risk," which contained, in addition to foreign agents, "persons of Jewish nationality who attempt to infiltrate and establish congenial relations with military personnel."[20]

On August 1, 1914, the day Russia entered the First World War, the commander of the Fifth Russian Army, Lieutenant General P. Pleve, ordered his counterintelligence service to step up antisubversive measures within the army's operational zone. Immediate attention, Pleve ordered, was to be paid to all non-Russians (*inorodtsy*). Instructions to security employees specified that evidence of wrongdoing might include "inconsistent" answers and a "vagabond" style of life.[21] Because financial rewards were offered for informing on a spy, the order opened the doors for mass denunciations, which poured in as the war progressed, and accorded the counterintelligence agents remarkable freedom in arresting hundreds of "suspects." As the most densely populated areas of Jewish residents in eastern Europe, the kingdom and Galicia, became battlegrounds, Russian spy hunters immediately began stalking Jews, who spoke Yiddish, a completely unintelligible language (for Russians), and looked suspicious in their peculiar garb.

Although the traditional anti-Semitic proclivities of the military were instrumental in the treatment of the Jews in the eastern front zone, the rapid militarization of political, social, and economic life in Russia played the most crucial role in the evolution of the imperial ethnic policies. On July 29, 1914, the tsar signed a document titled "The Regulations for Field Administration of the Army in Wartime" (*Polozhenie o polevom upravlenii voisk v voennoye vremia*), which set rules for waging war. Apart from specifying the chain of command, the *Polozhenie* stipulated that conquered territories should be formed into military general governments headed by governor-generals as the highest wartime authorities. The territory west of St. Petersburg and Smolensk and south along the Dnieper River to the Black Sea was placed under the jurisdiction of the supreme commander, who was to wage war by any means he deemed fit. The military became the absolute authority in the war zone and took over the civil administration. The powers invested in the army were vast, ranging from the setting of tariffs and prices to the imposition of military censorship and martial law; civil offices in the theater of operations were reduced to adjunct bodies. For example, the commander of the southwestern front (facing Galicia), General Nicholas Ivanov, forbade any civil officials and journalists to visit military units. Areas adjacent to the front line thus became virtually independent entities where the military received free reign in treating the civilian population according to its own conceptions of "loyal" and "disloyal" groups. The *Polozhenie* also abrogated all jurisdictional powers of the Council of Ministers and the War Ministry in the war zone. In early August, the Council of Ministers received extraordinary powers and could make decisions in the name of the tsar except for interfering in military affairs. This multiplicity of military and civil powers created difficulties in running the country in wartime and caused bitter rivalry among the Supreme Command, the Council of Ministers, the War Ministry, and the State Council.[22]

The transfer of civil powers to the military was neither new nor unique in Russian history. Historically, the army played a central role in Russia's policy making, especially in securing and governing newly conquered territories. During the reign of Ivan the Terrible, commanders (*voevody*) often assumed military and civil powers in territories within their jurisdiction. Later, in the seventeenth and eighteenth centuries, newly annexed regions in Siberia were also placed under military rule. During expansion into the Caucasus and central Asia, Russian generals became virtual rulers of new territories and exercised power by imposing high taxes, requisitioning grain and cattle, curtailing native languages and cultures, and resettling native populations. Russification policies in Poland were also accompanied by troop deployment in "restless" districts.[23]

The first measures undertaken by the army at the beginning of the war bode extremely ill for the population of the battle zone. On August 1, the chief of the Main Department of the General Staff, General M. Beliaev, ordered commanders of military districts to make all German and Austro-Hungarian subjects living or traveling in Russia prisoners of war. They and anybody else suspected of espionage were to be deported east of the Volga River. The Russian supreme commander, Grand Duke Nicholas, in a letter to Goremykin, explained that these measures were a response to Austro-German brutalities against the Slavs. "Delay [in countermeasures]," wrote Nicholas, would "cause a justified outrage [at Russian leniency]." No regard, therefore, was to be given to age, sex, or nationality. Thousands of Germans, Austrians, Poles, and Czechs (the latter being the very same Slavs on whose behalf the deportations were launched) were deported to Siberia, where many died in the course of the war.[24]

The portrait of the Russian military machine, which was soon to play a fatal role in the history of the *Ostjuden,*[25] would be incomplete without a few words about its commanders and men-at-arms. Described by several of his contemporaries as a "noble and cultured man," the supreme commander, who was also the tsar's uncle, enjoyed wide popularity within the Russian military as an able officer and a decent and strong-willed field commander. His strategic skills, however, were limited. The grand duke was also extremely religious and shared the anti-Semitic biases of the time. His chief of staff, General of the Infantry Nicholas Yanushkevich, a future nemesis of the Jews, was seen even in army circles as an extreme right-winger. Since March of 1914 he had served as the chief of the General Staff and had only an average military record. Therefore, his nomination to Stavka (General Headquarters) surprised many observers.[26] The supreme commander and his chief of staff were hardly prepared to fight a modern war. One might, therefore, assume that they would immerse themselves only in military issues and relegate civil affairs to their subordinates. Yet it was precisely civil affairs to which both leaders devoted much time, and they displayed remarkable zeal in presiding over the wholesale persecution of Jews in the battle zone.[27]

In July 1914, two-thirds of the Russian rank and file who were poised to engage the enemy in East Prussia, Poland, and Galicia had been drafted from the Slavic population of the empire.[28] Though not systematic, anti-Jewish indoctrination was strong among noncommissioned officers and soldiers, who had to memorize that Russia was threatened by the external enemies, "Germans and Austrians," and the internal ones, "Jews, students, and kikes."[29] The flat terrain of Galicia and the southeastern area of the kingdom accorded Stavka an opportunity to deploy the bulk of its cavalry, consisting of eighteen and one-half divisions (more than eighty thousand horsemen), against the Austrian-Hungarian army. Half this number were the Cossack and cavalry units of the Third and Eighth Russian armies positioned against East Galicia. Cossack troops from the Don, Kuban', and Terek territories (*voiska*) were especially known for their hostility to Jews. Although only a handful of Jews resided within these regions, the Cossacks despised the "inner enemies"—socialists, students, and Jews—who purportedly threatened the traditional way of life in Russia. Cossack anti-Semitism had also received a powerful impetus during the Russian revolution of 1904–1905, when the rightist political groups lumped together Jews and revolutionaries as a single subversive group.

After the declaration of war, Jews in Russian cities, alongside their Christian compatriots, were swept up in an enthusiastic frenzy. The most oppressed minority of the empire, they hoped that their participation on the front would grant them the rights of full-fledged citizens. In the atmosphere of general exultation, Jewish delegates to the Duma professed their loyalty to the tsar and swore, despite intermittent persecution over the centuries, to "stand up as a single man to shield [Russia] with their chests."[30] Jewish religious communities prayed for the victory of Russian arms and staged patriotic demonstrations, hoisting the scrolls of Torah, national flags, and portraits of the tsar. Some young Jews, including those whom *numerus clausus* forced to seek acceptance at foreign universities, returned to Russia to enlist in the army or volunteered with the Allied forces. Jewish expectations reached their highest peak when the tsar reportedly thanked Jews for their faithfulness to the crown in a dire time. The proclamation of the tsar, however, was a sham; Russian agents in Britain and France apparently invented the appeal to placate the Allies and procure loans and credits.[31]

The predominant atmosphere in the rural areas of the Pale of Settlement was, in contrast, that of gloom and doom. Jewish tradesmen, shoemakers, merchants, and innkeepers, most likely down-to-earth individuals, realized that the war would drastically alter their lives.[32] But even if they cherished illusions as to a better future, those dreams were soon dashed by the conduct of the Russian army. Already in early August, rumors of Jewish espionage in the kingdom and Kurland spread among the troops and reverberated in more distorted forms in Russia. Jews were accused of spotting for enemy guns, guiding Germans through front lines, cutting Russian telephone lines, firing at passing columns, and furnishing German intelligence with crucial information. Army commanders took matters in hand with arrests in Jewish communities, and divisional courts-martial feverishly tried alleged Jewish spies and saboteurs. Although the majority of cases provided no substantial evidence, some Jews were convicted of high treason.[33]

At this point, it should be stressed that Jews indeed served in the German and Austrian intelligence services. For example, in the Austrian intelligence branch in Czernowitz, three out of five agents were Jewish. Nevertheless, the chief of the Russian gendarme corps, General Kruglov, asserted that the numbers of Jewish spies did not exceed those of other nationalities. On the other hand, Jews also worked for Russian intelligence.[34] Yet, the Russian army was beyond such nuances, and the defamation campaign soon culminated in the first mass expulsions in the kingdom. In August 1914 Jewish communities in the Radom, Łomża, and Lublin provinces were ordered to leave within twenty-four hours on grounds of "security." After they left, their property was taken by local residents. In September, expulsions began in the Warsaw province and continued until November. Accusations of Jewish espionage reached such proportions that Jews of St. Petersburg appealed to the supreme commander not to smear the entire Jewish community, which stood loyally by the Russian cause.[35]

~

In the front zone Jews were not the only group singled out for imagined crimes. Russian Germans were equally blamed for seditious activities, and later, after Turkey entered the war, the Muslims of the Trans-Caucasus region were identified with the enemy. Nor were reprisals against potentially refractory groups a monopoly of the Russian army. Its Austrian counterpart was as susceptible to spy mania and arrested, imprisoned, and executed thousands of Serbs and Galician Ukrainians on charges of sabotage. In Belgium and France, the German army, spurred on by rumors of subversive activities of enemy irregulars, *francs-tireurs,* retaliated by shooting civilians and burning "suspicious" localities. In Macedonia, Serbian, Greek, and Bulgarian troops attempted to "cleanse" the region of potentially unreliable minority groups.[36]

Nevertheless, from the beginning of the war there was a difference between Russian treatment of Jews and other minorities. Although by virtue of cultural, ethnic, and linguistic links Germans and Muslims were associated with the specific belligerent states—Germany and Turkey—the fact that ethnic Germans had largely been integrated into Russian society initially mitigated the all-out assault on German communities. Similarly, the Muslim nobility had also retained its privileges and served in the army and bureaucracy. Although the Russian government classified Muslims as second-class citizens—*inorodtsy*—and was weary of Ottoman and Islamic influence in central Asia, at the time it did not deem them a secretive society with international connections. In addition, the Muslims resided in the areas that initially were outside of the front zone. Jews, on the other hand, as a traditionally isolated and despised minority, were viewed as connected to Jewish financial and industrial circles in Europe and America, and their capacity to wreak damage was, therefore, considered much greater. The main Jewish areas of residence, such as the kingdom, also became a battlefield instantly after the outbreak of hostilities. Accordingly, the vehemence of the anti-Jewish defamation campaign and the scope of violence inflicted on the Jews surpassed the experiences of Russian Germans and Muslims.

The Russian high command was particularly sensitive to information about Jewish sabotage submitted by frontline units and the counterintelligence service, and violence in Poland and Kurland became symptomatic of the troops' mindset. Russian generals and officers were convinced that if Russian Jews were assisting the enemy, their foreign coreligionists in East Galicia were even more hostile to the empire. Subsequently, having no inhibition in mistreating Russian citizens, the army would hardly show even less restraint toward subjects of the enemy state. Nonetheless, apart from beliefs in the perfidious nature and anti-Russian proclivities of the Jews, the army did not have a preconceived plan, nor was it guided by any principle of how to deal with foreign and Russian Jews in the war zone. The only clear concept in the minds of the Russian military was that Jews would inevitably pose a challenge to Russian rule. Therefore, from the beginning of the Russian occupation of East Galicia, the military began elaborating long-range radical plans to handicap Jews as a potential source of trouble.

2 / "Leveling" Jews
Ethnic Policies in Occupied Galicia

In early August 1914, the Russian and Austro-Hungarian armies clashed in several bloody frontier engagements, and on August 18, thirty-five Russian divisions under the command of Lieutenant General Alexei Brusilov penetrated deep into enemy territory. On September 2, hard-pressed by the superior Russian forces, the Austrians abandoned Lwów, and on September 11 the Austrian commander in chief, Conrad von Hötzendorf, ordered a general retreat beyond the San River. East Galicia, the main Russian military objective in Europe, was secured for the empire.[1] Until the spring of 1915, the Russian army governed the occupied territory, acting simultaneously as a military and a civil administration. From its inception, the occupation regime initiated a series of measures that aimed at turning Galicia into an imperial province. The disagreements between the army and the government in regard to the status of Galicia, however, seriously impeded the nationalization campaign. The army's drive to level Jews on a par with their Russian coreligionists was more successful. Numerous restrictions, reprisals, and expulsions severely crippled the socioeconomic foundation of the Galician Jewry at the time when it faced its most formidable challenge since the seventeenth-century Cossack wars.

The Russians Are Coming!
"Wild" Violence in the Summer and Fall of 1914

Long after World War I, the Jews of Galicia, like their contemporaries elsewhere in Europe, recalled with sadness the last peaceful days of the summer of 1914. The weather was cloudless, and a general atmosphere of serenity and relaxation reigned in the city and countryside. A contemporary described the summer streets of Lwów as radiating with "bright smiles, rustle of silk on women, and the whole ocean of flowers."[2] Even the Sarajevo assassination and the Austrian ultimatum to Serbia did not alter the popular mood. Therefore, when the news of the outbreak of hostilities reached Galicia, people still lent ears to government propaganda that kept boasting that the war would be quick and victorious. At the beginning of August, however, while official communiqués were still describing Austrian victories on the battlefields, rumors suddenly spread that the Russians had already crossed into Galicia. In a few days the peaceful atmosphere completely evaporated, panic spread, and the roads westward were flooded with hundreds of carts and thousands of refugees. By the second week of August, rail stations were overcrowded, seats were fought over, and departing trains were swarmed by a multitude of passengers. The chaos was exacerbated by rumors of sabotage on Austrian communication lines; denunciations piled up in police quarters, and the military carried out mass arrests of "unreliable" elements, especially among the Russophiles. Drumhead courts-martial were set up and meted out death sentences. In several instances, outraged mobs comprised of Jews and Poles assaulted columns of arrested "suspects." Some Jews also denounced Ukrainians suspected of "Russophilism" to Austrian authorities, who carried out swift and merciless justice.[3]

From the outset of hostilities, the news of the Russian invasion forced many Jews to flee Galicia. About one-tenth of the total, mostly individuals of means, managed to evacuate with the first wave of refugees. In September, when the Russian advance was not stemmed, the sound of battle generated the second wave, which continued unabated until the late fall of 1914. This time Jews from all walks of life trudged westward. Often without adequate clothing, "drawn by hunger and terror[,] . . . carts piled high with domestic utensils, furniture, poultry, women, and children," Jews crossed in thousands into West Galicia, Hungary, and, ultimately, Austria.[4]

The second wave of refugees was largely short of money because on August 1 the Austrian government imposed a moratorium on private and legal debts to allow the debtors to delay payment. Simultaneously, private accounts were frozen. Hence, when a multitude of refugees reached Krakow, the administration hurried to transport them farther, to Hungary and Bohemia. Thousands were arriving weekly, and by the fall of 1915 approximately two hundred thousand Galician Jewish refugees were to be found in Austria, Hungary, Bohemia, and Moravia. In Vienna alone, out of 137,000 refugees, 60 percent were Jews from Galicia and Bukovina.[5]

The Austrian government and the municipal administration tried to accommodate the refugees, using all resources at their disposal. It financed and organized soup kitchens and schools for children and granted subsidies to Jewish families. The population donated food, money, and clothing. Galician Zionists in Vienna set up aid committees, and Jewish press and parliament members publicized the plight of Galician refugees. Members of the Austrian parliament accused the Russian government of condoning the persecutions of the Jews and recited numerous instances of the Russian army's looting, rape, and destruction of Jewish quarters. Similarly, Zionist groups called for the collection of necessary funds to support Jewish refugees and denounced Russian atrocities.[6]

As economic conditions became harsher, the initially friendly atmosphere around the refugees began to dissipate. Concomitant with the gradual dwindling of supplies, the influx of the *Ostjuden* and their competition with local tradesmen increased ethnic tensions. The "alien" appearance and habits of Galician Jews made even their Austrian and Hungarian coreligionists very uneasy. Financial aid from Britain and the United States, although it kept many families afloat, was not sufficient to ameliorate the situation.[7]

Jews who stayed in Galicia faced far harsher adversities, however. Already in mid-August, under Russian pressure, Austrian troops and administration began withdrawing westward. The void of authority led to the first anti-Jewish outbursts among Ukrainians and Poles, who plundered and demolished government offices and assaulted Jews in several localities. These attacks reflected the wartime accentuation of ethnic and social identities whereby Poles and Ukrainians singled out Jews as the most "pro-government" and allegedly most affluent element. In addition, mass arrests and executions of Ukrainians by the Austrian military, and a conspicuously hostile attitude of Jews toward the alleged traitors, enraged large segments of the population, especially in the Galician countryside. Therefore, having suffered assaults by their compatriots, in some places Jews awaited Russian troops in hope that they would restore order and put an end to mob violence. The arrival of the first Cossack patrols in Galician towns and villages dashed their hopes, however, as the Cossacks joined local hoodlums in looting and burning. In Kołomyja, Berezów, and Myszyn (the Kołomyja district), Cossacks, soldiers, and local residents plundered and burned down German and Jewish houses and shops. In Husiatyn and Tłuste, Cossacks and peasants robbed the Jews and burned 716 Jewish huts.[8]

Pogroms soon engulfed many localities, causing widespread destruction in Jewish communities. From the outset, Russian officers were lenient toward the excesses of their subordinates and let them go on rampages as a reward for capturing a given locality, a method practiced along the entire eastern front. Looting with impunity, therefore, was a powerful incentive for violence. A Duma emissary mused to the prominent Jewish activist Solomon An-Ski (Rappoport), who came to the front on a relief mission to Jewish communities, that the alleged shots at Russian troops were always fired from shops and warehouses, which were immediately plundered in "retaliation."[9]

Lax discipline and the rapacity of the assailants, however, were but two driving forces behind the assaults. The effects of prewar anti-Semitic brainwashing also made Russian soldiers believe that the war against the Central Powers was likewise a crusade against the Jews. After all, many units that entered Galicia in the summer of 1914 were formed in central Russia and Siberia, whose residents had never had contacts with Jews prior to the war. The mindset of the Russian rank and file crystallized immediately when, on entering towns and villages, Cossacks and soldiers conveyed to the people that they had come to free Galicia from the "Jewish yoke." Often, the Cossacks stopped passers-by and inquired, *"Gde yevrei?"* (Where are the Jews?). Presenting a cross or showing a locket portraying Jesus Christ were sufficient ways to be let go; those who could not provide such "evidence" were unceremoniously robbed. To win popularity among the local population, in some instances the Russians incited the people to anti-Jewish excesses and, after having looted Jewish stores and houses, distributed the booty to Poles and Ukrainians.[10] Indeed, officers and soldiers were capable of making a clear distinction between "friendly" and "unfriendly" ethnic groups, and when in late November the army entered eastern Slovakia—inhabited by the "Slavic kin"—Russian troops displayed remarkable self-control rigidly enforced by the high command.[11]

At the same time, the rationale for the assaults on Jews derived from the genuine fears of saboteurs and shooters in the army rear. Army situational reports reflected a growing collective hysteria about the invisible enemy lurking behind Russian lines. Some commanders informed Stavka of secret Jewish organizations digging miles-long tunnels to Austrian positions; others reported that Jewish agents directed the enemy's fire from balloons, provided the Austrians with secret information, lured Russian troops into traps, burned their own houses before fleeing westward, and cut telephone lines. Only a few days into the war, rumors of Jews smuggling gold in coffins and signaling the enemy triggered collective reprisals against Jewish communities in the kingdom. A British observer of the Russian army took at face value a story that a Jew carried a German officer in his sack. In a letter to his parents in the Chernihiv province, Private Maksym Chepurnyi complained that "damn Jews were spying on our units; . . . if caught red-handed they are shot; therefore, we pillage and burn [Jewish quarters] for their offenses."[12]

A senior Russian officer recalled his encounter with the Cossacks who had rounded up a group of Jewish "suspects": "'Who are they?' I inquired of a Cossack NCO. 'Spies, sir,' he replied. 'They cut telephone wires.' 'Did you see them doing that?' I asked. 'No, sir,' answered the Cossack, 'but it is said they did. At any rate, all Jews, whether Russian or the local ones, are against the Tsar.'"[13]

Were Jews indeed engaged in subversive activities on a mass scale that endangered the Russian army? Russian reports rarely contain the names of individual culprits, but rather overwhelmingly refer to the collective image of "the

Jew" as a subversive force. It stands to reason, therefore, that such an obsession with the omnipresent Jewish foe was generated by psychological factors rather than by the real situation in the field. As demonstrated by two recent studies of ethnic violence, fear of real or potential opponents' intention suffices to generate a preemptive strike.[14] In the summer of 1914, retreating Austrian units blew bridges and railroads and burned houses, and some detachments found themselves cut off and tried to break through Russian lines. In addition to the general battle, sporadic fighting flared up in the territory already occupied by Russian forces. Simultaneously, on entering East Galicia, Russian troops encountered three ethnic groups—Ukrainians, Poles, and Jews. Collective perceptions—enforced by the conduct of commanders and official propaganda—that the first two were to be considered as friendly and the third as hostile had been imprinted in the mindset of the Russian rank and file and officers. Hence, Russian security concerns were immediately directed against the potentially dangerous group—Jews—and the *anticipation* of Jewish subversive activities, therefore, played a much more crucial role in inciting violence than actual acts of sabotage did.

In East Galicia assaults on Jews evolved along a classic formula: rumors of Jewish subversion served as a crucial precipitant to the chain of "complementary projections"[15]—the ascription of hostile intentions to the Jews and immediate reprisals for their alleged crimes. For that matter, anti-Jewish violence in the 1880s and in 1904–1905 was also precipitated or accompanied by rumors that either insinuated "official" consent to beating the Jews or provided sensational accounts of Jewish revolutionary activities and outrages against Christian children.[16] In the context of wartime, reports and rumors of Jewish sabotage thrived on each other and attained characteristics applicable to the situation. For example, in mid-August, a rumor of a female Jewish assassin who had allegedly shot a Russian officer in Brody caused an investigation by Russian authorities, who found no evidence of the crime. In addition, the army filed no report of an officer's murder. Nevertheless, on September 10 the newspaper *Russkoe slovo* asserted that a Cossack officer was shot on from a window in Brody. The rumor served as a signal for an assault on the Brody Jewish quarters, which were shelled and looted.[17]

Some contemporaries suggested that Stavka itself disseminated rumors about Jewish spies and sharpshooters. Undoubtedly, the conduct of the supreme commander and his chief of staff provided ample proof that Stavka was also swayed by anti-Jewish paranoia. Nevertheless, it neither planned nor coordinated the pogroms. Violence demoralized the troops, and discipline, never the strongest asset of the Russian army, became a grave concern for senior officers who attempted to stop the rampages. The Russian administration that arrived in urban areas restored some semblance of order by issuing commands to maintain discipline and reportedly executing several Russian soldiers and local hoodlums for robberies.[18] In the countryside, however, looting and burning continued unabated and soon began affecting non-Jewish quarters as well. Such situations compelled Russian generals to take strong measures. On August 20, 1914, the commander of the Eighth Army, Lieutenant General Brusilov, appealed to his troops to "honor the rights of residents [of Galicia] regardless of nationality" and ordered that marauding and pillaging be stopped. He blamed the cavalry and rear units for excesses, although he admitted that some officers encouraged the crimes. Apparently the appeal bore no fruit, for on August 23 Brusilov found it necessary to issue yet another order to the same effect.[19]

The situation within the operational zone of Brusilov's neighbor, the Third Army, was no better, and the army command also issued several orders threatening looters with courts-martial. Finally, on September 2 the supreme commander addressed the people of Galicia. He promised that the army had come to liberate Galicia from the "foreign yoke" and that Russia sought "nothing but the re-establishment of rights and justice, . . . peace and harmony" in the region.[20] The possible impact of the appeal was, however, nullified by a clause authorizing burning and "complete destruction" of localities in which shooting at Russian troops took place. Although the grand duke meant territories in East Prussia, the order was distributed among all the armies and was undoubtedly taken by all commanders at face value. Two days later, Nicholas's appeal was emulated by the commander of the southwestern front, General Ivanov, who issued a directive to his armies advising caution and tolerance toward the population of Galicia. The fury of the pogroms, once aroused, however, was not easily subdued, and both appeals, distributed amid the sounds of broken windows and screams of violated women, had no visible effect on the troops. On September 3, army units joined local thugs in Stanisławów in plundering stores and Jewish houses. Anti-Jewish attacks also took place in Bohorodczany and Tarnopol, where soldiers demolished houses, gardens, and backyards. The destructive frenzy even affected some Jewish soldiers in the Russian units, who took part in the excesses.[21]

The brutality of the Russian army also bore on the non-Jewish population, whose houses were looted by passing units. Cossacks and soldiers particularly targeted Galician Germans, forcing them to dig trenches, thoroughly plundering their possessions, and severely flogging those who delayed in giving up their goods.[22] Nevertheless, although Russian soldiers did not shy from looting and robberies, rape and murder were rare in Ukrainian and German villages. On the other hand, no such inhibition was displayed toward the Jews, who were often murdered on the spot. Eyewitnesses recalled that some Jews were killed immediately by the pillaging units. The assailants took special pleasure in group-raping women and girls; some victims later committed suicide. As attacks on Jews spilled over to non-Jewish houses, it became common for Poles and Ukrainians to display icons on doors and windows to avoid the intruders.[23]

One of the most violent attacks took place in Lwów after the Russian military administration set up its offices. At first nothing forebode trouble when on September 26 the newly appointed governor of Galicia, Lieutenant General Count George Bobrinskii, addressed the residents of Galicia, professing universal religious toleration. Therefore, when on the afternoon of the next day gunfire burst out in the city, it took both the administration and the population by surprise. The first shots were fired in the city center, and in an ensuing stampede several people were trampled and wounded. No sooner had the echo of the first salvos subsided than rumors circulated that a Jew had fired at soldiers in the Jewish quarters. The soldiers allegedly returned fire. Moments later, files of soldiers were seen to have rushed to the Krakow square, the hub of affluent Jewish residents in the city. At the same time, mounted Cossacks fired at windows on Wałowa Street, a district of Jewish professionals and tradesmen. In vain, civilians and officers searched the sky trying to locate an enemy airplane, which, in their minds, was the target of the shooting. When darkness covered the city and the gunfire died down, rumors spread that many people had lost their lives.[24]

At night, when the city was recovering from shock, large details of soldiers swarmed the Jewish city quarters. Streets were cordoned off by patrols, which shot at windows. Cossacks and soldiers, accompanied by a local mob, broke into Jewish apartments and wine warehouses, and, after indulging themselves, began indiscriminate shooting. They searched and looted Jewish houses and beat residents regardless of sex and age. About three hundred Jews were arrested and taken to military detainment, where they were badly mauled. Several Jewish adults and children were reportedly killed on the spot and left on the sidewalk. Some local residents guided soldiers to Jewish apartments and took part in sharing the loot.[25]

On the following day the scarce information that the administration had at its disposal was solely based on rumors. Although the reports varied widely as to who had fired the first shot and the number of casualties involved, the bottom line remained the same—Jews had instigated the unrest. Soldiers and Cossacks related to the residents that a Jew had attempted to rob a Russian soldier. When apprehended, the thief fired at his pursuers and hid in a house in the Jewish quarters. According to another version, the omnipresent Jewish female assassin shot at the troops from a window. The only tangible evidence of the events was the death toll of between twenty and fifty and more than one hundred wounded.[26]

Although the investigation by the authorities soon came to a standstill, rumors of Jewish culpability were sufficient to justify reprisals. The city chief, Major General Eiche, ordered a roundup of the "usual" suspects, and several prominent Jews, including the renowned politician Herman Diamand, were arrested. When on Saturday, September 29, the frightened Jewish community kept the synagogues closed, Eiche interpreted it as defiance and forced the Jews to open the temples and perform services. To keep at bay potential disturbances, he also imposed a curfew on the city and ordered garret windows to be bricked up.[27]

Eiche's accusations against the Jews as the main instigators were reiterated and magnified by the local Russophile newspaper, *Prikarpatskaia Rus'*. The newspaper replaced a mysterious Jewish shooter with a more imposing story of an abortive Jewish uprising and insinuated that a "Jewish mob" had fired at "peaceful" Russian soldiers. The alleged uprising was immediately quelled by the army.[28] In turn, Jewish contemporaries accused the military administration of staging the pogrom and even alleged that some Jews had known beforehand what was in the offing and warned leaders of the Jewish community. It is doubtful, however, that the administration had concocted disturbances that disrupted the life of the city. Of note, in his report to Brusilov (nominally Lwów was within the jurisdiction of the Eighth Army), Bobrinskii did not blame the Jews for the shooting, but cautiously addressed the matter as a "firing from windows" in the course of which several Russian soldiers and Jews were wounded. Bobrinskii's concurrent report to Stavka triggered the indignation of Yanushkevich, who already had his own version of the event. Yanushkevich, in his letter to Bobrinskii, insisted that Jews were behind the shooting and demanded that harsh reprisals "regardless of ramifications" be carried out immediately. Apparently, he gave corresponding orders to the garrison commander in Lwów, for army patrols began arresting Jews for "creating panic" and "spreading rumors." The arrests started without Bobrinskii's consent and marked the inauguration of a bitter conflict between him and the chief of staff that would continue throughout the Russian occupation of Galicia.[29]

There are some indications that at least some Russian officials were involved in instigating the pogrom. On October 4, Eiche summoned three prominent Jews to his residence. He was accompanied by his deputy, Captain Yatsevich, who was identified by Jewish contemporaries as an officer of Okhrana. Eiche and Yatsevich charged Jews with the shooting and demanded that they surrender the culprit. Should the demand be not fulfilled, three hundred arrested Jews would be held accountable. If Yatsevich was indeed a member of the political police, then given the rivalry among different Russian administrative and police branches and the history of Okhrana in staging provocations, its connection to the events in Lwów should not be excluded entirely.[30]

On October 4, another assault on Jews in Lwów ended with two fatalities. Rumor served as a trigger when word spread that a Jewish barber had slit the throat of a Russian soldier. The Cossacks again went on a rampage, mugging several and killing two Jews. This time, however, the intervention of a Russian officer prevented further excesses.[31]

The Russification Campaign

In the wake of the Russian offensive in Galicia, a large-scale propaganda campaign, which underscored public euphoria in the initial stages of the war, presented the victories of Russian arms as a twofold achievement: the vindication of the country's defeat in the Russo-Japanese war and the final stroke in the national unification of "primordial" Russian lands. Already in September 1914 the political status of the region became a crucial issue discussed at the highest echelons of power. The army and the government immediately engaged in an animated exchange of opinions, each reflecting the different priorities of the two institutions. Inebriated by victories, Stavka pressed for the immediate solution to the "Galician question" in the favorable conditions of wartime. Namely, the grand duke and Yanushkevich argued that the direct integration of East Galicia into the empire would solve all political, legalistic, and administrative problems. Winning the Polish and Ukrainian populations to the Russian cause would facilitate this process. To this effect, Yanushkevich suggested to the Council of Ministers that Galician Poles, who had previously been the dominant ethnic group in the region, retain their political and social privileges. At the same time, a systematic "re-education" campaign, which would include conversion to Orthodoxy and the imposition of the Russian language in the school system, would turn Galician Ukrainians into loyal Russian subjects. Stavka had already initiated several steps in that direction. In his September appeal, the grand duke underlined the kinship between Russians and Ukrainians and postulated Russian aims in Galicia. He emphasized that the Russian offensive in Galicia was a response to the long-cherished dreams of the Russian people—the unification of all Russian lands into one state. Nicholas also called on Poles to join the struggle against the Central Powers and implied that their national aspirations would be fulfilled—Polish territories would be united under Russian rule. Stavka also issued corresponding instructions to the troops in the field. As a proof of goodwill, Russian troops distributed to the Christian population foodstuffs, wood, salt, and oil appropriated from the stores (particularly Jewish ones) whose owners had fled before the invasion. Simultaneously, the Russian press emphasized the common roots of Russians and Ukrainians and insinuated that "alien elements"—Jews, Germans, and Poles—controlled the Galician economy.[32]

The Russian government remained lukewarm to Stavka's political initiatives, however. The Ministry of Foreign Affairs and the Council of Ministers realized that the future of Galicia was to be decided within the context of two larger issues—the status of all the conquered territories (including those still controlled by the Central Powers) and Russian territorial aspirations in conjunction with the Allied war aims. Hence, in mid-September 1914 the Ministry of Foreign Affairs and the Council of Ministers considered several drafts regarding the future administrative and political status of Poland and East Galicia. In spite of disagreements regarding whether the desired measures should be implemented immediately or only after the termination of hostilities, the majority of ministers consented to the treatment of East Galicia and West Galicia as two different political entities. After a series of deliberations with the Allies in regard to the postwar geopolitical reconstruction of eastern Europe, Russian ministers agreed to a blueprint for the conquered territories—East Galicia and Bukovina were to be integrated into the empire; West Galicia, Poznań, and Silesia were to be included in the kingdom. Similar to its enemies and allies, the Russian government thought that the war would not last long. Therefore, it decided that the implementations of immediate war aims should take precedence over political measures, which had to be postponed until the end of the war.[33]

Deliberating high politics, the government effectively left the issues of the regional policies and administration in the hands of the army, which for a while ruled Galicia alone. In Lwów the army commenced its rule by requesting sixteen hostages, four for each ethnolinguistic group—Poles, Ukrainians, Jews, and Russophiles. Despite equality in the numbers of hostages, other measures indicated that the military rule was clearly tainted by an ideological and ethnic approach. Although Stavka requested government subsidies for Ukrainian peasants, it was highly suspicious of nationally conscious Greek Catholic Ukrainians, whom the Russians labeled "mazepists."[34] Consequently, the Russian command ordered the arrests of Greek Catholic priests and prominent Ukrainian leaders suspected of a pro-Austrian orientation. By direct orders of General Brusilov, Metropolitan Andrej Sheptyts'kyi was deported to Russia. The attitude toward the Jews manifested itself on September 11, when the Lwów military commandant, General Sergei Sheremetiev, summoned five prominent Jews to his quarters. The general accused the whole Galician Jewry of cutting telephone lines, selling alcohol, and lowering the value of the ruble. Should these crimes continue, warned Sheremetiev, he would not hesitate to punish the Jews with all the severity of wartime laws.[35]

On September 18, the army promulgated an order that prohibited the sale of liquor and banned all clubs and educational facilities except regular schools. Publications in foreign languages of a "hostile disposition"—German and Yiddish—were forbidden. In addition, a special "Provisionary Statute" prohibited schooling in these languages and stipulated the dismissal of German and Jewish teachers. On September 19 a new order prohibited the sale and reading of books published outside of the empire and a ban on artistic performances and exhibitions without the permission of censorship. Simultaneously with the issuance of these orders, military commandants in Lwów, Tarnopol, and Stanisławów began the dismissal of Jewish civil employees.[36]

On September 18, the army rule officially ended when a newly appointed governor-general, George Bobrinskii, arrived in Lwów to assume his post. It appears that he owed his appointment to the good offices of the grand duke, with whom he had once served, and to the fame of his cousin Vladimir Bobrinskii, an ardent Pan-Slavist, whose name was popular among Galician Russophiles. Although some Jewish contemporaries portrayed Bobrinskii as a notorious anti-Semite, the governor-general displayed no special anti-Jewish propensities. The notoriety he attained among the Jews most likely occurred because in his capacity as governor-general he personified the hated Russian rule and because his cousin was known for anti-Semitic diatribes. In addition, although he shared the anti-Semitic prejudices of his time, Bobrinskii's disposition toward the Jews paled in comparison to the morbid anti-Semitism of his two superiors, General Yanushkevich and the grand duke.[37]

Bobrinskii was directly subordinate to the quartermaster-general of the southwestern front, Lieutenant General A. Zabelin (in December of 1914 he was replaced by Lieutenant General A. Mavrin). The general government was divided into four provinces—Lwów, Tarnopol, Czernowitz (Bukovina), and, later, Przemyśl—headed by provincial governors. Similar to the territorial organization of the empire, districts, cities, and towns were governed by chiefs (*nachal'niki uyezdov* and *gradonachal'niki*). In theory Bobrinskii enjoyed almost unlimited power in the general government and could impose martial law, collect taxes, and deport individuals considered hostile to the Russian cause.[38]

In reality, however, the army also retained its power in Galicia. In each province, district, and town it had its own representatives, commandants, who ran army supply depots, hospitals, and reserve units. The commandants were answerable to divisional and corps commanders, who, in turn, had their own superiors—army commanders Brusilov and N. Ruzskii (the latter was replaced in September 1914 by Lieutenant General Radko-Dmitriev). The two generals could issue their own directives and orders and often acted without the consent of the governor-general. A similar situation prevailed within the regional police and security branches. Headed by Colonel Alexander Mezentsov

(Mezentsev), the Temporary Gendarme Department became a part of the military administration and directly subordinated to Bobrinskii. The gendarmes, however, had their own commander, the chief of the Gendarme Corps, whose instructions would often run afoul of those of the governor-general and competed for supremacy with other police and security branches —the regular police and military counterintelligence. Therefore, Russian power in Galicia was based on two bodies—the front zone was within the army's jurisdiction, and the governorship-general acted as the civil administration in the rear. Their directives and actions with regard to the occupied territories were hectic, frequently contradicted one another, and lacked organizational planning.[39]

Russian protestations of fraternal unity among Slavs immediately conflicted with the realities of the occupation. A number of restrictions severely curtailed the cultural freedom and economic activities of the region. After forbidding liquor sales and banning educational institutions, the Russians made the opening of schools contingent on the political reliability of the teachers and their knowledge of the Russian language. Work hours of stores and restaurants were also limited, and travel was circumscribed. The Russian ruble was made a monetary medium at a much higher rate than before the war—thirty kopeks for one Austrian kron (in peacetime the rate was sixty kopeks for one kron). Correspondence was accepted only in the Russian, German, Polish, Czech, Romanian, French, and English languages; letters and telegrams in Yiddish and Ukrainian were destroyed. In several localities, the local administration began changing street signs from Polish and German to Russian.[40]

On September 23, Bobrinskii addressed the Russophile and Polish delegations and laid out his vision of Russian rule in Galicia. He assured the gathering that the Russian army had arrived to liberate "brother-Slavs" from the Austrian "yoke." Bobrinskii guaranteed all residents freedom of language and religion and promised that the inner life of Galicia's residents would not be disturbed. He also pledged to the Jewish representatives, two rabbis and the city vice mayor, Filip Schleicher, who temporarily retained his post, the safety of the Jewish community provided that Jews maintained law and order. It portended particularly ill for the Jews when Bobrinskii declared that Galicia was a "primordial" Russian land in which he intended to impose the Russian language and law. Two days later, on September 25, the clock on the Lwów city hall tower was switched to St. Petersburg time. A new era was ushered in for Galicia.[41]

From the beginning of the occupation, Russian treatment of local residents depended on whether a specific group belonged to a "friendly" or "hostile" ethnic community. Galician Germans were immediately targeted by the administration as unreliable and subjected to harassment and searches, and in the months of September and October the army arrested several hundred of the German intelligentsia and deported them to the empire. The property of the deportees was confiscated.[42] The Russians cracked down especially hard on the mazepists, whose anti-Russian propaganda activities and partisan struggle behind Russian lines greatly alarmed imperial authorities. To eradicate the danger, the Russian administration undertook several measures to extinguish the Ukrainian language. Teachers were brought from the empire to introduce the Russian language in schools, and the Council of Ministers financed teaching courses in Galicia, St. Petersburg, and Kiev, with emphasis on Russian language, literature, and history. Although initially shop owners were permitted to display signboards in Russian, Polish, and Ukrainian, the last of these languages was soon disallowed. Ukrainian newspapers were closed, and cultural organizations were disbanded and their property and assets confiscated.[43]

Professing religious tolerance, the military administration nevertheless assisted the Russian Orthodox Church in the forcible proselytizing campaign, which affected entire Ukrainian villages. In November 1914, the newspaper of the military administration, *L'vovskoye voennoye slovo,* proudly reported that in the course of two months, thirty thousand Ukrainians had converted to Orthodoxy. The Greek Catholic priests were expelled from parishes, and their houses were taken over by the Orthodox Church. Speaking in the Lwów Preobrazhenskii Church on December 7, 1914, the Russian archbishop Evlogii, who had arrived from Volhynia to "teach" Orthodoxy in Galicia, emphasized that "from the Pacific Ocean to the Carpathians the Russian people constitute one nation, one soul, one heart, one church, and one prayer. . . . The arrival of the victorious Russian army has ended the centuries-long separation between the Galician-Russians and Russia."[44]

Russian attitudes toward the Polish population were a continuation of the prewar carrot-and-stick policy. Although more than a century of Russian rule in Poland had convinced the government that Poles remained implacable enemies, the political situation during the war advised a more cautious approach to the problem. The Russian army appreciated the strength of Polish political groups and the economic power of the Polish nobility, and the appeal of the supreme commander in September 1914 was but one attempt at Polish-Russian reconciliation. The military administration kept close contacts with the Endeks, who advocated collaboration with Russia; retained the bulk of Polish civil employees in their posts; allowed Polish newspapers to function; and avoided confrontation with the Roman Catholic Church. Nevertheless, strict censorship controlled the press and schooling, and Polish politicians and officers suspected of anti-Russian orientation were deported to Russia. Nor was

Russia's claim to Galicia as the "primordial Russian lands" appreciated by the Poles, who did not fail to see the potential menace in such a declaration.[45]

Relations between Russian authorities and civilians were further aggravated by new prohibitions and regulations. Considering the property and belongings of those who fled Galicia—especially Jews and Germans—fair game, the military administration initiated steps for the mass appropriation of abandoned estates, houses, and financial assets. On October 23, Stavka authorized Bobrinskii to issue a decree stipulating the confiscation of property in several categories: individuals who had fled Galicia except those who had left managers in their estates, those suspected in anti-Russian activities, and "unreliable" and "fraudulent" Jews. The confiscated property was put at the disposition of the local administration. The same decree provided for the confiscation of the bank accounts of persons "hostile to Russia." Because the Austrians retaliated by announcing that the same measures would be taken against Russian deposits in Austrian banks, however, the Council of Ministers protested against this action. Although Goremykin supported Stavka's initiative, the ministers still debated whether Galicia should be treated as an integral part of Russia, as Russian propaganda maintained, or as an occupied territory. In the latter case, bank accounts could be "lawfully" confiscated. The ever-zealous Yanushkevich insisted that Galicia be immediately "equalized" with Russia and thus made liable to imperial laws. Stavka and the government reached a compromise whereby on November 23 the government newspaper *Pravitel'stvennyi vestnik* announced that the property of "hostile elements" in Galicia was liable for confiscation. Two days later it was announced that individuals who committed war crimes such as sedition and espionage and resisted Russian authorities were to be tried by courts-martial. Still, the government exercised caution. After a series of meetings, on November 28 the Council of Ministers decided that the confiscation of bank assets and the full implementation of Russian laws were to be put on hold until the end of the war.[46]

Nevertheless, Stavka was undeterred in its efforts to make Galicia Russian, and its nationalizing campaign struck the Galician Jewry particularly hard. Although all of Galicia's residents were subjected to economic regulations, arbitrary requisitions, limitation on movement, and prohibitions of language and schooling, Jews, unlike their neighbors, had to endure suffering of a different nature. If for the Russians the assimilation of Ukrainians and cooptation of the Poles seemed feasible, neither option was even considered with regard to the Jews. Stavka was determined to eradicate Jewish economic and cultural influence in Galicia as one of the last vestiges of Austrian rule, and, concurrently, the subjugation of Jews would herald the beginning of the full nationalization of Galicia. The campaign against Galician Jews was also consistent with a national drive against what were considered enemy aliens within the empire, which aimed at gradual elimination of foreigners from the imperial socioeconomic sphere.

Jewish landowning and land leasing in Galician villages were a special concern for the Russian administration. Within the empire, Russian laws restricted Jews from residing in villages and from owning property outside cities and towns of the Pale of Settlement. Jewish farmers, however, were allowed to settle in colonies in south Russia, Belorussia, and Bessarabia, where many engaged in agriculture. In Galicia, the number of Jews who owned land and made their living from agriculture was larger than in Russia, and Jews leased land from Polish landlords and Ukrainian peasants. From the Russian point of view, such a situation in the countryside constituted the sole basis of Jewish economic power in the region. The problem required immediate attention, and in mid-September Stavka sent the vice director of its diplomatic bureau, N. Basili, to Galicia to investigate the issue on the spot. On September 23, Basili sent his report to Yanushkevich. Knowing full well the expectations of his boss, Basili asserted that the Ukrainian population of Galicia was well disposed to the Russians and expected the Russians to free them from the "Jewish yoke." Jews, on the other hand, sabotaged the efforts of the Russian administration by withdrawing coinage from circulation and jacking up prices. Therefore, to strike at the Jews and to win over Ukrainians to the Russian cause, he suggested the application of Russian imperial laws in Galicia and the confiscation of Jewish landholdings. To make his point, Basili inflated Jewish landholdings, which averaged 8 percent of the total, to 35 percent.[47]

Basili's report made a strong impression on the grand duke, who wrote in the margin that the army should give the Jews a "lesson" (*ostrastka*).[48] The report also electrified Yanushkevich, who integrated it into his own memorandum to Prime Minister Goremykin on October 2. Yanushkevich relegated the Polish and Ukrainian questions to long-range concerns, which were to be approached gradually and cautiously. At the same time, he insisted that the Jewish question be dealt with instantly. Yanushkevich reiterated accusations that Jews were mortal enemies of the Russian state and that the war provided a rare opportunity to appropriate the property of Jews who had fled Galicia. The chief of staff insisted that the Russian government implement "every possible means" to combat the Jewish peril and said that the supreme commander and the tsar had already approved a plan to that effect. Yanushkevich suggested that the "ultimate" solution to the Jewish question in Galicia was to be carried out concomitantly with the same measures undertaken in Russia.[49]

War, stressed Yanushkevich, provided a rare opportunity for the official abolition of Jewish landowning once Galician Jews were "granted" Russian citizenship and treated as subjects of the Russian Empire. Their deportation east of the Pale of Settlement and the subsequent confiscation of land would then pose no legal problems. The urgings of the chief of staff, however, fell on deaf ears. Although in the fall of 1914 the Council of Ministers considered the expropriation of property belonging to foreigners and Russian citizens of German, Austrian, and Turkish extraction, the government was concerned that such measures in Galicia would antagonize Polish landowners, whose lands Jews leased. Despite a long-term goal to curb the economic power of Polish landowners in the kingdom, the complexity of Galicia's ethnic issues required a subtler approach. Therefore, much to the general's chagrin, Goremykin replied that it was premature to make decisions about Jewish citizenship, and Galician Jews, he implied, were still to be treated as the subjects of Austro-Hungary.[50]

Yanushkevich's appeals to the government were echoed by a broad propaganda campaign by the Russian right-wing parties, which fulminated about Jewish sabotage in the rear of the Russian army. They insisted that wartime was a godsend opportunity to solve once and for all the Jewish question by collecting all Jews in the cities that were about to be overrun by the Central Powers and stripping them of Russian citizenship. After the recapture of these cities, Jews should be expelled to Germany as foreign subjects and their property confiscated. As vitriolic was the Russophile press in Galicia, which portrayed Jews as a deadly threat to Russia and stressed that the liberation of the region would be complete only after the army eliminated Jewish influence in the region.[51] Prominent Russophiles such as Volodymyr Dudykevych and Roman Gerovskii were appointed as advisors to the army and the military administration and offered similar solutions to the Jewish issue through the complete Russification of the school system and the confiscation and redistribution of Polish and Jewish landholdings. Gerovskii, for example, assured the military administration that in Galicia and Bukovina "everybody was an anti-Semite" and that anti-Jewish measures would raise the popularity of the Russian regime. Nonetheless, the military administration realized that such drastic measures would disrupt the functioning of the regional economy and directly affect the army, which depended on supplies from Galicia. Bobrinskii, therefore, ignored the urgings of the Russophiles.[52]

In contrast, Yanushkevich was indefatigable in his efforts to cleanse Galicia of Jewish influence. He bombarded the government with other proposals, such as rewarding Russian soldiers who had distinguished themselves in battle with the land confiscated in Galicia. The Council of Ministers also turned it down. The rabid anti-Semitism of the chief of staff was shared by a significant number of Russian officials in Galicia, who were troubled by similar concerns. In a report to the chancellery of the general government, the chief of the Lwów district, Count Lamsdorf, complained of "pernicious" Jewish influences within the local administration and the police. The "Jewish danger," concluded

Lamsdorf, could be foiled only through the forcible sale of Jewish-owned land. He went as far as accusing Jews of inciting Russian troops to wreak destruction on the Galician countryside and corrupting the Russian police. Jews, according to Lamsdorf, had acquired compromising service records of Russian policemen who had been transferred to Galicia. Fearing blackmail, the hapless police became a mere tool in Jewish hands. Lamsdorf, therefore, insisted that only forcible sale of Jewish land through the Land Bank would amend the situation and deprive Jews of their economic power.[53] Lamsdorf's insinuations that Jews themselves provoked the pogroms became a routine method used by Russian officials to exonerate anti-Jewish brutalities. On the other hand, the allegations that Jews bribed the Russian police were not far from the truth, for imperial policemen had traditionally been known as greedy and corrupt. An observer from Russia noticed that corruption within all of Galicia's police and security branches was rampant, and prisons were crowded with people whose only fault was that they were unable to bribe the police. Policemen, especially on a district level, were individuals of low capacity and a dubious past, who, left without supervision, behaved like "little satraps." They launched a true hunt for Jewish peddlers and merchants, confiscating their property for alleged offenses and releasing it on being bribed. Accordingly, Galician Jews soon learned that bribes and gratuities were the most efficient tools to avoid arrests and confiscations.[54]

The Żółkiew district chief reiterated Lamsdorf's accusations, reporting to the Lwów governor that in the village of Żółtaniec, Jews and mazepists intimidated peasants by predicting a forthcoming return of the Austrians. The chief of the Rawa Ruska district, the collegiate assessor Golubev, went further than his colleagues and stated that in their anti-Russian zeal the Jews even forsook profitable deals in preference for sabotage in the army rear. Golubev claimed that after Rawa became the center of field and reserve hospitals, Jews refused to sell meat to the army, condemning wounded soldiers to starvation. Another Russian official, D. Chikhachev, in letters to General Zabelin and Goremykin, stressed the favorable moment for the "solution of the Jewish question"—the confiscation of Jewish land and the deportation of Jewish lessees and landowners to Russia. He pointed out that after the war the "philosemitic" stance of the Allies would impede any radical anti-Jewish measures. Chikhachev was also aghast at the prospect that the issue could be relegated to the Duma, where the abolition of Jewish landowning might be opposed by liberals and Polish landowners.[55]

Pressed by Stavka, on November 16 Bobrinskii, who kept maintaining that any measures in regard to Jewish landownership should be implemented only after the war, petitioned Zabelin to create a special committee to investigate the issue. In December the committee started collecting cadastres in the countryside and in January 1915 reported back to the administration. According to the collected data, in twenty Galician districts Jews owned 214,578 morg of land (one morg equaled 0.6 hectare)—or 8.1 percent of the total. The distribution of Jewish landownership was very uneven, however. In some areas, such as Rawa Ruska, Jews owned about 25 percent of the land, whereas in the Buczacz district they owned 4.3 percent and in Komarno 0.51 percent. The final findings were to be completed by the late spring of 1915.[56]

Bobrinskii's actions, however, did not satisfy his superiors, who believed that he did not pursue the Jewish question with sufficient zeal. The disagreements between the governor-general and Stavka soon erupted into an open confrontation. On December 16, 1914, General Zabelin demanded that Russian Jews be forbidden to enter Galicia and Galician Jews be barred from entering the empire. Bobrinskii opposed this measure on the grounds that due to the specific socioeconomic position of Jews who had been employed as army suppliers, such measures would instantly affect war provisions. In addition, driven to desperation, Jews would be more determined to engage in sabotage and resistance. Hence, he suggested that the prohibition of the Jewish movement in Galicia ought to be implemented gradually. Because the quartermaster-general was adamant, on December 26 Bobrinskii appealed to General Ivanov and complained of Zabelin's political shortsightedness. Zabelin was backed up by the chief of staff of the southwestern front, Lieutenant General Mikhail Alekseev, who informed Bobrinskii that the directive had originated from the supreme commander.[57]

Stavka intervened immediately. In an offensive tone Yanushkevich sharply reprimanded Bobrinskii for "toleration" of massive Jewish espionage in Galicia. The chief of staff insisted that the decree to limit the movement of Jews within the region be immediately carried out and that brutal reprisals against Jews were the only means to break Jewish resistance. As life in the general government became unbearable for Jews, it would prompt their mass exodus abroad. Finally, a compromise was reached whereby Yanushkevich and Zabelin consented to a discreet prohibition of the Jewish movement. Bobrinskii, in turn, was authorized to expel Russian Jewish merchants who had come to Galicia.[58]

While the generals battled each other over appropriate anti-Jewish measures, the middle- and low-level Russian officials effectively carried out their own "economic sanctions" against Jews, which in reality meant mostly uninhibited robbery and extortion. At least half of the Russian officials in Galicia appointed as city and district chiefs had previously served in the army or were recalled from the reserve; the commandants were cadre officers. For the majority it was the first time they held both military and civil power, and they apparently saw little difference between the two. Moreover, a sense of independence from distant superiors bred beliefs that they could rule as they pleased. As products of their time, many held anti-Jewish sentiments, and they did not hesitate to take from the Jews whatever struck their fancy or have Jews flogged for not complying with ransom demands. The practice of extorting money from Jews became a common occurrence. Jews were routinely accused of various transgressions, detained, and released on the payment of a ransom. In November 1914 the chief of the Czernowitz district, Yevreinov, reported to Bobrinskii that because many Jews left town with Austrian troops, it was impossible to collect "contribution." Yevreinov, therefore, suggested confiscating the Jewish National Home—an educational and cultural institution—whose worth was two hundred thousand rubles. Bobrinskii granted permission.[59]

In Lwów the administration used the September pogrom as the pretext to confiscate three buildings that belonged to affluent Jews and Poles. At the same time, the city commandant threatened the Jewish community with hostage taking and reprisals unless hefty ransom was paid. After telephone lines were damaged in the vicinity of Kołomyja (possibly by peasants who often used cable for household purposes), the governor, Lobanov-Rostovskii, demanded that either the Jewish community pay a heavy fine or be expelled from the town. The Kołomyja commandant, Sechin, went even further by imposing a fine on the Jews without giving any reason. Terrorized by plundering and constant requisitions by the commandant and passing troops, Jews paid the large sum of one hundred thousand kron in cash and gave up valuables. The army also imposed a heavy fine on the entire city of Stanisławów for alleged sabotage—thirty-six thousand kron for Jews and fourteen thousand for non-Jews. Professing goodwill toward Poles and Ukrainians, the local commandant collected only the fine imposed on Jews.[60]

Anti-Jewish policies along the eastern front received new momentum in the winter of 1914–1915. By this time the Russian advance westward had brought about a half-million Jews under Russian control, just at the time when Stavka was trying to get rid of Jews in Poland and Kurland. Yanushkevich and the grand duke had calculated that economic restrictions, requisitions of property, and loss of jobs would expedite voluntary Jewish migration abroad. Instead, these measures caused mass internal migration of Jews rather than exodus abroad. By December 1914, more than forty thousand Jews from the countryside had moved to Lwów alone. Other urban centers were also flooded with thousands of Jewish refugees, causing the outbreak of epidemics and drastic economic shortages.[61]

Nor did the government decree of December 16, 1914, which stipulated that all Austro-Hungarian and German subjects leave the Russian Empire, bring the desired results. Because the ways to implement this measure in the front zone were not specified, passage to Austria or Hungary through Russian positions was out of the question, and anyone apprehended near the front line was suspected of espionage. For example, on January 19, 1915, the Russians detained in a Lwów prison twenty-four Jewish families, altogether thirty-six adults and thirty-three children, who had tried to cross into Hungary. A voyage to a neutral country via Finland and Sweden required a substantial amount of money, and because the majority of Galician Jews had already been financially ruined, only a few could afford such a trip.[62]

Stavka stepped up its anti-Jewish drive after the tsar, on February 26, signed the so-called Liquidation Law prepared by the Council of Ministers. The law provided for the liquidation of landownership by Austro-Hungarian and German subjects within a 160-kilometer zone of the front line, and in Galicia the army began sequestration of land belonging to the Poles who had left the region at the beginning of the war. Concomitantly, Yanushkevich blamed the Galician military administration for being inexcusably lenient toward Jews. The chief of staff stressed to Bobrinskii that because Jews "terrorized" the local population, severe reprisals and confiscation of Jewish warehouses should be launched immediately. Visibly offended, Bobrinskii retorted that he professed no leniency toward Jews and that many Jewish leather, textile, and metal warehouses and storage areas had already been confiscated. The governor-general could not resist adding that if "Jewish terror" had indeed taken place, it could have happened *only* within the army's zone of jurisdiction. Nevertheless, he ordered that the compilation of data on Jewish property in the region be stepped up.[63]

On February 26, the supreme commander issued an order that, worded as a response to Jewish resistance, forbade Jews from entering Galicia and from moving from one district to another. Jewish spies and hostages would be hanged, and those who moved from place to place without permission would be liable to three months of detention. The order mockingly exempted Jews who wished to resettle voluntarily to Siberia. Because deported individuals were allowed to posses only five hundred rubles per family, the order dealt a severe blow to Jews, who would have only minimal means to support their families on a long journey. The war severed Jewish economic ties with Austria and Russia, and the limitation on travel drastically reduced Jewish trade in Galicia. The February prohibition effectively shut them off from markets in neighboring districts. On March 23 Jews were prohibited from buying and selling copper and other metals. An immediate result of these limitations was a rapid rise in prices, smuggling on an unprecedented scale, and shortages of war supplies. The army, in turn, bombarded Stavka with reports that Jews sabotaged Russia's war efforts.[64]

At the same time, Stavka stepped up its nationalizing campaign. The army was concerned that a number of Galician Jews still retained their positions in the regional civil service. Yanushkevich again appeared at the head of the struggle against "Jewish predominance" (*zasil'ye*). From the beginning of the war, he had written several letters to the Council of Ministers pointing to what he called a "deplorable" situation in Galicia's court system. He was particularly appalled by the fact that "non-Christian" employees were paid by the Russian state and, despite the shortages of competent workers, ordered that all Jewish employees be fired. In January 1915 Yanushkevich complained to the minister of justice, N. Shcheglovitov, about Jews employed in Galician courts and prisons. The minister suggested that Alexander Gesse, the procurator of the Warsaw court board, be sent to Galicia to investigate the situation. On March 2, 1915, Stavka prepared a memorandum that provided for the restructuring of the Galician judicial system and facilitated the dismissal of Jews. By that time, in the nine districts of Galicia (including the western districts of Lisko, Rymanów, Łańcut, Przeworsk, and Jarosław) out of seven hundred Jews previously employed in Austrian administration, only thirteen retained their posts. In the Tarnopol province all Jewish civil employees, including court doormen and firemen, were fired. The mass dismissal of Jews brought chaos to the regional civil service, and the administration, contrary to Yanushkevich's orders, still retained fifty-five Jewish employees in provincial and district courts, the fire department, hospitals, and the prisons. Gesse, who arrived in Galicia in March, "uncovered" these Jews and informed the chief of staff. On June 19, a day before the Russians pulled out of Lwów, Stavka issued the last orders to dismiss all Jews from the judicial institutions.[65]

How did Galician Jews react to the torments that befell them during the Russian occupation? After all, the utmost concern of the Russian military was a coordinated Jewish opposition, which allegedly included sabotage, anti-Russian propaganda, armed resistance, and international financial pressure on the Russian government. In reality, however, Jews were able neither to protect themselves from Russian persecution nor to influence any great power to apply pressure on Russia on their behalf. The outbreak of the war and the swift Russian advance took Galician Jews as much by surprise as their coreligionists in Kurland and the kingdom. Hundreds of thousands of Galician Jews, including political activists, fled to cities or to Austria, Hungary, and the Czech lands. Russian terror demoralized those who stayed in Galicia, and Jews were too deeply divided along ideological lines to offer any concrete counteraction to Russia. The traditional pacifism of Orthodox Jews effectively prevented the Galician Jewish community from engaging in any kind of resistance, and the most active elements among socialists and Zionists fled westward during the Russian invasion. Within the first six months of the occupation, Jews practically disappeared from any positions of influence, while confiscations, pogroms, and robberies left Jewish communities economically ruined.

The success of the Russian nationalizing campaign could be judged by the descriptions of An-Ski, who during his passage through Galicia in the fall and winter of 1914–1915 found no Jews on trains or in railroad stations. They moved at night on country roads, circumventing larger towns, often under guard of a soldier whom they had hired. Jewish shops, synagogues, and warehouses had been either plundered or appropriated by the local military; Poles and Ukrainians took over empty Jewish houses or simply dismantled them for firewood. A fear of reprisals and utmost despair gripped Jews exposed to exorbitant fines or conscripted into labor details. The third largest ethnic group in Galicia, Jews became pariahs in their own land, and in this regard, the Russian military indeed succeeded in "integrating" Jews into the imperial order. All forms of Jewish civil life disappeared. City mayors, often Russian-installed Russophiles, shut down Jewish schools, and children begged on streets or turned to prostitution.[66]

The Jewish leadership tried to alleviate the plight of their coreligionists by raising money to finance kitchens for the homeless and vocational schools for poor Jewish children. They also negotiated with Russian authorities. Due to these efforts, in January of 1915 Bobrinskii permitted the Lwów community to set up an aid committee headed by a Petersburg Jew, David Feinberg. The committee collected and distributed to Jews medical and financial aid, food, and clothing. The distribution of foreign aid, however, which was largely from American Jews, was taken over by the Russian administration.[67] The aid, moreover, was inadequate given the numbers of the needy. The majority of the Jews, therefore, tried simply to survive by any means. Some Jewish merchants learned the Russian language for economic transactions. Many turned to speculation, causing popular resentment. Others collected arms on battlefields and sold them to Russian merchants, who, free of ideological prejudices, came to Galicia in large numbers and bought on a wholesale basis everything of value.[68]

In some instances, Russian reports of Jewish resistance did contain a grain of truth. For example, in August 1914 prominent Galician and Bukovinian Jews issued appeals to their compatriots to participate actively in the anti-Russian struggle and to make all possible sacrifices for the victory of Austrian arms. These appeals made a strong impression on Yanushkevich, who hastened to send one copy to the tsar to demonstrate the ill intentions of the Jews toward the empire.[69] The resentment of the Jews toward the occupiers was also reflected in various forms of civic disobedience. Despite explicit decrees by the administration, many Jews, alongside Poles and Ukrainians, provided food, clothing, and tobacco to the columns of German and Austrian prisoners of war who were escorted through Galician cities and towns. In some localities, such as Brody, Jews sheltered Austrian prisoner-of-war escapees and Jewish deserters from the Russian army. After some Galician towns and villages were liberated, Jewish informants denounced to Austrian authorities Poles and Ukrainians who had collaborated with the Russians.[70]

Jewish merchants preferred the Austrian kron to the Russian ruble, and from the Russian point of view the refusal to accept the imperial currency was a particularly serious offense. Although some individuals may have acted out of patriotic considerations, however, for the majority of Jewish merchants and tradesmen it was unprofitable to operate in rubles, especially in the light of the fluctuating situation on the front. According to Russian reports, in addition to ignoring the ruble, Jews were also most active in spreading rumors of Russia's misfortunes on battlefields and predicting the inevitable return of Austrian troops.[71] Although it can be taken for granted that all residents of Galicia were prone to hearsay, Jews, subjected to the most brutal horrors of the Russian occupation, became a source of rumors as the way to defy their oppressors and verbalize hopes for forthcoming liberation.

All the aforementioned episodes, however, scarcely measured up to the wave of charges proffered against Jews by the Russian military. With little proof of Jewish resistance, the security branches and Stavka appealed to emotions rather than the reasoning capacities of generals and soldiers, stressing that all Jews, Russian and foreign, rich and poor, religious and secular, were hostile and intrinsically evil. Treatment of Jews, therefore, depended much on the willingness of a local commandant, an official, or a military judge to separate rumors from proven events and act on the latter. This the majority of Russian officials refused to do.

If by the end of 1914 the Russian administration had endeavored to evaluate its five-month rule in Galicia, it would have had little positive to report. Contrary to expectations, the relationship between the occupational regime and the Christian population was at its lowest point, and the latter was exasperated by fixed prices, restrictions, and requisitions. Promises of justice and order had long been abandoned for war necessities. Police surveillance and arrests of suspects had promoted an atmosphere of fear and instability in the region. Economic difficulties had resulted in the overcrowding of towns and cities.

Most ominous, however, was Russia's situation on the front and in the rear. Although by January 1915 East Galicia was occupied and the Hungarian plains lay exposed to Russian invasion, Russian armies had suffered a serious setback in northeastern Poland. A major offensive in the Carpathians had also bogged down. Huge casualties—in the first five months of the war Russia lost more than a million killed and wounded—clearly indicated to the Russian leadership that the war had just begun and that total war and economic mobilization was the only solution to the dire situation. Because military defeats had to be ascribed to reasons other than mere incompetence, poor discipline, and corruption of Russian military and civil authorities, the ethnic groups considered hostile were blamed for debilitating Russia's war efforts. Conceived as defensive measures, the nationalization campaign in the empire brought economic ruin to thousands of those regarded as enemy aliens, while the Russifying efforts of the military regime in Galicia effectively relegated the Galician Jewry to a pariah status.

3 / Russia's Internal Front
Expulsions and Deportations

During the first six months of the war, the Russian military's efforts to bring Galicia into line with the rest of the empire demonstrated the gap between grand imperial visions and the realities of occupation. Failure to achieve the envisioned plans was partially a result of more moderate policies of the Russian government, but it also derived from the lack of trained administrators and, ultimately, time. Although it was aghast at the unwillingness of the government to integrate Galicia into the empire, the military also attributed the difficulties in governing the occupied province to the machinations of internal foes, among whom Jews occupied a particular place. Although the initial stages of Russian occupation were replete with bloodshed and destruction in Jewish settlements and urban quarters, the assaults lacked an organized pattern. Eventually, however, the military began to mount more coordinated efforts in its struggle against what it saw as its internal enemies, displacing en masse Jews and Germans in the kingdom and Kurland. Concomitantly, Stavka and the army stepped up expulsions of Galician Jews.

The removal of "unreliable" ethnic groups from strategic areas was included in Russian contingency planning before the outbreak of World War I. On July 20, 1914, ten days prior to the declaration of war, the Russian General Staff and the Ministry of the Interior issued orders to the army to deport German citizens from several areas in Kurland, around Riga and Suwałki. Soon thereafter the command of the southwestern military district ordered the deportation of German and Austro-Hungarian citizens within its jurisdiction to beyond the Ural Mountains. Initially, the military aimed at preventing able-bodied foreign males from being drafted into enemy armies, but starting in mid-August deportations also engulfed women, children, and the elderly. At the same time, the first deportations of Russian Jews accused of assisting the enemy began in Poland. Russian suspicions were magnified by German propaganda directed at Polish Jews and the preferential treatment accorded to them by the troops of the Central Powers.[1]

The deportations aimed at achieving two objectives: depriving the enemy of potential recruits and "cleansing" the front zone of potentially unreliable minorities. Concurrently, the army also practiced hostage taking to ensure the security of Russian communications. Whereas large-scale deportations were planned by Stavka, local commanders increasingly expelled allegedly unreliable groups outside the areas of their jurisdiction as a defensive measure against potential saboteurs. At the end of October, Nicholas II visited the western front and listened to the litany of grievances about putative Jewish sabotage. Although the tsar may have approved harsh measures against Jews, the army needed no special permission to that effect because the "Regulations for Field Administration of the Army in Wartime" empowered Stavka to take any security measures it deemed necessary.[2]

Hostage taking accelerated in mid-October, and the first secretary of Stavka's diplomatic bureau, V. Muraviev, wrote to Foreign Minister Sazonov that these measures were "bearing good results." Publicly, Muraviev denied that atrocities were perpetrated against civilians and stressed that "strict means" were applied only to Jews who had persecuted the Russophiles during the Russian retreat from Bukovina. On October 3, General Ivanov issued an order that emphasized the increased "espionage activities of the Jews, German colonists, and the vagabonds of different kinds." Henceforth, troops of the southwestern front were authorized to act "with determination" and to use arms against individuals suspected of spying.[3] On November 27, the supreme commander proclaimed Jews the most resolute of Russia's enemies and authorized the execution of Jewish hostages "in case of necessity." At the same time, the military administration in Galicia ordered the first deportations of "unreliable" Jews to the Tomsk and the Yenisei provinces.[4] Because the authorities at first kept to perfunctory legal proceedings, the number of deported was initially small—sixty-five people in November and December—and after investigation, some charges were dropped. By the end of the year, however, Russian officials had increasingly thrown all legalities to the wind and deported Jews on trumped-up charges.[5]

The army's stigmatizing assertions were similar to the reports by the security and police branches. The Gendarme Department compiled lists of potential troublemakers in Galicia, listing Jews as the number one enemy. Nevertheless, besides engaging in anti-Semitic rhetoric, these "eyes and ears" of the tsarist regime possessed limited knowledge of the social and economic structure of the Jewish community in Galicia. This ignorance manifested itself in numerous reports in which the gendarmes lumped together Zionists, socialists, and the Orthodox as members of a single, united group. The gendarmes also claimed that secret Jewish organizations provided liaison between Galician conspirators—whether Jewish, Polish, or Ukrainian—and Vienna.[6]

The military counterintelligence branch, headed in wartime by gendarme officers, compiled reports of similar quality. Used to combat revolutionary groups in the empire, the gendarmes were less successful as a counterintelligence unit, and their merit in preventing espionage in the front zone was described by a senior Russian officer as useless. The general government had its own counterintelligence branch that was similarly ineffective and, in the words of Bobrinskii, did not "succeed in capturing a single spy."[7] Given the rivalry between different Russian administrative and police branches, such an appraisal was definitely biased. Nevertheless, it is certain that the gendarmes, the counterintelligence branch, and the police invented anti-Russian plots to substitute for the lack of empirical evidence of Jewish sabotage. Thus, in several Galician localities the police charged Jews with sheltering dogs that belonged to the Austro-Hungarian army. Arrests and deportations of Jews were also based on such charges as possessing a pocket mirror, which was classified as a signal device, or having a piece of barbed wire and telephone cable, which were purported to be evidence of subversive activities and intentions. Prisons were full of suspects who spent months awaiting investigation or trial. Even when the administration tried to investigate such cases, the consistent lack of evidence made the task impossible.[8]

The Russian government knew well of the army's abuses but tried to keep up appearances before its allies and public opinion and denied mass brutalities in the front zone. Observers from Russia emphasized the complexity of the Jewish issue in Galicia and the goodwill of the administration in trying to solve the question in the "most positive way for the Jews."[9] On February 8, speaking from the Duma rostrum, Foreign Minister Sergei Sazonov labeled charges of pogroms and persecution as German propaganda: "If Jews suffered, it was due to the exigencies of war, which do not differentiate [between Jews and non-Jews]."[10]

Russian authorities in Galicia marked for deportations Jewish politicians, teachers, rabbis, doctors, and merchants, depriving the Galician Jewry of its most advanced and needed leaders. The deportations were followed by the confiscation of property of the deportees, which was placed under the jurisdiction of the local administration. Still, the objectives of amassing and distributing the collected assets through the Land Bank were often impeded by the corruption and incompetence of commandants and district chiefs. Having come into possession of houses, horses, and various commodities, these officials often appropriated money and valuables and distributed less valuable goods to the Christian population. At times, the sentries posted at warehouses also helped themselves to the confiscated goods.[11] Packed in boxcars, entire Jewish families were directed to Kiev, which became a distribution point, and then as far as Turkestan and Kamchatka. Charges consisted only of a cover letter stating that the residence of an accused in a given locality was undesirable. The way the police and administration compiled evidence is illustrated by the case of Mark Kopelman. Kopelman was arrested in Lwów and deported on two counts—shooting at troops and the sale of alcohol. After his wife appealed the case, the Lwów governor admitted that there were no papers concerning Kopelman, nor was it known to what area in Russia he had been deported.[12]

Deportations in Galicia were only a small reflection of a larger campaign that was unfolding along the eastern front. In the winter of 1915 the deportations affected the areas along the Wisła River and near Kovno and Lublin. At the same time, Jews were expelled from the Płock district, and more than twenty thousand were forced from areas around Warsaw.[13] In February Stavka and the Ministry of Internal Affairs issued several circulars that specified places of exile for deported Jews: Tomsk and, later, Perm' and Yenisei provinces. The flow of anti-Jewish regulations was crowned by a decree of the supreme commander on March 12, ordering an expulsion of Jews toward enemy positions. As justification for such a drastic order, the grand duke blamed Jews for sabotage and for provoking Austrian reprisals against the Ukrainian population. The supreme commander stressed that the order marked the end of six months "of patience [of the army]" and was undertaken "only for the benefit" of the non-Jewish population.[14]

The deportations of Galician Jews immediately entailed difficulties for local commanders and administration. Between February 27 and March 3, 1915, the army expelled four thousand Jews from the town of Dobromil to its suburbs, where they were left under the open sky. The chief of the district, Colonel Eilis, complained to Bobrinskii that the expulsions "depopulated" the town and suggested that only Jewish males be deported. The colonel's pleas, as well as Bobrinskii's intervention with the army, resulted in the removal of the Jews from the Dobromil area to the Sambor district, whose chief, Krasovskii, in turn, frantically appealed to Bobrinskii for intervention. Krasovskii pointed out that Sambor had already been overcrowded by Jews expelled from other localities. Finally, on March 4, Bobrinskii was forced to accept the relocation of Dobromil Jews to Lwów.[15]

The army, however, was undisturbed by mounting complications and continued deportations, expulsions, and hostage taking. By the beginning of March, ten thousand Jews had been expelled from the front zone to the eastern districts of Galicia. The military administration had neither enough money to provide them with food and clothing nor adequate facilities to house them.

Only an outbreak of typhus forced Russian authorities to release some Jews to their places of residence. The rest eventually wound up in Russia without any documents, and the imperial administration was completely at a loss regarding issues of surveillance, place of exile, and supplies necessary for their upkeep. The appropriation of Jewish commodities, one of the principal objectives of the expulsions, also did not bring expected results because confiscated livestock and agricultural implements were immediately taken away by Poles and Ukrainians.[16]

As expulsions and deportations gained momentum, the army also launched a manhunt for laborers needed to build fortifications, dig trenches, and repair roads shattered by the war. Although peasants were paid for their labor, the military designated Jews as "enemy-aliens" not eligible for payment. Entire Jewish communities were pressed into labor battalions and worked under the supervision of Cossack guards. Any delay in completing tasks was attributed to Jewish opposition and resulted in deportations of whole details to Russia. For example, at the beginning of February Jewish workers in the vicinity of Stryj were deported on charges of inciting Ukrainian peasants to sabotage. Bribery, the only means to avoid labor service, became so widespread that the governor-general had to send special emissaries to investigate numerous cases. In turn, the administration blamed Jews for corrupting Russian officials.[17]

~

The irreconcilability of two mutually exclusive charges—the army insisted that Jews were of "cowardly" nature and yet a defiant and powerful foe—never seemed to trouble the military. On the contrary, the allegations of Jewish subversion fit perfectly well into the mental substratum of the Russian military, which convinced both itself and the general public of widespread Jewish resistance.[18] Indeed, the far-ranging destructive capacities ascribed to Jews were impressive. In April Mavrin insinuated that Galician Jews were secretly transferring copper to Austria, and General Brusilov accused Jews of Żydaczów of spreading rumors that caused such panic among the Russian administration that they hastily evacuated the town.[19] In a letter to Bobrinskii, Lieutenant General D. Shcherbachev, the commander of the Eleventh Army, offered a new solution to the Jewish "Gordian knot." The general pointed out that all previous measures failed to force Jews into submission. Hence, all Galician Jews should be collected in a gigantic dumping camp along the Romanian frontier. Left with no supplies, the Jews would cross en masse into Romania, which, in turn, would expel them to Austria proper. The arrival of multitudes of Jews would create havoc and economic shortages and thus severely undermine Austria's military capacity. Bobrinskii, however, rejected the plan on the grounds of potential complications with Romania and, more important, because of the fear that such an action would immediately trigger large-scale

Jewish retaliation. Among themselves, some Russian commanders and statesmen admitted that the army was scapegoating Jews. For example, Stavka's Quartermaster-General Yurii Danilov conceded that Jews "did not enjoy sympathy in certain circles," and Prince Shcherbatov, a member of the State Council, confirmed to his colleagues that Yanushkevich used Jews as an "alibi for his own failures."[20]

The removal of the Jews from the front zone culminated at the beginning of April after Russian troops captured Przemyśl. The Russian command immediately initiated a mass removal of "undesirable elements" to secure the conquered area. First Austrian POWs and then the Jews were designated for deportation. Transports with Jews from Przemyśl and the adjacent areas left for the eastern districts of Galicia on March 28. Hundreds of Jews were also sent on foot to nearby rail stations. Altogether, twenty thousand Jews were sent to Lwów and other localities to await deportation to the east.[21]

Deportations and expulsions sparked a new cycle of violence in Galicia. Although at the beginning of the war there was a slight chance that a perpetrator would be apprehended and prosecuted, by the winter–spring period of 1915 the Russian rank and file acted under the direct orders of their superiors and thus felt entirely immune to retribution. Indeed, the removal of Jews from the front zone was conceived as a part of military strategy, and the arrival of Russian units in Jewish settlements was marked by brutal assaults. What started as authorized actions inevitably degenerated into widespread murder, looting, and rape. Attacks mounted as the army either drove Jews toward enemy positions or shuffled them from place to place. In Bohorodczany, Sołotwin, and Porochy, Jewish quarters were burned, houses were looted, and some Jewish adult males were murdered. The future bard of the Bolshevik revolution, John Reed, recorded the expulsion of eight thousand Jews from the town of Zaleszczyki in April. Soldiers slaughtered male Jews and drove out women and children, who, without food and adequate clothing, were marched off from locality to locality. Some collapsed and died during the moves.[22]

The influx of deportees from Kurland, the kingdom, and Galicia generated an outcry from government and provincial officials in Russia proper. On March 6, Poltava provincial governor Baggovut protested against the deportation of three thousand Galician Jews into his province. He argued to Bobrinskii and Mavrin that the arrival of thousands of Jews would overburden provincial railroads. In addition, settling Jews in the countryside violated Russian imperial laws, and the governor agreed to accept only two thousand Jews at larger urban sites.[23] Stavka blamed the military administration for mismanagement of the deportation process and insisted that all Jews be driven toward enemy lines and that only politically "unreliable" Jews be shipped off to the

Poltava and Chernihiv provinces. Bobrinskii, in turn, refused to be a scapegoat and quite correctly responded to his superiors that from the beginning of the war they had repeatedly stressed the unreliability of *all* Jews.[24]

Indeed, by ordering expulsions of Jews toward the enemy lines, Stavka forsook its own instructions that Jews must be prevented from contacts with the enemy. Yanushkevich, however, was typically beyond such nuances and raved to Bobrinskii about the "lack of initiative" among Russian officials in pursuing anti-Jewish measures. His obsession with Jews was also reflected in a secret order sent to army and front commanders for collecting information that demonstrated Russian-Jewish soldiers' disloyalty and harmful influence on their comrades.[25]

The Great Retreat and Its Aftermath, May–December of 1915

Russian euphoria after the victory at Przemyśl and hopes for an offensive against Hungary received a devastating blow on May 2, 1915, when after massive bombardment three Austro-German armies shattered Russian lines at Gorlice and Gromnik (southeast of Krakow). The Russian retreat soon spread all along the eastern front. On June 3, Jarosław and Przemyśl were abandoned, and on June 22, Austrian troops entered Lwów. Unable to stop the retreat, Stavka deployed a scorched-earth strategy to prevent the enemy from capturing anything valuable. Orders were given to evacuate machinery, grain, and cattle to the east and to destroy whatever could not be taken along. Bridges, railroads, locomotives, and oil wells were burned or blown up. The evacuation was accompanied by wholesale expulsions of Germans and Jews from Kurland and Kovno and widespread looting.[26]

On May 11, the military announced that it had important evidence of Jewish collaboration with the enemy. Allegedly, in the village of Kuzhi in the Kovno province, Jews hid German troops, which ambushed a Russian infantry regiment. The news rapidly acquired momentum and circulated in the official press throughout the empire. Two Duma members, Aleksandr Kerenskii and Nikolai Friedman, traveled to Kuzhi and found, however, that Jewish residents had been evacuated on May 9, a day before the alleged ambush had taken place.[27] Nevertheless, the affair increased the zeal of Russian commanders to clear the front zone of spies and saboteurs. Expulsions gained momentum in Kurland and Galicia, where the populace of entire villages and towns was forced out and their houses set on fire. Thousands of people were driven eastward, adding to the general chaos of the retreat, while soldiers and Cossacks ran amok, destroying and burning Jewish settlements and acting like bands of thugs rather than regular units. That at least some officers tolerated the predatory instincts of their subordinates was demonstrated on June 6, when the grand duke was compelled to issue an order that subjected commanders who incited pogroms to courts-martial.[28]

As Russian armies kept reeling back, violence against Jewish communities became an outlet for battle-fatigued and demoralized troops. At the same time, executions of "suspicious" Jews turned into a fundamental principle of military justice. As the troops drove Jews out from the Galician towns of Delatyn, Sokal, Kamionka, Rawa Ruska, Żółkiew, Brody, Gródek Jagielloński, and Horodenka, their march was marked by pogroms, executions, and fires. In Śniatyń the Russians rounded up more than four thousand Jews in the city square. Then nineteen adults were publicly hanged for treason while soldiers looted houses and raped women. Similar atrocities took place in other localities. Driven on foot by Cossacks and soldiers, Jews often had neither food nor water, and anybody who tried to hand them a glass of water was mercilessly flogged by the guards. Having arrived at the places of exile near the Galician-Russian border, thousands of people were left under the open sky, and the army and the local administration denied any responsibility for their upkeep. Those who stayed behind after the Russian withdrawal were frequently robbed, and some were murdered by peasants and local hoodlums. Pillaging of Jewish houses continued until the arrival of the first Austrian patrols, which in several instances shot the looters on the spot.[29]

It should be noted that the entire population of the front zone was subjected to brutalities. Houses and crops were burned, and entire villages trudged eastward alongside the troops. Nevertheless, the army's attitude toward Poles and Ukrainians was not marked by ethnic prejudices, and Yanushkevich specified to Mavrin that the application of drastic measures should not be extended to non-Jews. Nor were mass deportations of Germans, which went on in May in Kurland, characterized by the atrocities prevalent during the expulsions of Jews.[30]

An example of ethnic differentiation in the war zone can be seen from an encounter between a Russian unit and refugees on a road in Poland: "When a soldier seeing another group of refugees made fun of the Jews he was greeted with laughter from his comrades. When a second soldier tried to join in on the fun saying that Poles were no better, no one laughed, and he was quickly corrected. 'Poles are a necessary people,' he was told. 'A Pole is a peasant, he's tied tightly to the land.'"[31]

On May 25, under pressure from the government, Stavka was forced to stop the expulsions of Jews from Kurland and the kingdom. In Galicia, however, expulsions eastward continued, and by May 30 the army had uprooted and shuffled from place to place some eleven thousand Bukovinian and Galician Jews. Bobrinskii, exasperated at the reports of thousands of people driven afoot to no definite destination, bombarded Mavrin with pleas to stop the expulsions. He insisted that because Jews would at any rate avoid being drafted into the Austrian army, expulsions served no purpose. At this time, however, the chaos at the front had reached such proportions that Mavrin was hardly in a position to influence local commanders.[32]

At the same time, trains with deportees from Galicia reached Kiev and were then sent back without providing food and water to the Jews locked in the cars. On one train carrying three thousand Galician deportees, seventy-six people died of exhaustion, and eighteen went insane. The city administration had no means to provide for the growing number of deportees, so the Kiev Jewish community obtained permission from the Ministry of the Interior to open kitchens and temporary facilities to house thousands of destitute people. Due to the intervention of influential Russians and Poles, some prominent Jews, such as the dean of the medical faculty at Lwów University, Adolf Bek, were sent to exile in Moscow. The rest were shipped farther, to Siberia and Turkestan, where local administrations dispersed them in towns and villages.[33]

On June 12, in a desperate attempt to stop the enemy's advance, Stavka ordered the mass evacuation of the entire population from the front zone. This time, as a concession to the entreaties of Russian ministers and Duma members, the grand duke stressed that Jews should be exempted from the evacuation and instead be driven toward enemy lines. Although in several instances the army carried out the instructions to the letter, during the hastened retreat some commanders still ordered that Jews be expelled eastward, contrary to the urgings of Stavka.[34]

~

Although in the summer of 1915 the assault on Jews rapidly escalated, it did not assume the genocidal proportions comparable to the Armenian genocide that was unfolding at the time of the Great Retreat. In fact, although expulsions of Jews continued even after the Russians stopped retreating, by August 1915 anti-Jewish violence had clearly passed its zenith. It is, therefore, important to mention forces that mitigated the destructive potential of the Russian military machine.

Despite the vehement anti-Semitism of the Russian military, it lacked two major prerequisites for a war of annihilation: an ideological doctrine of extermination and a unified effort of military and civil structures. The Russian government, although it shared the anti-Semitic biases of the army, vociferously objected to the army's brutal practices on the grounds that the influx of thousands of deportees into the empire undermined Russia's war efforts. In August 1915, during meetings of the Russian Council of Ministers, cabinet members agreed on the "sinister" role played by Jews in the revolutionary movement as well as on their "destructive" nature. Yet, they pointed out that mass expulsions eroded Russia's war capacity, and instead of containing Jews to the Pale of Settlement, the Ministry of the Interior had to expand Jewish settlements outside of longtime traditional boundaries.[35]

Russian public opinion also denounced the inhuman treatment of the Jews, and even rabid anti-Semites joined in protests against the heavy-handed rule of the army. A plethora of liberal-minded individuals, such as Maxim Gor'kii, Paul Miliukov, and Aleksandr Kerenskii, courageously criticized the army and the government for its barbaric conduct of the war. Vasilii Maklakov, a leader of the Constitutional Democratic Party, asserted that in view of the horrible carnage the Jews were subjected to they should be excused even "if the spy stories were found to be true."[36] In addition, because American, British, and French loans and credits were critical for Russia's war economy, the Council of Ministers was concerned that mistreatment of the Jews would reverberate abroad. Given the belief of the government that foreign banks were in the hands of the "international Jewry," expulsions in the front zone were thought to affect directly the efficacy of the Russian military industry. Fears that the mistreatment of Jews was alienating foreign public opinion came to the fore most vividly in April 1915 when a British delegation arrived in Galicia to organize aid to the population. The arrival of the delegation caused pandemonium in Stavka and in the staff of the southwestern front, both of which were alarmed that the delegation would investigate crimes perpetrated against the Jews.[37]

To the credit of the Russian officer corps, despite Stavka's pressure, not every commander endorsed the persecution of Jews. Some officers treated all ethnic groups on an equal basis and extended to the Jews protection against the depredations of troops and local assailants. In addition, hostilities between the army and the governor-general also reduced the impact of anti-Jewish actions. Bobrinskii repeatedly criticized the army's conduct as damaging to the economy and stability of the territory for which he was responsible. Thus in April 1915, in an interview with *Russkoye slovo,* he admitted that within his jurisdiction Jews "behaved quite correctly," although they did not sympathize with the Russian cause. Bobrinskii's revelations outraged the army, and the interview was excised from publications.[38]

The public outcry and protests of the government against the military's brutalities largely concerned the treatment of Russian Jews. Jews of Galicia and Bukovina as foreign subjects were less frequently referred to in the minutes of the Duma and the Council of Ministers. Nevertheless, as the generals caved in to the pressure, the situation in Galicia slightly improved. At the end of August the military allowed a number of deportees to return to Galicia and even made attempts to reimburse the victims of confiscations. Nevertheless, because petitions for restitution were to be accompanied by appropriate receipts from the army, barely a handful of petitioners were eligible. Out of 1,145 petitions directed to the governor-general, only 70 were approved. In fact, governmental instructions for restitution excluded the subjects of enemy states, giving the military an excuse to ignore the petitions of Galician Jews.[39]

At the end of September 1915, when the Russian army finally stopped retreating, the situation on the front was desperate. The kingdom and Kurland, with their densely industrialized areas, were lost. The once-proud army of the tsar was shattered, and casualties amounted to 1,500,000 killed, wounded, and taken prisoner.[40] In Galicia, the Russians managed to hold on to a small strip of land around Tarnopol, and the defunct general government retained a few dozen of its officials in the rear of the southwestern front. Such pressing issues as stabilizing the front and reorganizing the rear had temporarily rendered the Jewish question immaterial, and several Russian officials were tried for extortion from Galician Jews. The Jewish Central Aid Committee, with its seat in St. Petersburg, raised funds and organized medical care for Jewish refugees and deportees in the empire. It also traveled to the front zone and provided relief to Jews still under the jurisdiction of the army. The increasing role of civil institutions, the Zemstvo, in the war economy also contributed to the fact that the army outwardly mitigated its anti-Jewish fervor. No less important to the improved treatment of Jews was the influx of many new officers to substitute for huge losses suffered by the Russian officer corps during the first war year. The majority of new officers came from the Russian intelligentsia and at least initially displayed less anti-Semitic zeal than their predecessors.[41]

Yet, the improvement was limited. Local commandants continued confiscating Jewish property, and the new commander of the southwestern front, General Brusilov, insisted that the deportations of Jews in the spring and summer of 1915 were absolutely necessary. The threat of revolutionary unrest, deteriorating conditions in the trenches, economic shortages, and criticism by the Duma magnified the obsession of the high command with "internal enemies" embodied by revolutionaries, liberals, the Zemstvo, and, ultimately, Jews, who provided the Socialists and Bolsheviks with their most prominent members. These attitudes were reflected in the army's compilation of data on the "negative" influence of Jews in the army. In September and December 1915, Stavka ordered front, army, and corps commanders to collect information about the low moral qualities of Jewish soldiers, cases of high treason, and desertion of Jews to the enemy. With few exceptions, in their responses the generals repeated tales of Jewish sabotage and stressed that Jews spread revolutionary ideas in the army and murdered wounded Russian soldiers.[42] The collection of this data coincided with the anti-Semitic campaign in the right-wing press and a roundup of homeless Jews in Moscow in the winter of 1916.

Although the army kept secret the results of the surveys, it can be surmised that it planned to use them later to discredit Jews publicly and, perhaps, in future legislative measures.[43]

In Galicia, the army continued the practice of extorting ransom from Jews and hunted down Jewish workers for labor details. Sometimes Jewish workers were treated as concentration camp inmates. They were locked in barns, forced to sleep on the bare ground, and flogged for alleged transgressions. Because Russian troops suffered from malnutrition, the ration for Jewish laborers often consisted of a piece of dried bread and a bowl of steamed water. Living conditions were so appalling that in February 1916, out of three thousand Jews forced to work for eighteen days in low temperature outside Tarnopol, sixty-two died and only half were able to return home on their own. The rest suffered severe frostbite and had to be transported back in horse-drawn carts.[44]

Russia's Farewell to Galicia

The treatment of Jews in the front zone reflected the ebb and flow of Russia's fortunes in the war. By the spring of 1916, the efforts of the government, the Zemstvo, and the War Ministry to resuscitate the country's military strength had achieved considerable results. Great numbers of conscripts were drafted, and the war economy managed to produce impressive numbers of shells and guns necessary for large-scale operations. The improvement of the army's capability, the increasing dependence of Russia on her allies, and, most important, the worsening socioeconomic conditions in the empire brought about the lifting of some anti-Jewish regulations such as the prohibition of movement within Galicia. Russian officials and Zemstvo representatives distributed food and provided medical service to homeless Jews. A larger number of Galician refugees were allowed to return home from their places of exile, and many hoped that the worst phase of the Russian occupation was over.[45]

But these hopes evaporated in June 1916 when the entire southwestern front erupted in gunfire, and five Russian armies launched a gigantic offensive from Kremenets in the north to Bukovina in the south. Austrian-German troops were taken off guard and began a rapid retreat. By August 13, Buczacz, Brody, Stanisławów, Kołomyja, Delatyn, Nadwórna in Galicia, and Czernowitz in Bukovina had fallen to the Russians.[46] What came to be known as the Brusilov offensive activated a psychological code imprinted in the psyche of the army, and pogroms of Jews began immediately, concurrent with the Russian advance. Soldiers and Cossacks set aflame synagogues and Jewish houses and robbed, raped, and murdered in at least twelve localities. This time, however, the perpetrators rarely used rumors as a pretext for assault. Although Russian sources refer to the "excellent" fighting spirit of Russian troops, in the summer of 1916 the Russian rank and file were a different type of soldier in comparison to their compatriots in the beginning of the war and cherished no illusions that the war would end soon. Two years of combat completely divested these soldiers of any ideological motives for fighting, and this moral vacuum was filled with a short-range objective—survival by all means. For such troops looting and pillaging were the only rewards amid the drudgery of the trench warfare, and Jews provided a convenient outlet to discharge aggression with relative immunity. As the Russian army advanced, attacks on Jews rapidly escalated. To escape the Russians, entire Jewish communities wandered from place to place or fled with the retreating Austrian troops. Some localities became entirely divested of Jewish residents. For example, in Kołomyja, out of the prewar Jewish population of nineteen thousand, only five hundred were still there by the fall of 1916.[47]

Victories on the front forced Stavka to resuscitate the defunct general government. Bobrinskii, whose name was associated with Russian rule in Galicia, was dismissed, and on June 13, 1916, Fedor Trepov, the former governor-general of the Kiev province and the chairman of the Committee for Combating German Predominance, was appointed the new ruler of Galicia. Trepov vouched not to repeat the mistakes of his predecessor. He promised universal social and religious tolerance in the area under his jurisdiction and allowed Jewish deportees to return to Galicia; synagogues and Jewish schools were reopened, and Yiddish was allowed as the language of instruction.[48]

Although improved, however, the situation of Jews in the occupied parts of Tarnopol and Stanisławów provinces still left much to be desired. The army treated them with suspicion, and local commanders solved the problem of feeding thousands of wandering Jews by driving them to neighboring districts. Five thousand homeless Jews were crowded into Tarnopol alone, and with winter coming, the front command decided to remove them from the front zone. Reminiscent of the Great Retreat, in September and October the army began an evacuation of more than four thousand people from the front zone to Volhynia. Although the entire population within Russian-controlled areas suffered equally during these expulsions, Jews were still singled out and persecuted for allegedly abetting Russian deserters.[49]

The revolutionary upheaval in the spring of 1917 did not change the situation in Galicia. Although the provisional government in St. Petersburg did away with all civil and political limitations on Russian Jews, in the general government the military still had a decisive voice in civil affairs. After An-Ski visited Galicia in March 1917, he informed the government that Jews were still barred from city and district councils and courts and that the bulk of Jewish cultural and educational institutions were shut down. Multitudes of homeless

Jews wandered in the countryside, and their property, livestock, and agricultural equipment were either confiscated by the army or taken by the local population. Russian troops destroyed religious artifacts, used temples as latrines, and appropriated schools for barracks. Extortion by the administration and physical assaults by passing units were daily occurrences.[50]

An-Ski's pleas went unheeded. Even if the provisional government was willing to ameliorate the situation, it was hardly in a position to do so. By the spring of 1917, the Russian army was in a state of complete disarray. Outright banditry by the rank and file became endemic, and from March to August 1917, Russian soldiers deserted at an average rate of eighteen thousand per month. Eruptions of violence against officers and civilians were common, and the entire population suffered from frequent requisitions and confiscations. Intermittent conflicts between the army and the administration only underscored the atmosphere of chaos, incompetence, and corruption.[51]

Although the provisional government dismissed provincial governors and district chiefs, on a lower level the administration remained intact, and Galicia remained within the jurisdiction of the army. The main objective of the government was to keep Russia at war, and, therefore, it continued to play up to the military. Thus, on the one hand, the government tolerated the activities of Ukrainian and Jewish civil committees in Galicia, but at the same time in March it promulgated a decree giving the army the right to expel from the war zone prostitutes and individuals suspected of espionage and sedition. Barely had some Jewish refugees and expatriates returned to Galicia than they were immediately subjected to harassment and expelled on the grounds of security.[52]

The *acta finale* of the occupation came on June 30, 1917, when Russian armies launched their last offensive. As in the summer of 1916, Russians managed to break Austro-German defenses and on July 9 occupied Halicz and Kałusz. Yet, the majority of the Russian rank and file, according to a contemporary, were just a "mob of armed peasants," with little or no training and even less will to fight. On July 18, the advance bogged down, and under heavy fire Russian troops began a disorderly retreat that soon deteriorated into a mass flight of thousands of demoralized soldiers who inundated railroad stations and roads. The Russian administration hastily evacuated Galicia, taking along the last Jewish hostages. After the authorities left, mobs of soldiers assaulted towns and cities and started looting residential areas. Officers were killed on the spot, and looting of houses soon degenerated into savage pogroms accompanied by burning of buildings and stores. The cumulative effects of the fear of the advancing enemy, hate toward a government that did not deliver long-desired peace, and the overwhelming sense of hopelessness erupted in mass violent outbreaks as four thousand ravaging troops gave vent to their rage in Brody, Husiatyn, Buczacz, Monasterzyska, Podhajce, and Brzeżany. The Austro-German bombardment exacerbated the carnage, and the urban areas and the countryside suffered arson, pillage, and rape as Russian troops left Galicia. Moreover, though attacks were random, compact Jewish residential enclaves made them easily identifiable targets and attracted large numbers of looters, who turned them into heaps of charred ruins. Traditional images of "rich Jews," combined with ethnic resentment accumulated during the war, materialized in brutal assaults on the Jewish quarters in Halicz, Stanisławów, Zborów, Jeziernica, Kołomyja, and Kałusz, which were almost completely wiped out. Rape followed looting, and between 250 and 300 people (Jews and non-Jews) lost their lives.[53] In October and November of 1917 two more pogroms in Brody marked the final Russian evacuation from Galicia. The destruction of the Jewish quarters in Brody was so devastating that a Jewish activist in Vienna, Lazar Bloch, appealed to the Austrian foreign ministry to intervene with the Russian government.[54]

The war and the Russian occupation inflicted terrible carnage on the population and economy of Galicia. Ninety thousand houses were destroyed, more than half of all mills were rendered defunct, and by the fall of 1917 supplies of grain had become almost nonexistent. Although all Galician residents were subjected to the horrors of the war, the Jewish community suffered the worst adversities. Its economic base was completely shattered; between 50 percent and 70 percent of Jewish quarters lay in shambles; and pogroms, deportations, and forced migration reduced the Jewish population in some places to less than half of what it had been. Jewish schools, synagogues, and cultural institutions were badly damaged or ruined, and thousands of Jews were left homeless. Between twenty thousand and thirty thousand Jews were deported to Russia and dispersed around the empire from Brest-Litovsk to Krasnoiarsk, Khodzhent, and Kamchatka; up to fifty thousand were uprooted and shuffled within the region. In addition to approximately two hundred thousand Jewish refugees in Austria, Hungary, and the Czech lands, the war thus directly affected one-half of East Galician Jews.[55]

2
The Polish-Jewish Conflict

4 / Polish-Jewish Relations during World War I

When news of hostilities reached Galicia in August 1914, the reaction of Jews was strikingly similar to that of their coreligionists elsewhere in Europe. Although they feared and resented the war, Jews joined with Poles and Ukrainians in patriotic demonstrations and confirmed their loyalty to the Austro-Hungarian crown in public meetings. Old animosities were temporarily forgotten. Some Jews enlisted in the national armed unit, the Polish Legions, as well as in the Ukrainian formation, the Sich Sharpshooters, and took part in frontier battles during the first months of the war. Jewish political activists participated in the Polish National Committee, the body created to assist the formation of the legions, and individual Jews, as well as entire Jewish communities, donated to it large sums of money. Even the nemesis of Jews, the Endeks, for a time ceased its anti-Semitic agitation.[1]

Yet, as the Russian occupation soon laid bare old grudges, the Polish-Jewish rapprochement was short lived. From the beginning of the war, the Russian high command stressed its intent to liberate Polish lands from German and Austro-Hungarian rule. On August 13, 1914, the grand duke issued a declaration that stated:

> Poles! . . . A century and a half ago the flesh of Poland was torn to pieces, but her soul lived on. She hoped that the time would come for the resurrection of the Polish nation and its fraternal rapprochement with Great Russia. Russian troops are bringing you the sacred tidings of this rapprochement. Under the scepter of the Russian Tsar Poland will rise again, free in her faith, language, and self-rule. Russia, for her part, is hopeful that Poland would respect the rights of the people, whose destiny has been closely linked to her own.[2]

In the atmosphere of the fervent patriotism in the first days of the war, it was not surprising that Poles and Jews interpreted the declaration in completely different fashions. The Endeks hailed the grand duke's protestations as a first step on the road to Poland's independence. They expected that their support for Russia's war efforts would serve as a powerful lever in the bid for dominance in the political and social spheres of the country. On the other hand, Jewish political activists hoped that in the time of war the Russian government would ease anti-Jewish restrictions and perceived the last line of the declaration as the inauguration of more liberal imperial policies toward ethnic minorities.[3]

Both, however, were badly mistaken. The declaration had little practical effect because it was signed by the supreme commander of the armed forces, who exercised enormous power in the war theater, but lacked authority to change the political status of imperial lands. Consequently, the Russian government did not endorse the declaration officially. Moreover, a secret circular sent to the Russian provincial governors in the kingdom stressed that any potential political changes would affect only territories still held by the Central powers. At the same time, Russian authorities were eager to capitalize on the anti-Semitism of the Endeks as a common platform for political cooperation and as a means to channel Polish national aspirations into an internal Polish-Jewish conflict. Indeed, the declaration sparked a vehement reaction from the Polish right-wing press, which accentuated the need to *odżydzić* (de-Judaize) the country's socioeconomic and political spheres as a cardinal tenet of future Polish statehood.[4]

To encourage Polish-Russian cooperation, the military administration in Galicia left Polish officials in their posts. The latter, under Russian guidance or of their own accord, began dismissing Jewish civil and court employees. The Endek press increased its anti-Semitic propaganda, accusing Jews of speculation and pro-Austrian and pro-German orientation. As a wave of pogroms in the summer of 1914 swept through the region, Russian soldiers and Cossacks encouraged Polish and Ukrainian peasants to loot Jewish stores and abandoned houses and then distributed seized goods to villagers. Some Poles informed on their Jewish neighbors to the Russian police or guided the Cossacks to houses of affluent Jews. Polish officials often engaged in extortion of Jews, either on the pretext of punishing them for "misdeeds" or as a gratuity for protection against the depredations of Russian soldiers.[5]

Anti-Jewish animosities were exacerbated by economic shortages and social dislocation. The Russification campaign forced thousands of Jews from the countryside to move into urban areas. By the winter of 1915, about eighty thousand Jewish refugees had moved to Warsaw, where they lived in adverse sanitary conditions. Privation led to outbreaks of typhus. Jewish merchants and tradesmen competed with their Polish rivals, and many other Jews speculated on the black market, provoking popular animosities. Consequently, the Endek-led press campaign gathered momentum, which, in addition to traditional accusations of economic profiteering, highlighted the putative racial attributes of the Jews. Thus, the renowned Polish activist Aleksandr Świętochowski accused Jews of speculation, sabotage, and collaboration with the Central Powers. In the article *"Wojna trzydziesta czwarta"* (The Thirty-fourth War), he raised fears that Jews conspired to build an autonomous enclave—"Judeo-Poland"—inside the country. Świętochowski stated that the Polish nation would not tolerate a large ethnic group that associated itself with Poland's enemies and asserted that peculiar "nomadic" habits and biological traits made Jews incapable of assimilation. Hence, in ethnically "pure" Poland, Jews would have to be isolated from Polish society. Similar fears of "Judeo-Poland" were echoed by several Polish newspapers and journals.[6]

The Pawns of Realpolitik: The Ethnic Policies of the Central Powers

At the beginning of the war, the Central Powers had their own plans for the future of Poland. Berlin and Vienna took it for granted that the status of Polish lands within their respective jurisdictions would remain unchanged, but a buffer state might be created from the territories of the kingdom. Some Austrian and German officials also believed that the socioeconomic and cultural levels of Poles did not merit independence or even autonomy, and thus the country should be primarily considered a geographic entity and a pool of human resources and raw materials. Outwardly, however, the Central Powers made every effort to assure Poles that the liberation from Russian rule would open a new page in the history of Poland. In August 1914, at the time of the grand duke's declaration, the two governments issued appeals promising to resurrect the Polish state. Although extremely vague as to the territories and political status of the future Poland, these appeals galvanized Polish public opinion and revitalized hopes for independence. After the Russian retreat in 1915 the Central Powers divided Poland into two occupation zones. Territories of the kingdom were divided into the German general government, with its seat in Warsaw, and the Austro-Hungarian general government in the Lublin province. The military regimes guaranteed all national groups equality and civil liberties and retained intact the Polish administration.[7]

Ultimately, attitudes toward the Central Powers clearly delineated the different Polish and Jewish aspirations for the future. Following the hardships of Russian rule, Jews enthusiastically welcomed Austro-German armies. In Galicia, Jews expected that the prewar order would be fully restored. In the kingdom the discipline and conduct of German troops bolstered hopes that the days of oppression were over. Initially German and Austrian authorities believed that Jews might be used as a useful ally against Russia and a counterbalance to the Poles. The German military regime, therefore, allowed Jewish cultural, educational, and political organizations to resume their activities, and although it did not grant Jews the status of a national minority (as many Jewish activists had hoped), it fully restored their civil rights. Jews were excited over these developments. In the words of a contemporary, they "suddenly, as if by magic, ceased to feel like a pariah."[8]

But these events hardly signified a positive change in Polish-Jewish relations. On the contrary, German and Austrian rule exacerbated the confrontation between the two peoples. Poles resented Jews for their pro-German stance and particularly despised the activities of the German Zionist organization *Deutsches Komitee zur Befreiung der russischen Juden* (later renamed the *Komitee für den Osten*). Created in August 1914 by German Zionists, the organization proposed to the German foreign ministry the creation of a buffer state between Russia and Germany. The plan struck a responsive chord among some German officials, for the proposed state would include the former kingdom as well as Russia's western borderlands, and Jews, as the "most reliable pioneers of Germanhood in the East," would be recognized as an autonomous nationality on a par with other ethnic groups. The organization also propagated tight links between Polish Jews and German culture and argued that Poles lacked the "maturity" to have their own state. Germans rejected the plan, but it became known to and infuriated Polish political circles. The World Zionist Organization also criticized the *Komitee* on the grounds of aggravating the Polish-Jewish conflict.[9] The activities of the *Komitee* coincided with Jewish petitions to the German military regime in the kingdom to curb anti-Semitic propaganda in Polish newspapers. By the fall of 1915, the Polish press of different political affiliations had highlighted pro-German sympathies among Jews and accused them of speculation and draft evasion. The anti-Semitic propaganda took on such a scope that the German military governor of Warsaw warned an editor of the most notorious newspaper, *Gazeta Poranna 2 Grosze.*[10]

Charges that Jews speculated on the black market and avoided military service reflected the realities of the situation. Drastic economic shortages and destruction wrought by the war sharply increased prices. The population tried to make a living by means fair and foul, and Jews, due to their occupations as petty tradesmen and artisans, had more commodities to offer on the black market. Similarly, aversion to military duties was very strong among religious Jews, who dodged the draft into Austrian and German labor battalions.

As the war dragged on, political and military priorities made the Central Powers rely more on Poles, to whom German and Austro-Hungarian authorities eventually accorded a free hand in dealing with Jews. In the fall of 1915, the Polish administration in Galicia began a mass dismissal of Jews—reinstated after the Russian retreat—from public service. With the connivance of Austrian authorities, Polish officials supplanted Jewish employees in Komarno, Lwów, Rymanów, and Borysław. Even Polish civil employees who had been known for their collaboration with the Russians retained their posts. As a result, Jews frequently complained that Poles treated them on the "Russian model." Mutual accusations mounted as Poles and Jews competed to obtain positions in the administration and police.[11]

Anti-Semitic sentiments in Poland and Galicia mirrored the growing hostility of Poles toward Germany and Austro-Hungary. With the progression of the war the Central Powers increasingly treated Polish territories as a breadbasket and a source of raw materials. German military authorities dismantled Polish industry, requisitioned grain, cut forests, and imposed high taxation on cities and villages; able-bodied Poles were rounded up and sent to work in Germany's war industries. In the Austrian-held parts of Poland, the situation was not much different. To the chagrin of Poles, trade was in the hands of Jewish agencies from Austria. In the districts of Chełm, Hrubieszów, and Tomaszów, the home of a large Ukrainian population, public announcements were made in German and Ukrainian. Requisitions by passing troops, the mandatory delivery of food quotas, and mobilization for labor units exerted tremendous pressure on the civilian population in the Lublin province and Galicia. If Poles had any illusions as to the intentions of the Central Powers, by 1916 they had evaporated. Poles increasingly identified themselves in ethnic terms as a group oppressed and threatened by outsiders, Austrians, Germans, and Jews. Popular resentment was especially strong toward the Jews, who openly displayed their pro-Austrian and pro-German attitude and supported the military regimes. Moreover, because indignation at the Central Powers could be expressed only through clenched teeth, anti-Semitism became a convenient outlet for popular discontent. Polish-Jewish interests increasingly collided in all spheres of economic and social life. When the Austrian administration in Galicia forced Polish and Ukrainian peasants to return stolen Jewish goods, anti-Jewish animosities flared up in the courts. Many Jews informed on and testified against looters and those who had collaborated with the Russians. The Polish public reacted in outrage at what was seen as Jews settling scores with potential political rivals. Tensions also heated up when Jewish refugees and deportees returned to claim their houses and belongings, which had been appropriated by Poles and Ukrainians.[12] For its part, the Jewish press highlighted Polish anti-Semitic attitudes and professed the loyalty of Jews to the Central Powers as alone capable of protecting them from hostile neighbors. Yet, although Austro-German authorities effectively prevented public unrest, they often ignored anti-Semitic agitation. As the situation worsened, some

Jewish leaders, such as Herschel Farbstein, a leading Polish Zionist, feared that Polish independence would spell disaster for the Jews.[13]

The result of mutual hostility was predictable. Ideological anti-Semitism evolved into an integral part of Polish political life, and racial slurs became the norm as newspapers, booklets, and pamphlets referred to Jews as genetically treacherous, cunning, and intolerant. Anti-Semitism also made inroads into Polish political organizations that had advocated Polish-Jewish cooperation before the war. In July 1915, a leader of the Polish Socialist Party, Ignacy Daszyńsky, dismissed Jews from the party leadership and the editorial board of the party newspaper, *Naprzód.* To his Jewish colleagues, Daszyńsky explained that a "philosemitic" stance of his party would seriously undermine its political credibility after the war. Peasant organizations and liberal-minded politicians also voiced popular anti-Jewish resentments. For instance, a future foreign minister, August Zaleski, told a British activist, Lucien Wolf, that the entire Polish population would be opposed to equalizing Yiddish with Polish.[14] When some Polish politicians attempted to find accommodation with Jews, the two sides displayed mutually exclusive political views. For example, Leon Biliński, a member of the Polish Main National Committee (formed in Galicia at the beginning of the war) sought to persuade Jewish Orthodox leaders to form a joint voting bloc as a foundation for a future Polish-Jewish rapprochement. Jews, however, rejected this action, fearing that it would have clear anti-Austrian overtones. In addition, several Jewish organizations in Poland and abroad continued questioning the ability of Poles to have an independent state and portrayed them all as inveterate anti-Semites.[15]

Although economic exploitation of the country remained a trademark of the Austro-German occupation, and both military governments refused to grant Poland political concessions, setbacks on the front and fear of popular discontent forced the Central Powers to change these policies. On November 5, 1916, the two emperors issued a declaration that provided for a Polish state under German and Austrian auspices. Initially, the declaration sparked mass enthusiastic response by Poles and Jews. Jewish communities sent congratulations to Polish political representatives in Warsaw and Vienna and expressed hopes for a harmonious Jewish-Polish coexistence in independent Poland. When it became known that the new state would be deprived of Poznań, the Baltic Sea shore, Silesia, and Galicia, however, it caused an uproar in Polish political circles. The November declaration also signified a turn of the Central Powers' policies toward Jews because it effectively relegated internal affairs to the jurisdiction of Polish officials. In 1917 the German military regime passed control of education to the Polish administration, thus dashing Jewish hopes that the Yiddish and Hebrew languages would receive equal status with Polish. German and Austrian authorities ignored Jewish complaints about discrimination in the social and educational spheres, and economic shortages and inflation made Polish-Jewish competition in the administration and aid committees especially fierce.[16]

Meanwhile, leading Polish political factions had spawned different concepts of Polish nationhood. The Endeks promoted the resurrection of the prepartitioned Poland in which ethnic Poles would dominate politics and the economy. Dmowski argued that Ukrainians, Belorussians, and Lithuanians had not yet developed the prerequisites of a modern nation and that the "civilizing mission" of the Polish national state—*państwo narodowe*—was to assimilate and integrate these peoples. Jews, on the other hand, were a totally "alien" group that could not and should not be assimilated. *Odżydzenie* of the economic and social spheres would force mass Jewish emigration and thus effectively solve the thorny "Jewish question."[17] The followers of Józef Piłsudski advocated a confederation of Poles, Ukrainians, and Belorussians as a power capable of withstanding Russian and German aggression. Despite their differences, the two Polish leaders shared a broad consensus that ethnic Poles would constitute a ruling elite, whether in a national state or in a confederation. Therefore, as long as the country was occupied by foreign powers, any concessions to ethnic minorities were seen as untimely. In July 1917, a temporary ruling body, the Constitutional Committee of Temporary State Council, contemplated a declaration that would have guaranteed civil rights to national minorities in the future Polish state. Some committee members immediately hastened to stress that such a declaration was not legally binding, especially with regard to Jews.[18]

The Collapse of the Old Order

At the beginning of 1918, the economic situation in Poland and Galicia was extremely dire. Hunger, inflation, and requisitions by the military regimes forced thousands of people to move into urban areas, where populations increased dramatically. These drastic demographic changes coincided with the refusal of Hungary—a major supplier of agricultural products—to sell foodstuffs to Austria and Germany. Therefore, the burden of supplying the Central Powers fell entirely on the kingdom and Galicia. Economic shortages aggravated popular attitudes, and in January demonstrations and unrest took place in Krakow. At a time when socioeconomic tensions ran high, Polish public opinion was shocked by the news of the Brest-Litovsk treaty. Signed on February 9, 1918, between the Central Powers and the Ukrainian National Republic (a new state that arose on the ruins of the Russian Empire), the treaty stipulated the cession of the Chełm province to Ukraine in exchange for grain supplies. Although the province contained a large Ukrainian population, it was located on the left bank of the Bug River and was considered by the majority of Poles as an integral part of historic Poland. Outrage at the treaty was universal, and mass strikes and demonstrations took place in cities, towns, and villages. The treaty marked the final rupture of Polish-Austrian and Polish-German relations. Vehement indignation was also directed against Jews, who were blamed for complicity with the Central Powers, especially because Ukrainian and Jewish employees appeared at their workplaces while their Polish colleagues went on strike. The fact that the Zionists and Assimilators joined their voices against the treaty did not alleviate the situation. The traditional Jewish pro-Habsburg and pro-German attitudes were the main factor behind Polish grievances. Although popular resentment was also directed against Ukrainians, they were still perceived as politically immature and incapable of independent action. Leaflets disseminated by the nationalist press portrayed Poles standing alone and surrounded by external and internal enemies; some booklets also predicted that unless Jews emigrated en masse, the "day of reckoning" was inevitable. Anti-Jewish riots broke out in Krakow and Lwów, and in other localities the energetic police intervention prevented further excesses. The joint protests of Jewish and Ukrainian parliament members in Vienna against the attacks were interpreted as yet more proof of Jewish-Ukrainian collaboration.[19]

Popular indignation at the Brest-Litovsk treaty marked the political mobilization of all layers of Polish society. Although this society was deeply divided along social, economic, and political lines, commoners and politicians came to believe that the Polish nation was betrayed by the Central Powers and sabotaged by disloyal ethnic minorities, especially Jews. The treaty became a junction at which the ideological anti-Semitism of politicians and the popular anti-Semitism of the masses coalesced into a powerful drive for national independence. Such anti-Semitism became both functional and genuine, for it encapsulated the rational dissatisfaction with existing socioeconomic conditions and emotional appeals to build a nation on common ethnic and historical foundations. In Warsaw, the Endeks gained mass support for a boycott of Jewish stores, and at the end of October a series of anti-Jewish riots erupted in the kingdom. The riots soon spilled over into more than ninety localities in West Galicia, where peasants and soldiers made up the backbone of the mob. Attacks on Jews and anti-Jewish agitation coincided with the influx of thousands of deserters and prisoners of war from Russia who poured into the countryside in the spring and summer of 1918. Armed gangs terrorized the population and particularly targeted Jews, who on several occasions armed themselves and beat off the attackers.[20]

Although Austro-Hungarian troops were able to put down these disturbances, the decline of the Central Powers underscored the rapid mobilization of ethnic identities, whereby linguistic, cultural, and religious differences amplified political divisions and separated Poles, Jews, and Ukrainians along "us" and "them" lines.[21] At the same time, the riots demonstrated that large segments of the Polish population would welcome the collapse of the old order. Jews, on the other hand, foresaw the end of the empire as an unmitigated disaster and hastened to seek accommodation with Ukrainians, whose national aspirations made them the only possible counterbalance to Poles.

Indeed, already by 1914 the Ukrainian national movement had made remarkable progress. Ukrainian financial, cultural, and educational institutions had grown in number, and the Ukrainian intelligentsia unequivocally considered themselves a distinct ethnic and national group. The war also gave a powerful impetus to the national aspirations of Ukrainians, who hoped for a favorable postwar territorial settlement and more political representation in Bukovina, Transcarpathia, and East Galicia. Thousands of Ukrainians served in Austro-Hungarian armies and fought on all fronts of the empire. The Ukrainian volunteers who formed the Sich Sharpshooters incurred very heavy casualties. In the postwar settlement, Ukrainian political activists were determined to build an autonomous unit within the Habsburg monarchy. East Galicia, it was hoped, would serve as a nucleus around which other areas inhabited by Ukrainians would amalgamate. Ukrainian objectives, however, collided with those of the Poles, who had dominated the regional administration and politics before the war and would accept nothing less for the future. Thus, after the declaration of the two emperors in November 1916, a committee of the Polish parliamentary group, *Koło Polskie,* worked out a new constitution, sharply reducing the number of Ukrainian deputies in the parliament. For Ukrainians, given their numerical superiority in Galicia, such an arrangement was unacceptable. The Ukrainian political representation in Vienna retaliated by succeeding in appointing Volodymyr Detsykevych as deputy governor of Galicia and announcing that it would never recognize Polish predominance in the postwar political establishment.[22]

As the Polish-Ukrainian confrontation gained momentum, the Ukrainians began preparations for the postwar political contest. On October 18, 1918, several Ukrainian political groups in Lwów formed the National Council, which was to act as a constituent assembly. The council, headed by Yevhen Petrushevych, claimed its authority over Ukrainian ethnic lands within the Austro-Hungarian monarchy and, recognizing the possibility of Polish counteraction, called for national autonomy for ethnic minorities—Poles, Germans, and Jews. More important for the evolution of Ukrainian-Jewish relations, the council recognized Jews as a distinct nationality, the notion long denied to them by Vienna.[23]

Ethnic tensions were rapidly approaching their boiling point. On October 20 a gathering of Jewish students in Lwów demanded national rights for Jews, and on October 26 a rally of Zionists, Orthodox, Poalei-Zion members, and socialists requested that Jews be represented as a separate group in future peace talks. In Warsaw, the most popular peasant newspaper, *Piast,* called for the economic boycott of Jewish businesses, and clashes between Jews and Poles took place in Warsaw, Lwów, and Krakow. As a result, in West and East Galicia, Austrian troops, the field police, and civil guards were put on high alert.[24]

In the late fall of 1918 Jews in the kingdom and Galicia were perhaps the only ethnic group that sincerely grieved over the collapse of the old order. As the press burst out with such headlines as "Terrible News from Galicia," "Murder and Plunder in Przemyśl," "Attacks in Łańcut," "Pogroms in Brzesko," and "De-judaisation of Poland," they recalled with sadness the "good old days" of the Austro-Hungarian and German empires. Polish-Jewish competition in the socioeconomic sphere, fierce in the first decade of the twentieth century, had been further aggravated by the war. The rule of the Central Powers sharpened mutual antagonisms as Poles and Jews tried to win concessions from the military regimes.

As the end of the war drew near, the two peoples had entirely different viewpoints in regard to the future. Before World War I ideological anti-Semitism was a prerogative of Polish right-wing parties, and anti-Jewish sentiments of the population emanated mostly from socioeconomic discourse. Although resenting the competition with Jewish peddlers and merchants, common Poles still perceived them as legitimate "others," a traditional part of ethnically diverse Polish life. The war witnessed the evolution of traditional anti-Jewish sentiments into a xenophobic ideology of the masses. The heavy-handed rule of the Central Powers strengthened national ties among the Poles, contributed to the development of highly introverted popular consciousness, and reinforced the beliefs in the putative racial distinctiveness of the Jews. Placed within a doctrine of national unity, anti-Semitism became an important constituent of the Polish struggle against foreign oppression.

The war also witnessed a major psychological transformation among Jews. In 1915–1916, it seemed that the rule of the Central Powers would eventually actuate Jewish national aspirations, civil and political equality. But these illusions did not endure for long. As the situation on the front and in the rear worsened, the Austrian and German military regimes found it expedient to support Poles at the expense of Jews. Nevertheless, the Jewish leadership had become convinced that only strong external pressure on Poles would guarantee Jewish national and civil rights. Therefore, it was imperative to seek the support of the Allies, whose voice would be decisive in the postwar world political settlement.[25]

5 / The Lwów Pogrom, November 22–24, 1918

At the end of World War I a horrified Jew saw Habsburg emblems being ripped off building walls in Prague and desperately cried out: "Who will shield us now?"[1] Indeed, as the Austro-Hungarian and German empires crumbled, state institutions that had traditionally protected Jews from the pent-up fury of local nationalisms ceased to exist. New countries emerged on the map of Europe, and independence was soon followed by violence against Jews in Czechoslovakia, Hungary, and Poland. Polish Jews had more reasons to fear for their future than did their coreligionists elsewhere in eastern Europe. Viewed as "outsiders," they were blamed for siding with Poland's enemies. As the war came to its end, attacks on Jews escalated. In November 1918, news of a pogrom in Lwów spread around the world. Polish-Jewish relations entered a critical stage, pregnant with long-lasting consequences.

The Ukrainian Coup d'etat and the Issue of Jewish Neutrality

As the war progressed, chances for the Polish-Ukrainian rapprochement dissipated, and Vienna's vague and mutually exclusive promises made conflict almost inevitable. In this situation, in order to win major powers to their respective causes, Polish and Ukrainian representatives in Vienna claimed to have secured Jewish support for their respective plans for the future political settlement in Galicia.[2] On October 19, 1918, the Ukrainian National Council declared the creation of a Ukrainian state that included East Galicia east of the San River, the Lemko area,[3] northwestern Bukovina, and parts of Transcarpathia. The declaration also stipulated the equality of all nationalities. Most important for Jews, it granted them equal national status with Poles and Ukrainians as well as a proportional number of seats in the council.[4]

The creation of the Ukrainian National Council coincided with Polish preparations for a takeover in Galicia. By October 31 Polish paramilitary groups had assumed power in Krakow, and the Polish Liquidation Committee, as a temporary governing body, was called into existence. In Lwów, the Polish Military Organization (POW) and the Union of Freedom subordinated themselves to a war veteran, Captain Czesław Mączyński, who had strong ties with the Endeks. In the meantime the collapse of the Austro-Hungarian army resulted in the mass desertion of multinational troops, who flooded towns and villages. Thousands of deserters formed armed bands and ravaged the countryside. Robbery, murder, and looting became endemic.[5]

In this situation, on the night of November 1, Ukrainian forces in Lwów under the command of Major Dmytro Vitovs'kyi seized the initiative by arresting Polish officers, disarming Austrian soldiers, and detaining the Austrian military governor, Count Karl Huyn. At daybreak, the Ukrainian National Council declared itself to have assumed power in Galicia. The council proclaimed Ukrainian statehood and guaranteed civil equality and political rights to all national groups. The Ukrainian coup, however, was only the beginning of widespread turmoil, for the mobs of civilians and soldiers in Lwów and Przemyśl went on rampage in munitions depots and warehouses, smashing shop windows and robbing passersby. Jewish stores and houses especially attracted roaming gangs. The Austro-Hungarian command was incapable of preventing excesses because multinational units refused to obey their commanders and joined the looters. The police and gendarmerie were equally powerless as the spirit of anarchy penetrated their ranks.[6]

To add to the spreading chaos, the Polish-Ukrainian confrontation turned into an armed conflict. When the news of the Ukrainian coup spread in Lwów, strongholds of Polish resistance were hastily organized. High school, gymnasium, and university students, augmented by civilians, barricaded themselves in schools and barracks. The Polish Civil Committee was formed, and in cooperation with the POW it endeavored to establish a uniform command among the defenders. Both bodies became spearheads of resistance and rallying points for Poles of all political persuasions, sex, and age. The heroic stance of the Polish youth soon reverberated around the country, and the struggle in Lwów was universally perceived as the ultimate showdown for independence. Even elements of the city underworld joined the defenders, and the fighting effectively separated the city into two hostile camps. Although some Jewish officers and soldiers sided with the Poles, the Jewish majority, who lived in Ukrainian-held parts of Lwów, were determined to await the outcome of the struggle.[7]

The Jewish leadership also tried to avoid being involved in the conflict. On the evening of November 1, representatives of several Jewish political parties formed the Committee for Public Safety. The committee announced that Jews would stay neutral and, to protect the Jewish quarters from criminal attacks, organized a militia. The committee also informed the Polish vice president of the city, Marceli Chłamtacz, and the Ukrainian commander, Major Vitovs'kyi, of these facts. The militia was armed and wore white armbands; later it was provided with identification cards in Yiddish.[8]

The declaration of neutrality triggered a wave of outrage among the Polish population, who interpreted it as an act of treachery, the proverbial last straw of Jewish wrongdoing. By the time the fighting erupted in Lwów, Polish-Jewish relations had already deteriorated to the point where the majority of Poles perceived Jews as hostile bystanders, if not open enemies. Because in partitioned Poland Jews had tended to side with what was seen as the stronger party, whether Austrians or Germans, the refusal to support the Polish side meant that Jews again were waiting to jump on the winner's bandwagon. In addition, an antiquated story of Poland's hospitality in accepting thousands of Jewish refugees in the Middle Ages was accentuated by the Polish press, which pointed to what was perceived to be the ingratitude and perfidy of the Jews. Moreover, Poles saw the Polish-Ukrainian conflict not only as an ethnic struggle but also as a confrontation between the city and the unkempt Ukrainian countryside, which invaded Lwów, the cradle of superior Polish culture. Jews, who composed a significant portion of the urban population, unequivocally sided with the Ukrainians. The Ukrainians, on the other hand, welcomed the declaration of neutrality because it effectively divested Poles of financial and human resources available in the Jewish quarters.

Polish and Ukrainian viewpoints failed to appreciate the situation confronting the Jews, for whom the escalating conflict had offered few alternatives. The wartime Polish-Jewish conflict and violence at the end of World War I portended grim prospects for Jews at the dawn of Poland's independence. On the other hand, as attractive as Ukrainian promises were, traditional Polish political dominance in Galicia and the relative fragility of the Ukrainian national movement advised caution in siding with the Ukrainians. Therefore, the Assimilators and the Orthodox protested against the declaration of neutrality as dangerous for the future of Jews in Poland. It also mattered that Ukrainian troops controlled the Jewish quarters in Lwów and that the *shtetlach* in the countryside were surrounded by Ukrainian villages. It can be surmised, therefore, that even if Jews nourished any desire to support the Poles (which the majority definitely did not), such a move was fraught with dangerous consequences. Therefore, on November 1, Jewish communities throughout Galicia also proclaimed neutrality, which seemed to be the only sensible course of action.

Although the Assimilators correctly assessed the potential ramifications of neutrality, their protestations of loyalty toward independent Poland did not change the situation. On November 6, the Committee for Public Safety in Lwów reiterated its intention to use any means to prevent the Jewish population from being dragged into the conflict. From this moment on, ethnic divisions were marked by the Polish-Ukrainian frontline through the city, rendering Polish-Jewish understanding impossible. Similarly, the announcement by the Polish government on November 7 that it guaranteed civil rights and liberties to all citizens made no difference as the fighting rapidly escalated.[9]

The Course of Events

In light of the events that unfolded in Lwów in November of 1918, it is no surprise that the issue of neutrality, and especially the activities of the Jewish militia, would later become the subject of heated debates. Jewish contemporaries and historians argued that the militia observed neutrality to the letter, whereas their Polish counterparts insisted that it broke neutrality from the start of the fighting. As law and order in Lwów crumbled at the end of October, the main Jewish district, Zamarstynów, which was situated on the fringe of the city, was targeted by roving bands of robbers. Lawlessness was aggravated by the fact that Austrian authorities had opened prison gates and set free about eight hundred criminals.[10] As the only protection for the Jewish population, the militia engaged these bands, often in pitched encounters. The militia also stopped and frisked Poles who were trying to cross over into Polish-held parts of the city. According to eyewitnesses, the militiamen vividly displayed their anti-Polish attitudes. Such stories aggravated the already-charged atmosphere in the city.[11] It should not be doubted that by the end of World War I anti-Polish resentments were strong among Jews and that militiamen released their long pent-up anger and mistreated Poles on the streets. Furthermore, the size of the militia was a matter of concern for the Polish command. By the standards of street fighting—initially Ukrainian and Polish forces did not exceed fifteen hundred men each (among the latter a large number were untrained youth)—the militia was a power to be reckoned with. By early November it comprised some 200 armed men; by mid-November it numbered 45 officers and 302 soldiers. Deployed in its entirety, such a force would be able to turn the tide in any local encounter.[12]

Nevertheless, despite misgivings on both sides, on November 10 the Committee for Public Safety and the Polish command signed a formal agreement that recognized the neutrality of Jews as well as demarcated Polish and Jewish respective zones of operation. By that time, the activities at the militia's checkpoints had already triggered numerous protests from the Polish side. Convictions that Jewish neutrality was a mere facade were reinforced by the main Ukrainian newspaper, *Ukrains'ke slovo,* which on November 3 announced that

"Jews act hand in hand with Ukrainians."[13] Jewish contemporaries argued that such a presentation of facts was erroneous. But from the Ukrainian point of view the militia's actions explicitly showed where Jewish sympathies lay. More important, the announcement aimed to underscore the legitimacy of Ukrainian claims—allegedly supported by Galicia's large ethnic minority—and to bolster the spirit of Ukrainian troops, who were largely drafted from the countryside and felt uncomfortable in a large and unfamiliar city. The presence of an ally most likely strengthened their resolve.

At the same time, the Ukrainian command recognized Jewish neutrality and let the militia maintain order in the Jewish quarters. It was an uneasy task. Ukrainian patrols carried out unauthorized searches of Jewish apartments and houses, and armed gangs preyed on residents. Robberies and assaults became daily occurrences. Already in the first week of November the militia had engaged armed bandits in several clashes. Maintaining neutrality became even more difficult because Polish and Ukrainian detachments often crossed into the militia-controlled districts. In addition, supplies were at a premium, and Jewish detachments also violated the demarcation lines, confiscating foodstuffs on the fringes of the city. The motley uniforms of the belligerents—in the dark of night, Polish, Ukrainian, and Jewish insignias were difficult to differentiate—fueled rumors, which added to the general confusion of the street fighting. Conversely, in the Polish-held parts of the city, rumors of Jews attacking Polish details and murdering wounded soldiers became especially persistent.[14]

However active the Poles believed the Jewish militia to be, in truth it constituted only a minuscule fraction of the Jewish population. The majority of Jews in the city as well as in the entire Galicia area wanted only to wait out the storm. In the midst of the conflict, however, this attitude went largely unnoticed. The official newspaper of the Polish forces in Lwów, *Pobudka,* published every instance and rumor about the militia's violation of neutrality. Resentment against "treacherous" Jews flared up on November 12 when a Jewish delegation approached a Polish position at the Sienkiewicz school, one of the Polish strongholds. Only the intervention of a commanding officer, Karol Baczyński, saved the envoys from swift and brutal reprisal by his troops. For more perspicacious members of the Committee for Public Safety, this incident must have served as the first premonition of what would happen should there be no restraining force in the city.[15]

Other developments added new ingredients to the vilification of the Jews. The nature of street fighting allowed only for a loosely unified command among Polish units, which often fought without support and instruction from Mączyński. Such a lack of coordination resulted in the disarmament and detention of militiamen because some Polish commanders refused to recognize the militia as a legitimate force. Although the Polish command and the Polish Civil Committee confirmed the neutrality of the Jews in a formal agreement, arrests of militiamen continued.[16] The social makeup of Polish troops also facilitated anti-Jewish animosities. Within their ranks petty criminals constituted a tangible component. Criminal elements were reported even among the Polish gendarmerie, the main order-keeping force. Although they displayed good fighting qualities, they abhorred any disciplinary limitations and often engaged in activities diametrically opposite to any military code. Thus the thin line between patriot and looter became very difficult to detect. To curb criminal activities, on November 8 the Ukrainian command introduced drumhead courts-martial, and the next day the Polish command followed suit. The enforcement of these measures, however, was a different matter, and the Jewish militia often fired on bandits wearing the Polish insignia. The Polish rank and file, for whom the criminals were good comrades and valiant compatriots, took the militia's shots as undisguised acts of hostility.[17]

Initially the Polish-Ukrainian conflict was fought according to the accepted rules of warfare, and the wounded and prisoners of war were treated humanely. Soon, however, such behavior gave way to undisguised atrocities on both sides. Four years of fighting desensitized large segments of Galicia's population, and the privation and chaos at the end of World War I reduced any moral and psychological constraints, resulting in bloodshed. The enemy was increasingly identified in ethnic terms as Poles and Ukrainians ascribed the violation of military conduct to each other's specific negative characteristics. The Polish press called Ukrainians "blood-thirsty Cossacks," referring to the Ukrainian Cossack armies that in the course of the seventeenth century annihilated thousands of Poles, and Ukrainian papers reminded their readers of the worst aspects of the centuries-long Polish rule in Ukraine. Accordingly, the two sides blamed each other for executing civilians and prisoners of war and retaliated in kind. On November 14, Ukrainian units murdered captured Polish soldiers, and a day later, Poles responded in kind, killing captured Ukrainians. Similar instances also took place elsewhere in East Galicia, further facilitating reprisals and counter-reprisals. In the confusion of city fighting in Lwów, all the belligerents reported being fired on by "saboteurs and subversives" from roofs, basements, garrets, and windows and called for immediate retribution. Polish forces, which in the first two weeks of fighting found themselves in particularly difficult situations, inevitably linked unidentified shooters to the "internal enemy," Jews.[18]

Further proof that Jews directly participated in fighting came on the night of November 15, when in a clash between the militia and Polish detachments two militiamen lost their lives. According to various sources, the militia tried to curb the activities of an armed gang that was robbing residents in the Jewish quarters. Having received reports of these events, the militia command dispatched a unit of thirty men under the command of an officer, Maximilian Straub. The unit attacked and dispersed the looters. In pursuit, it approached the Polish lines with a white flag, but the Poles opened fire and killed two militiamen, including Straub (some sources claim four militiamen, and others say only Straub). The rest were taken prisoner. Although Jewish sources insisted that the militia had informed the Polish command about the impending operation, the Polish side alleged that at least one Ukrainian supported the militia with gunfire. A Ukrainian newspaper, *Dilo,* also reported that a Polish offensive had been thwarted by a joint effort of the Jewish militia and Ukrainian forces.[19]

Meanwhile, *Pobudka* kept announcing that Jews attacked Polish units and that caches of munitions and arms were concealed in synagogues. Alleged witnesses related stories of Jews guiding Ukrainians to Polish positions, strafing Poles with machine guns, and pouring boiling water on soldiers. On November 17, *Pobudka* warned Jews not to "provoke anti-Semitism" among the Polish population.[20] In such a psychological climate, fear of possible pogroms compelled the Jewish leadership to appeal to the Allies. On November 14, the Committee for Public Safety wrote to President Woodrow Wilson and explained the situation of Jews caught in the midst of the Polish-Ukrainian conflict. A Jewish delegation also approached a French officer, Henry Villaime, a member of an Allied mission in Galicia, and asked him to mediate between the belligerents. Villaime agreed to convey the message to the Polish side.[21]

The Pogrom: Close-Up, Part I

On November 21, Polish forces, reinforced by units from Przemyśl, launched an offensive that decided the fate of Lwów. After sporadic fighting, Ukrainians withdrew from the city, and the next morning was recorded in Polish popular memory as one of triumph and glory. On a clear day with a light frost, singing Polish troops marched in. An eyewitness recalled the jubilation of Polish crowds: "Streets, dead quiet just a moment before, suddenly erupted with . . . people shouting, hysterically sobbing, and singing. . . . The marching columns were showered with flowers, cigarettes, and tobacco; . . . an unbelievable rush of joy swept house after house, street after street."[22]

At the time of the victorious celebration, a mob of civilians and soldiers rushed into the Jewish quarters, smashing windows, breaking into houses, and murdering people regardless of age or sex. Referred to by Polish sources as the "dregs" (*szumowiny*), the elements who attacked Jews indeed had all the trappings of a mob in that they were excited, disorderly, and brutal. The assailants' mood was fortified by the rumors that the attack was a "punitive" expedition and that the Polish command had "granted" the defenders of Lwów a free hand in the Jewish quarters. Discipline in the Polish ranks had never been too strict, and there were many drunken soldiers around. Immediately after Polish troops entered Lwów, the defenders of one city sector, Bem, went to a prison and released inmates. Although some were later apprehended and returned to their cells, about seventy escaped and more than likely joined the crowds.[23]

The makeup and lack of discipline among Polish troops were but two ingredients in the tragedy. The attitude of the Polish command was also a crucial factor that contributed to the spread of violence. On the morning of November 22, according to his memoirs, Mączyński had inspected Polish positions around the city. In his communiqué issued after the tour he asserted that Lwów was in Polish hands but for Żółkiewska Street—the hub of the Jewish quarters—and the area around a historical hill, the High Castle. At both sites, he reported, Jews and Ukrainians, armed with submachine guns, fought until late that evening. Resistance had been fierce, and Jewish defenders had allegedly poured boiling water on Polish soldiers. His report was corroborated by another Polish contemporary, who stressed a "very strong" resistance by the militia until afternoon.[24]

But these allegations were contradicted by the Supreme Command of Polish troops in Galicia, which on November 23 issued an order stating that Ukrainian troops had left Lwów on the night of the twenty-first. The order confirmed the presence of armed gangs dressed in uniforms and the establishment of drumhead courts-martial to punish bandits. Several Polish and Ukrainian contemporaries also stressed that there had been no Ukrainian forces in the city since the last Ukrainian soldiers left early in the morning of November 22, and there were no incidents of "boiling water, attacks with axes, and [Jewish] shooting" at Polish soldiers. In addition, there was no trace of fighting in the Jewish quarters. Moreover, Major Roman Abraham, who commanded the Polish position adjacent to the Jewish quarters, failed to mention Jewish resistance.[25] Other Polish sources reported that the Jewish militia had been disarmed around eight in the morning on November 22 and that after that time no fighting was recorded. If Ukrainians withdrew from the city on November 21, and the militia had been disarmed on November 22, what fighting was Mączyński referring to?

The events must be reconstructed step by step to answer this question. According to contemporaries and the investigative committee set up by the Polish government, the pogrom had started on the morning of November 22, when soldiers and civilians with the Polish insignia had broken into Jewish houses and stores, searching for firearms. Shots had been fired everywhere to intimidate residents or to finish off victims. Women were raped, furniture was destroyed, windows were smashed, and walls were ripped apart in search of gold. After thorough looting, the attackers tossed hand grenades into stores and apartments. According to rumors, the Polish command had given the assailants forty-eight hours to loot with impunity. The pogrom had come in waves, with one group of looters followed by another, shouting anti-Semitic slogans and leaving the impression of a systematic assault.[26] Three synagogues were set on fire, and Jews who tried to save religious artifacts perished in the flames. This later led to accusations that Poles deliberately prevented the residents from escaping the burning buildings. In some instances, after having looted an apartment, the attackers locked up residents inside and set it afire. Soldiers constituted the bulk of the looters, and Jewish witnesses maintained that the area had been tightly sealed by troops and police, a sign that the pogrom was organized.[27]

Nevertheless, from documentary sources it becomes evident that the Polish command neither ordered nor coordinated the brutal acts of its subordinates. The mob consisted of groups and single individuals who seem to have acted on their own, although Jewish sources reported the presence of noncommissioned men and officers among the assailants. Yet, given the anti-Jewish mood of Polish troops during the fighting in Lwów, one can conclude that anti-Jewish violence required no organization. It was enough to let things go, and this is exactly what Polish commanders did. On November 22, a deputation of Jews had approached General Bolesław Roja, who had assumed the general command of Polish forces in the area. The deputies informed Roja that armed groups were breaking into Jewish stores and asked for protection. Roja consented to the request and sent the deputies to Mączyński, who as the immediate officer on the scene was responsible for carrying out appropriate measures. Another officer, the commander of the relieving force, Lieutenant Colonel Michał Karaszewicz-Tokarzewski, tried to convince Mączyński to give restraining orders to the troops. When Jewish deputies reached Mączyński, he promised immediate action. His order to maintain law and discipline, however, was issued only the next day, November 23. In his memoirs, Mączyński attributed the delay to the fact that the publisher was late with printing out the order and that Roja had forbidden its publication. Yet, on November 21 Polish civil authorities had published an appeal to the population to maintain calm and not engage in "outbursts of hate." Therefore, Mączyński's version that it was the publisher who had bungled his orders does not hold up under scrutiny.[28]

That Polish commanders anticipated disturbances can be deduced from the actions of General Roja. On the afternoon of November 22 he requested reinforcements from the Polish Liquidation Committee in Krakow to "uphold law and provide protection against bands of robbers." Several hours later, he repeated the request, stressing that with no additional forces it would be impossible to stop the excesses. Polish units in and around Lwów numbered about three thousand frontline officers and soldiers—a sufficient force to put down armed resistance save for large-scale unrest or popular disorder. Yet Roja requested reinforcements, appreciating the difficulties in restraining his subordinates. The next day, Roja issued an order authorizing the use of arms against any "individual, civilian or uniformed, caught red-handed in robberies and violence." On November 24, courts-martial were introduced, which sentenced to death two men and a woman. Later, several dozen persons received prison sentences.[29]

Although the printing house allegedly botched Mączyński's good intentions, it did not fail to publish another announcement on November 23. As Lwów celebrated its liberation, an address signed by Mączyński and directed to the Jewish community appeared on city walls. It accused Jews of shooting Polish troops in the back, attacking them with axes, and pouring boiling water on passing soldiers. The address told Jews that the Polish command tried to

> restrain the natural impulses of the Polish population and the troops. All residents regardless of confession have the right for lawful protection. To this end drumhead courts-martial and summary punishment have been introduced.
>
> Nevertheless, the bulk of the Jewish population should be obliged to constrain those of their co-religionists who still conduct themselves in such a manner as if trying to bring an unpredictable disaster upon the entire Jewish community.
>
> The Polish Command hopes that the Jewish population, primarily in its own interest, would restrain its co-religionists from any display of hatred toward Polish rule, and by correct and loyal conduct would make it possible for the authorities and the rest of the population to introduce and uphold law and order.[30]

Whatever Mączyński had in mind, Jewish and Polish contemporaries agreed that at the time when the pogrom was in full swing, the appeal further incited the mob and effectively exonerated its deeds. At this point it suffices to say that the pogrom went in waves until November 24. Then drumhead courts-martial were finally established, and after the Polish gendarmerie and officer patrols arrested several looters, order was restored. One can conclude, as did some Polish officers, that the pogrom could have been prevented, or at least tamed, but for a lack of will on the part of the Polish command.[31]

This conclusion seems fully justified if one looks at developments that took place in Przemyśl exactly at the time of the fighting in Lwów. The Ukrainian takeover of Przemyśl also started on November 1, and the Polish-Ukrainian conflict soon engulfed the entire district. The Jewish community declared neutrality, and the Jewish militia protected the Jewish quarters from roving bands of marauders. The closer proximity to Krakow allowed the Polish Liquidation Committee to dispatch reinforcements to Przemyśl promptly and tip the tide of the battle.[32] The Polish command accused the Jewish militia of fighting on the Ukrainian side. On the evening of November 11, once the Polish offensive cleared the city of Ukrainian units, there were sporadic attacks on Jews and looting of Jewish shops, and military details and police began searches in Jewish and Ukrainian houses, terrorizing the residents. The excesses, however, were stopped by the energetic intervention of the Polish commander, Major Julian Stachiewicz, who dispatched officer patrols to the Jewish quarters.[33]

The Pogrom: Close-Up, Part II

When daylight settled in on November 25, the Jewish quarters in Lwów presented a miserable sight. Houses, synagogues, and buildings were still smoldering, black smoke was pouring through empty windows, and streets were littered with pieces of furniture, utensils, and linen. Fifty-four houses were completely burned or destroyed, and material losses amounted to more than one hundred million Austrian kron (approximately $200,000). Precious religious artifacts, manuscripts, and Torah scrolls perished in the flames. One of the city's oldest synagogues, built in 1630, was burned to the ground. Accounts of human losses varied, and the total number remained controversial, but between 73 and 150 Jews were murdered, and 463 were wounded. The number of rapes remained unknown. Because Polish casualties reached between 200 and 210 and Ukrainian casualties were similar during the three weeks of fighting in Lwów, even the lowest estimate of Jewish losses—seventy-three dead civilians—was high by the standards of street fighting.[34]

The gap between the lowest and highest estimate of victims was conditioned by the provenance of the sources. The Polish side tried to minimize Jewish losses, whereas Jewish sources stressed the extent of the tragedy and inflated the numbers. The Polish military, for example, reported that between November 1 and November 24 seventy-eight Jews were killed. It argued that between November 23 and 24 more Poles and Ukrainians were killed than Jews.[35] Yet, the government commission sent to Lwów by the Ministry of Foreign Affairs to investigate the events on the spot came to a different conclusion. It estimated that 150 Jews were murdered, some fifty houses were partially or completely burned, and more than five hundred stores were looted. They reported that the pogrom directly affected seven thousand families. The commission concluded that the army "craved for revenge and was absolutely sure that Jews collaborated with Ukrainians; [appropriate] orders were given for reprisals."[36]

~

As horrible as the Lwów pogrom was, it paled in comparison to the Russian pogroms of 1904–1905 and even more so to the carnage that befell the Jewish communities in Ukraine during the Russian civil war. Yet, the uproar the Lwów tragedy generated worldwide suggests that its impact was much out of proportion to the number of casualties. Why?

The pogrom drew much public attention and became a watershed in Polish-Jewish relations less for what it actually was than for what it meant and symbolized. The complexity and consequences of the pogrom should be measured and understood only against the situation of Poland in European politics at that time. After more than a century of foreign domination, Poland had emerged as an independent state. The three partitioned parts, with different political traditions and different social and economic structures, had to be integrated into one unit. These political, social, and economic difficulties were compounded by military conflicts on all Polish frontiers—in East Galicia with Ukrainians, in the Poznań province with Germans, and in the northeast of the former kingdom with Lithuanians. In Belorussia and southern Lithuania, the simmering Polish-Soviet confrontation would soon erupt into a full-scale war. Therefore, Poland's international standing, economy, and defense depended greatly on the support and goodwill of the Allies to finalize the postwar borders. The Polish struggle for independence had won many sympathizers and supporters in the West, and it was paramount to maintain Poland's image as a democratic and freedom-loving country rising from the ruins like the proverbial phoenix. Reports of the Lwów pogrom came as a thunderbolt, badly damaging the country's reputation.

From the Polish point of view, Jews had willfully distorted the events in Lwów. Indeed, Jewish agencies in Europe and America had widely publicized the pogrom and highly exaggerated its scope. Thus, on November 30, 1918, the *Manchester Guardian* referred to it as "one of the worst pogroms in Polish history, and a device of the old Polish oligarchy to counter the new democratic tendencies [in Poland]." The communiqué of a Zionist organization in Lwów published the number of victims as six hundred. In December, the *Jewish Chronicle* in London asserted that thirty-two hundred Jews had died in the pogrom. Other sources came up with 956, 1,000, or 1,600 casualties. These stories were echoed by the Ukrainian press in Galicia and Ukraine. Almost all reports insinuated that the pogrom had been organized, that soldiers and officers murdered Jews in cold blood, and that the majority of Poles rejoiced at the news of the pogrom.[37]

Various Jewish organizations in the West sent protests to the Polish government, and prominent politicians, renowned religious leaders, and businessmen in Britain, France, and the United States pressed for economic sanctions against Poland. In January of 1919, under the influence of the news of pogroms in Poland, the newly created League of Nations made recognition of the new states of eastern Central Europe contingent on guarantees of civil rights for national minorities.[38] Such conditions were interpreted in Poland as vivid proof of an international Jewish conspiracy. The Endeks were convinced that Woodrow Wilson and Lloyd George were under strong Jewish influence and that a clandestine international organization headed by Jews was seeking world domination. Jews, they alleged, used the Lwów pogrom merely as a device to destroy Poland.[39] Galvanized by these events, the Polish media proceeded to dispel what it considered to be "Jewish slander." But in an atmosphere of anxiety and hatred, the Polish version of the pogrom was, not surprisingly, much further from the truth than the Jewish one. On November 25, 1918, the Lwów City Council blamed criminals released by Ukrainians as the main culprits. *Pobudka,* which had played such a conspicuous role in inciting anti-Jewish sentiments, bluntly declared that the Jewish militia had been formed illegally and without Polish approval. To add insult to injury, Jews themselves were blamed for inciting the pogrom or participating in it. Thus, on November 29 the Polish Telegraph Agency released a communiqué claiming that criminals released by the Ukrainians and Jewish hoodlums had staged the pogrom. It asserted that the Polish military rigorously prosecuted the culprits and executed fifty bandits. The Polish Liquidation Committee, the Department of Mail and Telegraph, and the Polish embassy in Kiev reiterated the same story.[40]

In December 1918, Polish sources reported on the ethnic makeup of the pogrom participants: 60 percent Ukrainians, 30 percent Poles, and 10 percent Jews. Criminals were pointed to as the main evildoers. These criminals allegedly even had armored cars at their disposal, and Polish troops had arrested as many as sixteen hundred offenders. Moreover, according to these sources, Jews who actively participated in the pogrom should blame only themselves because one "who sows wind, will reap tempest."[41] Spearheading anti-Jewish agitation, the Endek press maintained its ideological pattern established during World War I. *Słowo Polskie* explained the pogrom as the natural outburst against Jewish vices and crimes such as speculation, collaboration with Poland's enemies, and espionage. Further accusations were adjusted to fit the current political situation. Jews were alleged to have tortured wounded Polish soldiers or to have spearheaded the Ukrainian coup.[42] Even moderate Polish politicians joined in refuting what they saw as the Jewish anti-Polish campaign. The former viceroy of Galicia, Michał Bobrzyński, asserted that in Galicia the Polish administration had always treated Jews on an equal basis. Instead, Jews sided with Ukrainians, and that triggered popular Polish outrage. Bobrzyński accepted, however, that the dregs of society and soldiers had staged the pogrom and that its consequences had severely damaged the reputation of Poland.[43]

The question of who had perpetrated the pogrom and why it had not been curbed immediately became the focus of further nebulous charges against the Jews. Criminals released from Lwów prisons featured most prominently in every Polish report. Ukrainians followed next. Jews, as militia members, petty criminals, or willful individuals dressed in Polish uniform, consistently emerged as the third factor. Mączyński's chief of staff, Antoni Jakubski, insisted that Jews were demoralized by the Ukrainian defeat and, having "completely lost sense," turned against Polish units.[44] Roja and Mączyński blamed one another for not acting more effectively in stopping the pogrom. Mączyński also argued that because he had subordinated himself to the commander of Polish reinforcements, Lieutenant Colonel Michał Karaszewicz-Tokarzewski, the latter was responsible for all appropriate measures. The colonel, in turn, contended that Mączyński was on the spot when the pogrom began and should have dealt with the trouble on his own.[45]

Reports by foreign observers who came to Lwów to investigate the pogrom were primarily based on information presented by both sides and reflected Polish-Jewish mutual accusations. Captain Antony Wright, a member of the Allied mission to Galicia, stressed that at the root of Polish anti-Semitism was German-Jewish cooperation during World War I. Wright asserted that Jews had violated neutrality by siding with the Ukrainians. But he also stressed that the poor discipline of Polish forces had promoted violence and that the Polish command was able to maintain order by promising its troops forty-eight hours of looting in the Jewish quarters. Polish officers and soldiers, reported Wright, perceived looting as an integral part of warfare, and anti-Semitism played no major role in the pogrom. Wright concluded that sixty Jews had been killed and that many more were robbed, wounded, or raped.[46]

In much stronger words, Israel Cohen, a British-Jewish observer, stated that the pogrom had been carefully prepared and that there was another attack on Jews at the end of December.[47] A report by an American diplomat, Henry Morgenthau, asserted that the Lwów Jewish quarters were in the Ukrainian-held territory and that it was hard to verify the facts of Jewish-Ukrainian collaboration. He gave the number of deserters and criminals at large as fifteen thousand, identified sixty-four Jewish casualties, and alleged that seven thousand people were charged with participating in the pogrom. Morgenthau ascribed the tragedy to the lack of discipline among Polish troops and pointed out that determined actions by officer patrols ended the violence.[48]

Pandemonium generated by the Lwów pogrom prompted Polish authorities to take measures to prevent the leak of further compromising evidence to the press. Jews who tried to collect data on the pogrom's human and economic losses were apprehended by army patrols or gendarmerie and reported to the Polish command. The military was especially concerned about the activities of the Jewish Aid Committee, which gathered information on the pogrom and raised funds for relief efforts. On November 27, alarmed by rumors that Jews were preparing an armed uprising, the Polish command in Galicia put the Lwów garrison on high alert. After the Assimilators also joined in the chorus of protests to the government, Polish authorities interpreted this apparent shift of a previously loyal group as a unified Jewish opposition. Fears of Jewish retaliation were also reflected in several appeals issued by the military command, which warned Jews that any anti-state activities would cause "unforeseeable consequences" for the Jewish community. The government and military officials were also concerned that Galician Jews closely collaborated with the "international Jewry," which pulled strings at the Paris Peace Conference. To put a stop to unified Jewish actions, on December 12 the military detained five prominent Jewish activists. A Zionist newspaper, *Togblat,* was shut down, and its reopening was made contingent on printing the texts in Latin.[49]

The Lwów pogrom marked a rising combativeness of Jews in that they vociferously protested to the Polish military and, more important, appealed to world public opinion. From the Jewish point of view, the very inception of Poland was marked by brutal and undisguised murder, which augured a grim future. Accordingly, political, economic, and military difficulties of the state were brushed off as merely a justification for an organized anti-Jewish campaign. Such views were voiced by the newspaper *Ha-tsfira,* which stressed that the new Poland was "re-born with bloodstains on [its] forehead."[50]

Of note, some Polish political and religious leaders attempted to ameliorate the results of the Lwów tragedy. In fact, during the pogrom several Polish officers were reported to have protected Jews from ravaging bands. The Roman Catholic archbishop of Lwów, A. Bilczewski, appealed to the Polish population, stressing that "whatever the transgressions of the Jews might be," looting and mob law had to stop. Deputations of Polish *szlachta,* the Polish Liquidation Committee, and the Lwów City Council donated money to the Jewish community to help repair damages.[51] These protestations of goodwill, however, were drowned out in the chorus of anti-Semitic diatribe that engulfed the country. Besides charges of collaborating with the enemy, Jews were accused of conducting an anti-Polish defamation campaign abroad. Most offensive, however, were attempts by Polish authorities to blame Jews themselves for the pogrom. In spite of the fact that none of the Lwów hospitals and doctors ever reported patients treated for burns, the Polish press kept insisting that Jews had poured boiling water on soldiers and that there were Jewish criminals in Polish uniforms among the mob. The charge that Jews hid munitions and arms in Lwów synagogues resulted from a controversy over whether a round slot in the roof of a synagogue was a submachine gun port, as the Poles insisted, or a ventilation hatchway, as the Jews maintained.[52]

Although Jewish and Polish versions of the pogrom diverged sharply on every point, some facts can be ascertained to provide a more or less complete picture of the events in Lwów. When the Jewish leadership probed into a possible Jewish-Ukrainian alliance in November 1918, the majority of Jews remained passive. Furthermore, the Orthodox, who composed the largest contingent among the Galician Jewry, refused to join the Committee for Public Safety and protested against the creation of the militia. Therefore, accusations that Jews maintained a unified and monolithic anti-Polish front were highly exaggerated. Equally ungrounded were charges that the entire Jewish militia in Lwów actively participated in fighting on the Ukrainian side. Indeed, before November 21 neither the Polish command nor the Polish Civil Committee presented official charges to the Committee for Public Safety about the militia's violation of neutrality. In addition, although it is unquestionable that some militiamen actively supported Ukrainians, the militia was disarmed on the morning of November 22 and ceased to exist as the only armed Jewish detachment. Hence, "heavy fighting" in the Jewish quarters on November 22–23 as referred to by Polish sources was impossible unless one assumes that the entire Jewish population was heavily armed. Of significance, between November 1918 and March 1919, Polish courts tried only eight militiamen and two Jewish civilians for collaborating with the Ukrainians during the fighting in Lwów. The two civilians were sentenced to prison, and the militiamen were acquitted.[53]

Polish sources gave disproportional weight to the role of criminals in the pogrom. It is true that the Jewish area of the city, Zamarstynów, a habitat of the poor, had a bad reputation before the war. Nevertheless, the number of criminals—some Polish contemporaries referred to thousands of felons—seems absurd.[54] After all, such a force could have easily attacked the Jewish quarters in the beginning of the fighting when general chaos and confusion made it much easier. The Jewish militia, which numbered about three hundred men, would not have been able to repel the attack of such a horde of armed villains. Instead, Lwów thugs allegedly waited until the fighting was over and the Polish military was in control of the situation.

It stands to reason, therefore, that the conduct of the Polish command was the main factor behind the violence. Common soldiers were convinced that they had permission to loot the Jewish quarters, and some Polish commanders believed that Jews were to be punished for their treachery. Jakubski, for example, admitted that the assault on the Jewish quarters had all the trappings of a punitive expedition and that "Jews received an exemplary punishment. The whole area had to be pacified in a military way."[55] The motley composition of Polish troops also contributed to their propensity to violence. Criminals who had joined the Polish side displayed good fighting qualities, but they did not necessarily abandon their primary trade. Clashes between them and the Jewish militia became the main basis for the accusations of Jewish violation of neutrality.[56] Still, according to Polish court records, the mob that attacked Jews represented all walks of life, were of different ages, and had varied incentives for participating in violence. Some perpetrators were professional criminals, whereas the others were regular city residents. For example, Włodzimierz Żeliński, who faced trial in June of 1919, was a retired accountant. Jan Łotowski and his two companions, sentenced to three years of severe imprisonment in September of 1919, had no definite trade. Katarzyna Bołuchówna and Stefania Maksymowicz were housemaids who had directed Polish soldiers to an allegedly rich Jewish family. Tried in 1921, twenty-two-year-old Leon Marek had no occupation. Dressed in Polish uniform during the pogrom, he threw a hand grenade into a Jewish apartment. The explosion killed one and wounded four.[57] By February 10, 1919, the Lwów Police Department announced that it had arrested seventy-six individuals implicated in the pogrom. Out of this number, forty-three were women, and, because the bulk of the mob in the Jewish quarters were armed men, this proportion of women among the arrested indicates that the majority of the assailants escaped justice.[58]

The Lwów pogrom was arguably one of the most consequential episodes in Polish-Jewish relations in the first half of the twentieth century. For Jews, it marked the beginning of a new Poland where anti-Semitism held sway in the political establishment and among the population. Jewish political leaders, therefore, became convinced that only a widely publicized campaign in Poland and abroad would ensure the security and safety of Jews. On the other hand, the Polish political leadership as well as large segments of Polish society viewed Jews as a uniformly hostile and intractable ethnic group poised to sabotage the new state. In this situation, when Poland, surrounded by hostile neighbors, was desperately trying to build a viable state machinery amid the chaos of war, such attitudes were bound to breed more violence as the Polish frontier wars got under way.

6 / The Polish Frontier Wars, 1919–1920

By the beginning of 1919 Poland had faced tremendous challenges. As a main battlefield of World War I, the country had been devastated by the years of fighting, the unbridled robberies of its natural resources and requisitions of foodstuffs by the belligerent armies, and the forcible relocation of its population. The bulk of Polish industry and trade had ground to a standstill; inflation, speculation, and crime were rampant; and only rudimentary state institutions were functional. In addition, regional political and economic differences among the three partitioned parts made the process of integration extremely difficult. The military situation was just as menacing. In the west, the Germans still held West Prussia, Silesia, and the eastern Baltic shore. In the east, the forces of the newly created Western Ukrainian National Republic (ZUNR) controlled two-thirds of East Galicia, except the Lwów and Przemyśl districts. In early January the Red Army captured Vil'nius, and in February it set up the so-called Soviet Lithuanian-Belorussian Republic. At the same time, the Polish-German confrontation in the Poznań province exploded into a full-scale armed conflict that continued until the spring. In cities and the countryside the nascent Polish Communist Workers' Party carried out anti-state propaganda and promoted the establishment of Communist rule.

In such a situation, ethnic conflicts were directly entangled with the country's external politics. In the international arena, American, French, and British Jewish organizations attempted to influence Allied decisions regarding the minority rights in central and eastern Europe. In Poland these attempts were popularly perceived as a "Jewish plot," an image that was facilitated by Jewish support for the ZUNR as well as by the prominence of Jews in the Bolshevik governments in Russia and Hungary. Exacerbated by economic shortages and social unrest, anti-Semitic attitudes grew in intensity concomitantly with the escalation of fighting on the frontiers.

The Minority Rights Treaty

From the inception of independent Poland, the Polish government realized the potential of the Polish-Jewish confrontation for Poland's international reputation and tried to smooth the seething ethnic tensions. On November 12, 1918, Józef Piłsudski, the most popular political figure and provisional chief of state, received a Jewish delegation in Warsaw. The delegation pledged cooperation in the reconstruction of Poland and voiced its concerns about widespread anti-Jewish violence and anti-Semitic propaganda in the country. The delegates requested that a department of Jewish affairs be created as one of the governmental agencies and that the internal life of Jewish communities be regulated by communal councils.[1] Piłsudski promised to give thorough consideration to these requests and to take measures against anti-Semitism. The Polish leader, however, was in a difficult situation. To establish law and order, he needed a centralized administrative apparatus and regular armed forces. Both branches were still in the making, and communication with many units engaged on Poland's frontiers was almost nonexistent. Moreover, anti-Jewish sentiments were shared by different social layers of Polish society, and, consequently, any public statement contrary to popular convictions would only strengthen the position of Piłsudski's archrivals, the Endeks. Eventually, in January 1919, facing growing opposition to his government, Piłsudski struck an agreement with the Polish right and appointed Ignacy Paderewski, affiliated with the Endeks, prime minister of the new cabinet. From this point on, the Endeks would largely dominate Polish nationality policies.

In Paris, the Polish delegation, headed by Dmowski, hastened to depict the pogroms in Poland as merely Jewish fabrications. In turn, the American Jewish Congress, the Zionist Organization of America, the Alliance Israélite Universelle, and the Joint Foreign Committee actively advocated the imposition of sanctions on Poland and promoted civil and national rights for Jews in central and eastern Europe. Simultaneously, in Warsaw the Jewish National Council (Żydowska Rada Narodowa [ŻRN]), formed in December 1918 by the members of several Jewish political groups, requested the recognition of Jews as a national minority. Its branch in East Galicia claimed to represent the East Galician Jewry in the ZUNR government and announced its intentions to strive for Jewish national autonomy.[2] The Jewish organizations, however, failed to work out a common course of action. American and British representatives disagreed on whether guaranteeing Jews religious and cultural liberties would suffice or whether Jewish national autonomy would automatically secure these rights. The ŻRN pressed for national and individual autonomy for Jews in eastern Europe, their admission to the League of Nations, and sanctions against the governments that did not take measures against economic boycott and violence.[3]

Jewish diplomatic activities caused popular indignation in Poland, transcending all social cross-sections and mirroring official and popular views on the issues of ethnicity and national identity. The experiences of World War I had strengthened psychological bonds among ethnic Poles, whose notion of nation and ethnicity was based on common ethnic and religious distinctions. For that reason the popular majority was reluctant to accept Jews—"alien" by religion, culture, and language and known for their wartime pro-German and pro-Austrian leanings—as a part of the Polish nation. The Endeks especially accentuated the discrepancy between Jewish demands for civil and political equality and minority rights, which allegedly entitled Jews to specific rights and privileges and laid the groundwork for a Jewish substructure inside Poland. Such perceptions were voiced by a prominent Endek, Stanisław Grabski, who claimed that he had been approached by an emissary of the American Jewish Congress. The emissary indicated to Grabski that Jews would support Polish territorial claims in Paris on two conditions—an administrative enclave in *Kresy Wshodnie,* where Yiddish would receive equal status with Polish, and Jews would hold at least 50 percent of all positions in the local civil institutions. Although the authenticity of Grabski's claims may well be doubted, it is certain that the Polish leadership interpreted Jewish autonomy as a dangerous precedent for other ethnic minorities. In an interview with the newspaper *Dziennik Nowy,* therefore, Grabski asserted that the creation of the so-called Judeo-Polonia was out of the question.[4]

Meanwhile, the Allies were divided about minority rights in eastern Europe. President Woodrow Wilson was inclined to place Jews as a national minority under the aegis of the League of Nations. The French argued for political and civil rights without, however, national autonomy, and the British considered supporting the rights of minorities for self-administration in schools and cultural institutions under the auspices of the state. In addition, the Allies considered Poland a key element in the *cordon sanitaire* around Soviet Russia and were reluctant to apply too much pressure on the Polish government. The Polish delegation in Paris skillfully utilized these concerns by highlighting the role of Jewish revolutionaries in the Bolshevik movement.[5]

A group of Polish literati and intellectuals associated with the National Democrats made the same insinuations to the Allied mission in East Galicia, presenting the Jewish-ZUNR alliance as the forefront of Bolshevism. Such association of Jews and Bolsheviks was not, however, merely a device to influence international public opinion. Various religious and political organizations in Poland expressed fears that "Judeo-Bolshevism" (*Żydo-komuna*) was a part of an international Communist conspiracy. In December 1918, in a letter to the

ŻRN, Krakow bishop A. Sapiecha stressed that the Polish-Jewish confrontation could be resolved only after Jews ceased their efforts to "infect [Polish society] with Bolshevism" and terminate a "slanderous anti-Polish propaganda campaign" around the world. The bishop asserted that in Polish popular opinion, "after the collapse of the partitioning empires, a new enemy has arisen in the international arena, Jews." Such perceptions, concluded Sapiecha, would heavily influence the future coexistence of Poles and Jews.[6] The facts that in Poznań the Jewish community sided with the Germans in the Polish-German conflict and that the Gdańsk Jews vehemently protested against the potential integration of the region into Poland appeared as further proof of a unified Jewish front against Poland.[7]

The Sejm, which opened in January 1919, became a public podium from which similar accusations were hurled against the entire Polish Jewry. After Paderewski solemnly opened its first session and promised that in the "radiance of Polish liberty [national minorities] would freely develop their own [cultural] forms, sentiments, and thoughts," inflammatory invective became the tone of the day. Polish right-wingers and members of the clergy accused Jews of promoting Communism, murdering Polish children and soldiers, and "provoking" international sanctions. Jewish deputies were vilified and interrupted, and requests for Jewish national autonomy sparked a new cycle of anti-Semitic vitriol. The majority of deputies were especially appalled at the supervision of the League of Nations over Jewish autonomy, believing that this supervision curbed Polish sovereignty and effectively relegated the country to a second-class state. Paderewski himself fulminated that the minority rights treaty was "specifically tailored for Jews—the people without a defined territory, for whom the Jewish street will substitute the Motherland."[8] In response, Jewish deputies maintained that the government was unable to stop the excesses and consequently adopted an attitude of benign neglect on the issue. As another spiral of mutual Polish-Jewish accusations gained momentum, Paderewski appealed to President Wilson, complaining about anti-Polish agitation in the United States and requesting that a special foreign mission be sent to Poland to investigate Polish-Jewish relations. He said that Poland "has always been a bastion of tolerance" and that violence was largely generated by "Jewish arrogance and agitation."[9]

At the end of May, the Allied representatives finally prepared the draft of the Minority Treaty. Similar to the situation after the Brest-Litovsk treaty, a wave of protests swept the country. Polish public opinion was especially bitter over the fact that Germany did not have to sign the document. Although the treaty was to apply to other national minorities in Poland, such as Germans and Ukrainians, popular wrath was particularly directed against Jews, whose "insinuations" in Paris were seen as the prime moving force behind the Allied decision. On May 31, 1919, Paderewski complained to the Sejm that Poland was being treated

> as a small barbarian people. . . . This great and civilized nation, the champion of tolerance and progress[,] is forced to accept law and internal rules imposed from outside. Honest, decent, and wise people, who imposed these rules, wanted not to insult us.
>
> They were egregiously misinformed. . . . These rules we would have instituted on our own. . . . However, if our friends overseas wish to placate certain co-nationals of ours, so much the better, as long as it would help establish internal order and end the slanderous and insulting campaign.[10]

On June 28, 1919, Poland (along with Romania, Greece, Czechoslovakia, and the Kingdom of Serbs, Croats, and Slovenians) signed the treaty and guaranteed her national minorities civil, religious, and political rights and the right to use native languages in communal life. In regard to Jews, the Polish government pledged to place Jewish school committees under state control and thus make them eligible for state funds. Jews were exempted from work on the Sabbath and religious holidays, and the Polish government would not hold elections on Saturdays. Yiddish was to be used in Jewish schools, although Polish could be made mandatory. As citizens of the Polish state, Jews were made liable for military service and obliged to contribute to national defense as well as maintain public order. The implementation of the treaty was placed under the supervision of the League of Nations and its tribunal. Still, the treaty did not provide either for a representative Jewish body in the Sejm or for a Jewish department in the Polish government.[11]

On the surface, the supervision by the League of Nations curtailed Polish sovereignty because it allowed Jews to lodge complaints to a foreign institution. Nevertheless, a provision in the treaty explicitly stipulated that Jews could appeal to the League only through the Polish government. Hence, direct contact with the League was out of the question. Although civil and political rights of Jews were guaranteed, Jews officially remained a religious minority; their hopes for national autonomy were thus effectively dashed. In addition, in light of Poland's potential contribution to the struggle against Bolshevism (which seemed more threatening after the establishment of the Communist regime in Hungary), the Allied Supreme War Council was willing to grant Poland the right to administer East Galicia until further decisions were made on its status.[12]

In spite of these limitations, the treaty was denounced by every political group in Poland as the veritable proof of the influence Jews wielded in the international arena. Although a handful of intellectuals argued that granting Jews equal civil and national rights would lessen the Polish-Jewish confrontation, the overwhelming majority of politicians and commoners were outraged at the putative exceptional privileges for Jews. The leader of the Polish Socialist Party, Daszyński, fulminated that although Jews were not a national, but a religious community, the treaty accorded them a special status. In the Sejm, anti-Semitic deputies raved that the treaty imposed a Jewish occupation on Poland and lay the country open to Bolshevism and the "Red Terror."[13]

In the summer of 1919 several foreign missions arrived in Poland to investigate anti-Jewish excesses. Henry Morgenthau, who headed the American mission, wrote a memorandum in which he concluded that the violent outbreaks were largely spontaneous and resulted from anti-Semitic propaganda. Morgenthau admitted that Jewish sources tended to inflate the number of casualties. The Polish government, on the other hand, had not acted effectively to stop the disturbances. Morgenthau also asserted that instead of making the life of Polish Jews easier, the Minority Treaty only escalated Polish-Jewish animosities.[14] Two other members of the mission, General Edgar Jadwin and Professor Homer Johnson, pointed to the pro-German and pro-Bolshevik sympathies of Jews as the grounds for anti-Semitism in Poland and expressed hopes that peace and stabilization of the economy would change the situation for the better.[15] A British observer, Sir Stuart Samuel, did not mince words, accusing Poles of instigating the economic and social boycott of Jews and blaming the Polish government for its inability to stop anti-Semitic agitation and violence. In the course of conversations with Paderewski and Dmowski, Samuel implied that the treatment of Jews would resonate in the international arena and thus have a direct effect on the availability of foreign credits to Poland. Quite naturally, such allusions only vindicated public convictions that Jews were plotting against the Polish state.[16]

Although these reports reflected the personal views of foreign observers and indicated the complexities of Polish domestic politics, they were completed after the treaty was signed and had no further impact on the Allied policies toward the Jewish question in Poland. Since the end of the summer of 1919, other pressing issues drew the close attention of the West. The civil war in Russia was entering its decisive stage, and the Allies were hastily organizing a joint Romanian-Czechoslovakian offensive against revolutionary Hungary.

Jews and the ZUNR

In a desperate search for the most viable solution to secure the safety and rights of Jews, Jewish political parties endeavored to arrive at a common course of action. These efforts, however, were impeded by profound divisions among several factions, each offering its own way out of the predicament. In early February of 1919, the representatives of Jewish political mainstreams held debates in Lwów to discuss the common course of action. The Assimilators promoted the full integration of Jews into Polish society and the emigration of the "surplus" of Jews to Palestine and vehemently opposed national autonomy as "Jewish separatism." The Zionists and the Orthodox argued that although Polish Jews did not nourish any territorial aspirations, they nevertheless should demand national and individual autonomy, which would embrace religious affairs, schooling, and the recognition of Yiddish as the internal language of Jewish communities. The Socialists, although supportive of national and individual autonomy, emphasized that only social reconstruction would positively solve the "Jewish question."[17]

Given such a variety of opinions, it was only natural that many Jews in the Ukrainian-controlled areas gave at least moral support to the ZUNR, which granted all national groups equal civil and national rights. Although ZUNR promises were intended more to emphasize the legitimacy of the Ukrainian rule than its acceptance by the population, ZUNR ethnic policies attracted sizeable numbers of Jews to the Ukrainian cause. The West Ukrainian government officially recognized Jewish neutrality in the Polish-Ukrainian war, granted Jewish communities the status of self-governing bodies, and guaranteed Jews national and cultural autonomy, the notion denied to them by the Poles. Already in November 1918, with the approval and encouragement of the ZUNR administration, Jewish national councils were formed in the entire territory of East Galicia. Between December 18 and 20, representatives of the councils, including the Zionists, who were in the majority, the Socialists, the Poalei Zionists, and smaller Orthodox factions, met in Stanisławów. They established the Central Jewish National Council—CŻRN—which was to represent Jews with the Ukrainian government and at the Paris conference. The council petitioned the Allies to grant national and individual autonomy for Jews in eastern Europe, to accept a Jewish representative body to the League of Nations, and to impose sanctions on the countries that violated Jewish civil and political rights.[18]

Although initially the bulk of the Galician Jewry tried to abstain from becoming enmeshed in the Polish-Ukrainian conflict, further steps by the ZUNR eventually drew more and more Jews to its colors. Besides recognizing the Jews as a distinct nationality and acknowledging Yiddish as an official language, the Ukrainians called for the creation of a parliament (*sojm*) as the judicial organ of the republic. The *sojm* was to be elected in June 1919 and would comprise 160 Ukrainians, 33 Poles, 27 Jews, and 6 Germans, thus giving every ethnic group proportional representation. In April of 1919, the Ukrainian government also approved the creation of the Department for Jewish Affairs, which was to promote Jewish interests and to have exclusive jurisdiction in Jewish matters. Although the course of the war soon buried these plans, at a time when the Polish government consistently refused to heed Jewish requests, Ukrainian protestations of good intentions won over a substantial number of Jews of different political persuasions. The Jewish and Ukrainian press maintained a mutually friendly tone, and Jewish publishing houses, cultural institutions, and Hebrew and Yiddish schools functioned without interruptions. The ZUNR Council of Ministers also raised money to purchase textbooks and visual aids in Yiddish for Jewish schools and collected money to assist the victims of the Lwów pogrom.[19]

Jews responded favorably to these gestures of goodwill and provided financial help to the ZUNR. Jewish political groups also supported the republic, and in March 1919 the Poalei-Zion professed to support a "free, independent, and united Ukrainian Republic." The Bund and the Jewish Social-Democratic Party followed suit, refraining, however, from declaring full military participation in the Polish-Ukrainian conflict. In return, the ZUNR government confirmed the status of the CŻRN as the main Jewish representation in the region.[20] Jewish assistance for the ZUNR was particularly important in the financial sphere and administration. The CŻRN donated money to Ukrainian hospitals and provided aid to Ukrainian soldiers, and Jewish merchants received numerous concessions from the government, which was eager to revitalize the shattered Galician economy. As crucial for the ZUNR was the cooperation of Jewish civil employees. Starting in November of 1918, Polish functionaries who refused to take the oath of allegiance to the ZUNR either quit their jobs or were fired by the Ukrainian administration. The newly created vacancies provided professional opportunities for Jews, who willingly filled these positions and took the oath of allegiance to the Ukrainian state. They accorded the young Ukrainian republic invaluable help, especially in the post office and transportation departments and the court system. In Stanisławów Jewish railroad workers handled the huge traffic of the one hundred thousand Russian prisoners of war who were returning from captivity and kept the railroad operational. Jews also served in town councils; Jewish lawyers acted as judges and legal consultants in the courts of Kołomyja, Stanisławów, and Tarnopol. Although some Poles and Germans also served in the Ukrainian administration and the army, Jews made up the largest non-Ukrainian contingent in all state branches of the ZUNR.[21]

Jewish assistance for the ZUNR was not limited to the financial and political spheres. In some localities, the Ukrainian administration delegated matters of security and order to the Jewish militia, which operated as a police force. In Brzeżany and Kołomyja, Jewish war veterans enlisted in Ukrainian units and earned distinction in battle. In Stryj and Tarnopol, Jews served in military intelligence, the administration, and the medical department. In February of 1919, in the areas adjacent to the front line, Jewish committees began the mobilization of able-bodied males into the ZUNR armed forces—*Ukrains'ka Halyts'ka Armiia* (UHA). In Radziechów and Sambor, Jewish officers and civilians made up 33 percent of the gendarmerie; Jewish youth served as scouts for the Ukrainian army.[22]

In the late spring and early summer of 1919, when Polish troops launched an offensive in East Galicia, hundreds of Jewish volunteers enlisted in the UHA and participated in the fighting. In June a Jewish "shock" battalion was formed in Tarnopol under the leadership of First Lieutenant Solomon Leinberg. The battalion numbered seven hundred Jews and Ukrainians and became a part of the First UHA Corps that took part in heavy fighting near Tarnopol and Skałat. By the end of July, the battalion had crossed the Zbrucz River with other UHA units. Several other Jewish detachments also fought in the UHA ranks and crossed into eastern Ukraine in the summer of 1919. The Jewish units then fought the Red Army near Fastov, Koziatyn, and Berdychiv. Together with their Ukrainian comrades, Jewish officers and soldiers captured by the Red Army were sent to concentration camps. Those who survived would return home only after the Soviet-Polish war.[23]

Jewish-ZUNR relations, however, were not without problems. Although the ZUNR did its best to promote Jewish-Ukrainian cooperation, attitudes on the local level were at times marked by old prejudices and erupted into violent outbursts. In November and December of 1918, Ukrainian peasants robbed Jewish merchants and looted Jewish houses and shops in Śniatyń, Kołomyja, and Sambor. In the southeast districts of the Stanisławów province, where attacks on Jews were more frequent, Jewish communities were reluctant to collaborate with the ZUNR. Jewish craftsmen and merchants who had refused to accept Ukrainian money were heavily fined, and Ukrainian authorities conducted illegal searches and confiscated goods in the Jewish quarters.[24]

In January of 1919, Ukrainian military officials in several localities began forcibly drafting Jews into the UHA and labor details. The poor discipline of the Ukrainian troops and the weakness of the Ukrainian administration resulted in a rise in anti-Jewish assaults. Between January and April, robberies and murders in the Jewish quarters mounted in Tarnopol, Brzeżany, Buczacz, Stary Sambor, Drohobycz, Sokal, Złoczów, Stryj, Bełz, Jezierzany, and other places. Peasants and soldiers attacked Jewish stores and warehouses, and in several places only the executions of the rioters reestablished order. In Przemyślany, Ukrainian officials had to protect Jews from the depredations of the eastern Ukrainian units, which had arrived to succor the ZUNR. Nevertheless, anti-Jewish excesses in Ukrainian-controlled territories were far fewer in number and less brutal than those in Polish-held areas. The Ukrainian government also publicly condemned the excesses, and Ukrainian authorities often intervened on behalf of the Jews, imprisoning and executing a number of perpetrators.[25]

Nevertheless, the ZUNR government was disappointed that Jews refused to declare themselves openly on the Ukrainian side. Already in December of 1918, the Ukrainian press threatened that if Jews did not take part in the Polish-Ukrainian conflict, they would lose their rights as Ukrainian citizens. Such charges mounted as the war progressed, and Jews were increasingly blamed for waiting to wager on the stronger party. Symptomatic of Ukrainian attitudes was an article in a Ukrainian newspaper in Kołomyja, *Pokuts'kyi visnyk,* which in February of 1919 stated that "the Ukrainian government granted [Jews] political, national, and civil rights. And yet, they retained shop signs in Polish and speak Polish. Are Jews ashamed of [speaking] Yiddish or Ukrainian? If they so lavishly dispensed money to the Polish Legions during World War I, why don't they finance Ukrainian troops? Don't they believe in the just [Ukrainian] cause?"[26]

From the beginning of its struggle against Poland, the ZUNR could count only on its own skills and resources. Although in January 1919 it joined forces with the *Dyrektoriia*—the Ukrainian national government in Kiev—this government, hard pressed by the Whites and the Bolsheviks, could spare only a few units and little money to aid the ZUNR. Ukrainian diplomatic efforts with the Allies also proved unsuccessful, and the Polish delegation managed to convince the Western powers that the ZUNR was just a Bolshevik springboard to Hungary. Hence, the ZUNR turned to the Jews and, by granting them national rights and political representation, hoped for their active participation in the war. Until the spring of 1919, however, the majority of Jews exercised caution and refused to commit themselves openly to the Ukrainian side. This passivity, while in line with Jews' traditional attitudes in East Galicia, greatly impeded Jewish-Ukrainian collaboration.

Still, liberal ethnic policies and, more important, the determination of the Western Ukrainian government to guarantee the safety of the Jewish communities in Galicia spurred many Jews to throw in their lot with the ZUNR. The Western Ukrainian intelligentsia and officer corps had been accustomed to the traditions of tolerance of the Austro-Hungarian Empire. Though sharing traditional anti-Jewish biases, they recognized and accepted in principle the national, political, and civil equality of Jews. Therefore, notwithstanding the short-lived existence of the Western Ukrainian National Republic, and contrary to the long-standing reputation of Ukrainians as pathological anti-Semites, the history of the ZUNR provides a fascinating example of the two peoples' participation in a state-building process.

The *Odżydzenie* of the Borderlands

In the spring of 1919 the Polish army launched a decisive offensive against the ZUNR. In spite of desperate resistance, the UHA was gradually giving ground, and the territory controlled by the Ukrainians was inexorably shrinking. Simultaneous with the Polish advance, a wave of anti-Jewish violence erupted in wartorn East Galicia and *Kresy Wshodnie.* In comparison to the mob-dominated assaults in the fall of 1918, this time regular units led the way in beating and robbing Jews in cities and the countryside. Humiliation of religious Jews became the main amusement of the rank and file, who, with tacit approval of officers, cut the beards of Orthodox Jews and forced them to clean streets and latrines. Jewish apartments, stores, and synagogues became fair game as military and police detachments looted them under the guise of searching for arms. In Lwów and its surrounding areas, search details looked for alleged arms hidden in Jewish cemeteries. The "searches" evolved in a similar pattern: as long as officers were present, their subordinates more or less maintained discipline. Once the commanders departed, however, soldiers returned and crashed through houses and apartments in search of money, jewelry, and food. Often at gunpoint, residents gave up anything valuable to the extortionists, who cut mattresses open and smashed doors, windows, furniture, and mirrors.[27] Searches were accompanied by the forcible induction of Jews into labor details. In Sambor, Monasterzyska, and Stanisławów, Polish units forced Jewish men, women, and children to clean streets and public latrines and dig fortifications. Some Jews responded by organizing the production of falsified certificates that exempted their recipients from labor duties. Such offenses were classified by the army as anti-state activities and were punished by imprisonment.[28]

Concerned with the morale and discipline of the troops, the Polish command tried to stop the spread of violence, threatening culprits with court-martial, and in Drohobycz, Borysław, and Stryj, the energetic intervention of officers, the gendarmerie, and army patrols stopped anti-Jewish disturbances. Some socialist groups and progressive intellectuals such as Dr. Leon Biliński and Andrzej Strug also condemned the violence in strong words. Nevertheless, public statements made by prominent Polish politicians frequently were too ambiguous to have any effect on ravaging troops. Thus, Daszyńsky flatly denied that the pogroms took place and referred to Jewish victims as unfortunate results of the war. Piłsudski, in an interview with *Time* magazine, stated that the violence emanated from the collapse of the partitioning powers and was driven by popular animosities toward wartime Jewish profiteers. For looters, these and similar utterances sounded as official sanctions to attack Jews with impunity. Accordingly, when in the spring of 1919 anti-Jewish riots broke out in the Rzeszów and Lublin provinces, leaflets allegedly signed by Piłsudski and stamped by what was called the Committee of Jewish Pogroms were distributed to the crowds.[29]

The assaults on Jews in the borderlands also took place within a context of intense socioeconomic tensions. Polish peasants resented the government's unwillingness or inability to carry out land reforms, and a sense of class-based economic injustice generated popular frustration. As a result, peasants attacked manorial houses, and slogans such as "Down with landlords and Jews!" reflected the traditional association of Jewish land tenants with the landlords.[30] In addition, mass mobilization rapidly expanded the national army, which by the spring of 1919 had grown to three hundred thousand men. The Polish command, however, was unable to provide its ranks with sufficient amounts of clothing and food supplies. Soldiers starved and had no boots, and their willingness to fight decreased concurrently with poor pay. For them, therefore, looting Jews served as partial compensation for the hardship at the front and presented no moral dilemma. This situation was reflected in a report by the commander of the Third Infantry Division in East Galicia, who complained to his superiors that because his soldiers had no supplies, he renounced any responsibility for their transgressions.[31]

The situation in *Kresy Wshodnie* and Galicia also reflected the psychological imprint of the four years of continuous warfare, for World War I and the frontier wars made the residents of these areas inured to brutalities and suffering. The violence not only served the immediate needs of personal enrichment but also provided a legitimate and relatively easy target—Jews—upon which to unleash personal frustrations. Looting and robbery, therefore, were consistently accompanied by beatings, rapes, and wanton destruction of prayer books and sacred scrolls in the synagogues. The congruence of ethnic and ideological animosities also precipitated assaults. Two Polish units—Poznań regiments and General Józef Haller's army—especially earned the reputation as notorious Jew baiters and staged brutal pogroms in Sambor, the Lwów district, and Grodek Jagielloński. The anti-Jewish zeal of these soldiers derived from the situation in the Poznań province, where Jews sided with the Germans during the Polish-German conflict in the winter of 1919. Similarly, the actions of Haller's army, which had arrived from France, might be explained by the fact that some contingents came from the United States, where Jewish-Polish relations went from bad to worse during World War I.[32]

To a large extent, the influx of many Russian-trained officers into the Polish army explains its ideological predisposition. Between just November and December of 1918, 990 Polish officers of the Russian imperial army, including 47 colonels and 12 generals, took service with the Polish armed forces. These numbers steadily grew in 1919. Nonetheless, because the largest contingent—

6,426 officers—came from the relatively tolerant Austro-Hungarian officer corps, the "Russian" origin of many officers provides only a partial explanation of their ethnic biases.[33] Popular association of Jews with Bolshevism also gave violence a powerful momentum, and the Endeks and their allies especially promoted the "Judeo-Bolshevik" connections. In the spring of 1919, in his address from Paris, Paderewski stressed that Bolshevik propaganda was especially successful among "radical Jewish elements." In several instances Polish troops engaged in reprisals against the alleged Jewish-Bolshevik conspirators. For example, a local Polish commander in Pinsk ordered the execution of several Zionists on charges of Bolshevik activities. Similarly, more than ninety Jews lost their lives in Lida and Vil'nius when Polish soldiers staged "reprisals" in the Jewish quarters. Twenty-three Jews were murdered in the Stanisławów province during the march of General Julian Żeligowski's division, which had previously fought the Bolsheviks near Odessa.[34]

~

Concurrent with the offensive in East Galicia and *Kresy Wshodnie,* the Polish administration and the military hastened to use the favorable moment to "de-Judaize" the reconquered territories. In comparison to the Russification campaign, which had aimed at "leveling" Galician Jews on a par with their coreligionists in Russia by integrating them into the traditional imperial order, *odżydzenie* was designed to "de-Polonize" Jews by excluding them altogether from Polish political, socioeconomic, and cultural life. Backed by the military and the administration, the Polish middle class—public employees, merchants, and the intelligentsia—became the spearhead of *odżydzenie.* Determined to eliminate their main socioeconomic rival, they petitioned the government, complaining about the predominance of Jews in trade, commerce, and professions and demanding their replacement by ethnic Poles. In Galicia, an "initiative group" comprised of university professors, writers, and teachers, known as the Committee for National Defense—*Komitet Obrony Narodowej* (KON)—headed the anti-Jewish drive.

Polish professional unions acted in a similar manner. At the end of 1918, the Union of Polish Railroad Employees sent a telegram to the government, protesting the employment of "alien" Jews and demanding "bread and jobs only for Poles!" The government responded to the plea by withholding state aid to Jews and dismissing allegedly disloyal Jewish employees from the railroads department. In Lwów the military began firing Jewish police employees who had served in such a capacity during the fighting in the city. In January 1919 the Polish Liquidation Commission in Krakow ordered the registration of all Jewish employees in public service as well as the compilation of data about their attitudes toward the Polish state.[35]

The Polish military rejected Jewish volunteers and simultaneously accused

Jews of draft evasion. In March 1919 the Liquidation Commission ordered all public employees to take the oath of allegiance to the Polish state, which, if taken, contravened provisions of Jewish neutrality proclaimed in November 1918. Jews, Ukrainians, and Germans who did not take the oath were fired. The Ministry of Justice demanded that Jewish and Ukrainian lawyers profess Polish nationality, and the Union of Attorneys in Lwów issued the same request to jurists, judges, and clerks. At the time, the definition of nationality—*narodowość*—embraced more than just citizenship. In the context of the post–World War I state-building process, *narodowość* implied full assimilation into Polish society by forsaking one's own culture, language, and tradition. Traditionally advocated by Jewish Assimilators, such a notion was rejected by the majority of Galician Jews, who under the Austro-Hungarian Empire enjoyed full cultural and religious freedoms. Consequently, out of ninety Jewish defense attorneys in Lwów, only nineteen signed the declaration. The rest lost their jobs. The KON, however, appealed to the government commissar in East Galicia, requesting that all Jews and Ukrainians, regardless of whether they took the oath of allegiance or not, be dismissed from civil service. When on March 5 an explosion demolished an ammunition depot at the Lwów railroad station, the KON sounded the alarm as to the potential disloyalty of "alien" postal and railroad employees.[36]

On April 30, 1919, the presidium of the Council of Ministers decreed that all civil employees who had not taken the oath of loyalty be fired. In East Galician districts under Polish control, the administration ordered Jewish public functionaries, railroad workers, and teachers to account for their activities during Ukrainian rule. In Stanisławów and Brody all Jews in public service were fired. Medical personnel were also purged; Jewish teachers and students were expelled from public schools. In May, in spite of the severe shortage of doctors and nurses, the local administration in Skole fired all Jewish employees from hospitals. The KON triumphantly announced that the "Jewish problem" in the medical sphere in Skole was thus successfully "solved."[37]

Although the Minority Treaty officially secured the civil rights of Jews, its implementation completely depended on the position of the local administration, which used the charge of "political subversion" to detain or fire Jewish teachers, lawyers, and public employees. Various restrictions, such as the requirement of a certificate of baptism, effectively barred Jewish applicants from positions in post offices and railroads. In Stanisławów, the district administration removed all Jewish civil workers. The city mayor, Dr. Dobiński, stated to the Jewish delegation that he did not recognize the Jewish National Council—despite the declaration to the contrary in November 1918. The council was disbanded, and Jewish students were expelled from public schools. In Drohobycz the administration removed seventeen Jewish teachers, five city council functionaries, seventeen other civil employees, and four hundred students from the local gymnasium despite the efforts of its Polish director, Dr. Jan Jarosz. In Sambor, where Endeks dominated the administrative apparatus, Jews were removed from the city council, police, railroads, and post office.[38] By October 1919, according to the Sejm military commission, seventeen Jewish and fifty Ukrainian gendarmes were still employed in the entire area of East Galicia and the kingdom. Despite the shortage of professional railroad workers, the Department of Railroads demanded the certification of baptism as the prerequisite for hire. By early January 1920 the Railroad Department in Stanisławów proceeded with replacing Jewish employees at restaurants and cafés with ethnic Poles; all contracts with non-Poles were to be terminated by May.[39]

In western Poland, the Polish government had begun the nationalization of German-owned land, but it did not follow the same pattern in the borderlands. Although a substantial number of Jews owned or leased the land in these areas, the bulk of estates remained in the hands of Polish landowners, and any attempt to alter the status quo was tantamount to a direct assault on private ownership—a basic foundation of the Polish state—and hence would produce far-reaching internal and external consequences. Only in light of peasant unrest in the spring of 1919 did the government decide to consider the limitation of landownership to 60–180 hectares. The implementation of this reform, however, was postponed until further investigation and did not affect Jewish landowners, the majority of whom owned just about the prescribed limits. Only in the areas where the land estates of absentees were nationalized did the administration make a specific effort to distribute land exclusively to ethnic Poles.[40]

Jews, Bolshevism, and the Polish-Soviet War of 1920

After the defeat of the ZUNR and the establishment of Polish rule in the borderlands, the administration, vigilante groups, and the nationalist press did not cease anti-Semitic agitation, blaming Jews for political subversion, speculation, food shortages, and petty crime.[41] Nevertheless, the country finally received some breathing space as the embattled borderlands—Poznań, Cieszyn, and East Galicia—were partially or completely integrated, and in Belorussia and southern Lithuania the Polish-Soviet war came to a standstill. This relative tranquility coincided with a sharp decline in anti-Jewish violence. Polish authorities took more stringent measures against excesses, forcible mobilization of Jews into labor details became less frequent, and Jewish activists who in 1918 and 1919 had been detained for anti-state activities were released. These acts imbued Jews with hopes that the termination of military conflicts would bring stability and peace to the country and, correspondingly, would soothe anti-Jewish animosities.[42]

The escalation of the Polish-Soviet war brought these hopes to naught, however. Initially, in April and May of 1920 successful Polish offensives in Belorussia and Ukraine culminated in the capture of Kiev. Soon, however, the Soviets managed to rally their forces. They shattered Polish defense lines and by July had crashed across the Berezina River. In early August the Red Army was closing in on Warsaw. The Polish retreat reverberated in a wave of anti-Jewish pogroms in cities and towns along the frontline. Especially brutal were attacks in Białystok, Siedlce, Płock, Łyków, and Drohiczyn, where more than sixty Jews lost their lives. The brutalities reached such a scope that in July the Council of Ministers and the Ministry of Military Affairs felt it necessary to appeal to the troops to stop pogroms, threatening the culprits with courts-martial. In August 1920 fourteen Polish soldiers were sentenced to death for attacks on Jews in Minsk. Yet, while trying to uphold the discipline of the army, at the same time the government greatly contributed to the upsurge of anti-Semitic hysteria in the country. War Minister Władysław Sikorski appealed to the Poles to fight "Moscow gangs led by Jewish commissars," and the gendarmerie in Warsaw distributed posters that associated Jews with Bolsheviks to the public. Mass arrests of "unreliable" elements targeted not only Jewish Communists but also socialists, Zionists, and civil activists. Jewish soldiers and officers in the Polish army were disarmed, sent to labor battalions, or detained in the Jabłonna and Dąbie camps set up for isolating "suspicious" elements.[43]

The notion of "Judeo-Communism" gained its most powerful momentum in the period of 1917 to 1919, when during the revolutions in Russia, Germany, Austria, and Hungary, many Jews became prominent in Communist movements. In the context of the tumultuous European politics of the period, when the empires collapsed and new national states came into being, anti-Communism and anti-Semitism amalgamated into a powerful myth of the world Jewish conspiracy, which instilled fear in various social and political groups. Unquestionably, Communism, as the only ideology that offered fundamental social change and ethnic equality, attracted many Jews to its banner, and the Jewish membership within the ranks of the European Communist parties was certainly impressive. Among the ten leaders of the Communist Workers' Party of Poland, seven were of Jewish descent. In Hungary, these numbers were even higher. Nevertheless, scholars who have offered various interpretations to gauge the role of Jews in the Communist movement have reached a general consensus that although Jewish revolutionaries made up a high proportion of the Communist elite, the Jewish masses in general remained hardly sympathetic toward Bolshevism.[44] Although such an argument is valid in general, the situation in the multiethnic areas of *Kresy* and East

Galicia was much more complicated, and the conduct of Jews during the Soviet invasion was far from uniform and varied depending on the place.

In the borderlands many Ukrainians, Belorussians, and Jews accorded an enthusiastic welcome to the invading Red Army. In the Galician districts of Zaleszczyki, Jaworów, Dolina, and Podhajce, Ukrainian peasants were especially receptive to Bolshevik slogans. Such a reaction derived from the dire economic shortages caused by the war as well as from the Polish army's frequent requisitions of grain and horses and its brutal treatment of the civilian population. The conduct of the army also antagonized ethnic Poles. In contrast, Soviet troops were relatively well disciplined and, as Polish reports admitted, behaved almost "impeccably." Bolshevik slogans of social equality as well as promises of land reform also attracted large numbers of Ukrainians, Belorussians, Poles, and Jews to support the new regime. For the Ukrainian intelligentsia, Soviet aspirations to unify Volhynia and East Galicia with Ukraine also sounded appealing.[45] In *Kresy Wschodnie* these attitudes were also facilitated by specific socioeconomic conditions prevalent in this region. During World War I, many Polish landlords and Jewish land tenants fled their estates affected by the fighting. After the Polish offensive in the spring and summer of 1919, they returned home and claimed their estates and possessions. Social tensions, therefore, erupted immediately as the Polish administration and police sided with the landowners and land tenants against the peasants. After the arrival of the Red Army, local village councils set up revolutionary estate committees, which distributed agricultural implements—confiscated from large estates—to poor peasants. In addition, the unwillingness of the Polish government to carry out socioeconomic reforms made large numbers of Polish peasants reluctant to enlist in the army, and large numbers of recruits deserted and hid in the countryside.[46]

The reactions of Jews were similar to their Polish and Ukrainian conationals and varied according to political affiliations, social background, and geographical location. At the beginning of the war, a splinter Bund faction announced its entry into the Third Communist International. The most radical elements within the Poalei-Zion also welcomed the Soviet model of dictatorship of the proletariat. More important, however, was the fact that by the time of the Soviet invasion, Jews, especially in the border areas, felt out of place in the new Polish state. For them the relatively tolerant Polish-Lithuanian Rzeczpospolita of the old times was a long bygone era, and the new emerging Poland was a proto-national state characterized by aggressive nationalism and virulent anti-Semitism. In contrast, Bolshevik policies of civil and political equality for ethnic minorities drove scores of Jews in the *Kresy Wshodnie,* Galicia, Białystok, and Płock districts to enlist in the Red Army and the Bolshevik militia and to serve in the administration. The Polish Communist Party and its Jewish members took an active part in the Soviet administration and the political police, the Cheka. Jewish functionaries were especially active among the propaganda detachments of the Polish Revolutionary Committee, a temporary governing council in the territories captured by the Red Army.[47]

Some Polish observers admitted that the conduct of Jews varied according to political affiliation and social background and that Jews served in the Polish army and irregular units or as informants and guides for Polish troops. Yet, the anti-Semitic propaganda highlighted the instances of Jewish-Bolshevik collaboration, passing in silence the cases when ethnic Poles colluded with the Soviets. Such an approach to press releases was to convince the country that only "alien" elements—non-Catholic and non-Polish—were receptive to Bolshevik ideology. To this end, the government propaganda omitted the facts that the Soviets cracked down on the Zionists, closed Jewish religious and cultural institutions, confiscated stores and workshops, and subjected "bourgeois elements"—Jewish tradesmen and merchants—to heavy fines.[48]

The initial response of the Galician Jewry to the Bolshevik invasion was remarkably similar to the situation in August of 1914, when the outbreak of World War I temporarily extinguished Polish-Jewish antagonisms. Jews volunteered for the Polish army, the Jewish community donated money to the military, and synagogues staged religious services to pray for Polish victory. Nevertheless, analogous to the failed rapprochement of 1914, the enthusiasm for national defense among Jews soon evaporated. As the Bolshevik First Cavalry Army closed in on Lwów, the Polish military cracked down on the Jewish intelligentsia suspected of pro-Bolshevik sympathies. Bund and Poalei-Zion members were arrested, and the headquarters of these parties were shut down; Jewish civilians, officers, and soldiers were interned at a camp in Dąbie near Krakow. In Lwów, Borysław, Krakow, Sanok, and Drohobycz, army and police details searched Jewish quarters. Although no empirical evidence of subversive activities was found, the military portrayed Jews as the spearhead of Bolshevik activities. At the same time, Polish officials complained that thousands of Jewish refugees who fled the Bolshevik offensive moved to the cities and countryside, causing economic shortages.[49]

The presence of Jews in the short-lived Soviet government of East Galicia seemingly lent credence to the popular identification of Jews with Communism. In July 1920, in the eastern districts of the Tarnopol and Lwów provinces the Red Army set up the so-called Galician Soviet Socialist Republic. Its governing organ, the Galician Revolutionary Council—*Galrevkom*—established its headquarters in Tarnopol and was initially headed by Feliks Kon, a professional Jewish revolutionary. Besides Kon, three of seventeen Galrevkom members were of Jewish background: K. Litvinovich, the commissar of the post service, telegraph, and communications; A. Baral', the commissar of trade and industry; and one Kulik, the head of the Council of Arts. In the dreaded Cheka, Jews constituted approximately one-third of the personnel. The Bolshevik "class" approach to recruitment of the local population was also reflected in the makeup of the militia, where many poverty-stricken Jews and Ukrainians were the most suitable applicants.[50]

Yes, despite accusations of mass collaboration with the enemy, only 24 Jews out of 642 suspected Bolshevik sympathizers wound up on the blacklists compiled by the Polish police and gendarmerie in East Galicia after the retreat of the Red Army.[51] How, then, do we account for two seemingly irreconcilable facts—these numbers and the popular conviction that "if most Jews were not communists, most communists were probably Jews"?[52] As important as these numbers are, they were less relevant in the turbulent atmosphere of post–World War I Poland, where ethnicity became the key determinant of one's patriotism and loyalty to the nation. Whereas in the former kingdom and *Kresy Wschodnie* Russian imperial laws had confined Jews to traditional occupations in trade, small artisanship, and tavern keeping, and after 1918 the *odżydzenie* further barred them from careers in state and public sectors, the Bolshevik reliance on class rather than ethnicity opened numerous vacancies for Jewish applicants in politics, the civil service, and the army. Their better educational background guaranteed Jews positions in the Soviet hierarchy. For that matter, Bolshevik recruitment policies were similar to those of the ZUNR and drew many young and educated Jews to serve in the Soviet administration, the Cheka, and the militia. Although these positions guaranteed Jewish functionaries a relatively high social status, they simultaneously made them extremely visible to the eyes of Poles and Ukrainians. The fact that Jews owed their positions to the foreign intruder magnified their guilt and underscored the status reversal whereby Jews, who had been limited in social mobility, suddenly were elevated to the positions of power. Such perceptions played a crucial role in facilitating the image of the omnipresent "Jew-Bolshevik."

Soviet economic policies, however, soon alienated even those who had initially welcomed the Soviets. Because many Galician Jews were classified as *sobstvenniki* (private owners), they were considered intrinsically alien to the dogma of the classless society. In August 1920, the *Galrevkom* abolished private property; nationalized banks, factories, plants, and agricultural implements; and confiscated the property of churches and other religious institutions. The Cheka arrested "bourgeois elements" such as the Jewish intelligentsia, rabbis, and Catholic priests. The Soviets particularly cracked down on merchants and craftsmen, who were subjected to searches and requisitions. Outright extortion was used to "expropriate the expropriators," and special labor details were set up for the "reeducation" of hostile elements. Soviet commissars who had arrived with the Red Army incited the local poor against rabbis and religious Jews. Physical assaults, especially by the units of the First Cavalry Army, were also not uncommon. In Stryj, where the Bolsheviks ruled for only sixteen hours, Soviet troops, with the assistance of peasants, looted Jewish shops and houses. The harshness of Soviet rule and its militant anti-religiosity and economic policies turned the majority of Jews decisively against the invaders.[53]

As the Soviet-Polish war was reaching its zenith in the mid-summer of 1920, however, Polish propaganda rarely made a distinction between pro-Bolshevik and anti-Bolshevik Jews. Consequently, the more desperate the situation became, the more often Jews were targeted by Polish troops. Charges of sabotage preceded attacks on Jews in the Płock, Białystock, and Kielce districts as soldiers ran amok, looting and burning Jewish houses. Dozens of Jews were murdered and maimed. The partial paralysis of the Polish administration and the mass desertion of the Polish rank and file, which swelled the ranks of criminal bands, exacerbated the general chaos and confusion.[54] In East Galicia, Jews were fair game for Polish troops passing to the frontline. The situation became especially precarious with the arrival of Ukrainian units subordinated to Symon Petliura, the leader of the *Dyrektoriia,* and the White Cossacks. These remnants of anti-Bolshevik armies were recruited in Polish internment camps or volunteered for the war as the last opportunity to return home and escape adverse conditions in camp barracks. The majority of these individuals had long lost any ideological motives and fought only for short-range objectives—revenge and profit. Some had already participated in anti-Jewish pogroms in Ukraine in 1918 and 1919. Of varying fighting abilities, but notoriously destructive, they became an embarrassment rather than an asset to the Polish military. But for the moment, when the fate of the country hung in the balance, the Polish command was eager to use them, turning a blind eye to their predatory habits.

Between August and October the Ukrainians and Cossacks carried out brutal anti-Jewish pogroms in more than sixteen localities. Although they singled out Jews, the non-Jewish population was also subjected to rape and murder. The Ukrainian Eighth Brigade wrought death and destruction in the Stanisławów and Żółkiew districts, where 114 Jews and more than 30 Ukrainian and Polish peasants were murdered. Only the determined intervention of Ukrainian and Polish commanders prevented the further spread of violence. In other localities Ukrainian units and the White Cossack brigade led by Captain Frolov murdered more than 170 Jews and wounded 190 more; 350 women and girls were raped. The conduct of Poland's allies became so infamous that a number of Galician Ukrainians who had joined the anti-Bolshevik forces deserted for "not wanting to be labeled beasts."[55]

In the fall of 1920 the guns finally fell silent on Polish frontiers. With the termination of the Polish-Soviet war, anti-Jewish violence visibly decreased. In November 1920 the Sejm publicly acknowledged that the attitudes of Jews during the war varied in different regions and especially praised the East Galician and Volhynian Jewish communities for having loyally performed their citizen duties. Following anti-Semitic barrages, such a sudden extolment did not, however, signify a positive shift in Polish-Jewish relations. Instead, it stemmed from pure political pragmatism. The Allies had declared that the future political status of East Galicia was to be decided by a public referendum, and, consequently, the Polish government was determined to secure a favorable Jewish opinion in the country and abroad. In a like manner, although the majority of Jews voted for Galicia's integration into the Polish state, their response was compelled by practical rather than patriotic considerations. Six years of warfare severely crippled the Galician Jewry, whose pre–World War I population was reduced by 124,099 people, or 19 percent, in 1921. The bulk of these losses came from mass evacuations in 1914, Russian deportations, and the changing fortunes of the Polish frontier wars. After such a long period of violence and persecution, Jews of different political affiliations and social backgrounds yearned for any semblance of peace and would settle for any government capable of delivering stability, law, and order.[56]

Although the lives of Jews were no longer threatened, the anti-Semitic propaganda did not cease. In the fall of 1920 the *Protocols of the Elders of Zion* made its first appearance in Poland and found its way to America, where it was disseminated among Polish communities.[57] *Odżydzenie* continued unabated, and in December 1920 the Ministry of Military Affairs made the commissioning of officers contingent on a candidate's ethnicity. In response to the protests of Jewish deputies in the Sejm about the dismissal of Jewish officers from service, the ministry responded that "the army is the embodiment of the state's vitality and strength, and, therefore, the officer ranks must be filled by individuals known for and capable of love and sacrifice to their motherland. Such sacrifice can be offered only by those whose citizenship and ethnicity [*narodowość*] bind them inseparably to the state."[58]

In the six years of warfare, the ethnic profile of Galicia's socioeconomic sphere was dramatically and irreversibly altered. In comparison to the pre–World War I period, by 1921 the number of Jews engaged in trade had been reduced by 9 percent, in industries and artisanship by 20 percent, and in transportation and communication by 43 percent. Altogether, the number of Jewish state and civil employees fell from 12,312 in 1912 to 5,186 in 1921. Out of the 6,000 Jewish railroad and postal employees before the war, only 670 retained their posts in 1923. A similar situation prevailed in the police, education, and legal professions. Because the number of Jews with school and university diplomas had traditionally been higher than in other ethnic groups, the Jewish professional elite were especially impacted by these changes. Although discriminatory practices achieved their primary objectives, they simultaneously backfired in that more Jews were forced to engage in the areas still open to them—trade, commerce, and artisanship—thus aggravating the Polish-Jewish rivalry during the interwar period.[59]

Conclusion

In his authoritative study *Warrant for Genocide,* Norman Cohn suggests that the

> deadliest kind of anti-Semitism, the kind that results in massacre and attempted genocide, has little to do with real conflicts of interest between living people, or even racial prejudice as such. At its heart lies the belief that Jews—all Jews everywhere—form a conspiratorial body set on running and then dominating the rest of mankind. And this belief is simply a modernized, secularized version of the popular medieval view.[1]

Such a definition of anti-Semitism certainly elucidates the roots of anti-Jewish violence in wartime East Galicia. At the same time, however, it does not explain why the violence did not remain a constant, but rather erupted in certain circumstances and remained dormant in the others. Indeed, why did most ferocious attacks on Jews take place during Russia's military victories in the summer and fall of 1914, during the Great Retreat of 1915, and at the height of the Polish offensive in the spring of 1919 and in the summer of 1920 when Poland's fortunes reached their nadir? In this book, I have attempted to demonstrate that the "conspiracy theory" is most relevant only when placed in the context of a specific political, social, and economic situation.

World War I and its aftermath witnessed the dramatic radicalization of ethnic policies, reflected in official and popular perceptions of ethnicity as firmly defined affiliation based on common genetic roots and cultural and religious values. Such assumptions reinforced group self-identity and effectively placed the "others," who did not share similar extraction, into the category of outsider. In eastern Europe the "host" nations turned increasingly against the "inner enemy"—allegedly disloyal minorities—whose potential destructiveness equaled that of the classic enemy, Germany, Austro-Hungary, or Russia.[2]

Among these minorities Jews occupied a special place. Traditionally, their distinct religion, culture, and language separated them from their Christian neighbors, and popular resentment toward the customarily Jewish occupations of landlords' proxies, moneylenders, and petty tradesmen at times sparked violent assaults. Only in the conducive atmosphere of wartime, however, did centuries-long animosities explode into large-scale violence. War reinforced popular beliefs in the secretive and destructive nature of Jewish communities and created a highly charged atmosphere of anxiety and fear, whereby Jews were blamed for political and economic subversion.

In East Galicia, Russian ethnic policies mirrored a larger campaign that unfolded along the eastern front and targeted potentially dangerous minority groups—Jews and Germans. Having received extraordinary powers in the war theater, the Russian military, which had traditionally treated Jews with disdain and suspicion, proceeded to govern Galicia in accordance with the imperial ethnic order. To this end, the Russians attempted to win or co-opt the potentially "friendly" ethnic groups—Ukrainians and Poles—and simultaneously to relegate Jews, perceived as security threats, to second-class citizens. Nonetheless, although Russification severely crippled the Galician Jewish community, it also backfired because obsession with the alleged "Jewish threat" amplified collective social paranoia within the Russian military and society. Accordingly, the military committed badly needed resources and manpower to the anti-Jewish campaign, seriously undermining Russian war efforts.

In a similar way, the attempts to resurrect Poland as a national state in which ethnic Poles would dominate all spheres of public life dovetailed with the potential resistance of ethnic minority groups. By 1918 Polish public opinion had classified Jews as the hostile "others" whose assimilation was not only impossible but also highly undesirable. In the atmosphere of collective fears of internal and external enemies, it was an interaction of reality and myth that gave anti-Semitic sentiments their fullest expression. Whereas the Germans, Ukrainians, and Lithuanians asserted their national aspirations with arms in hand, Jewish diplomatic and political efforts were popularly perceived as underhanded, conspiratorial, and extremely damaging to Poland's independence. Viewed as a unified and monolithic foe, Jews suffered physical assaults, and the *odżydzenie* campaign aimed at eliminating them as political and economic competitors.

In reality, however, Jews were too deeply divided along social, economic, and political lines to pursue a unified policy, and their wartime associations with the Central powers, the ZUNR, and the Allies were a sign of weakness rather than strength. In fact, the traditionally precarious situation of Jews among the "host" nations guaranteed their loyalty or at least submission to the governing elites, and they, if grudgingly, would most certainly have opted for any government that would grant them equal rights and assure their safety. Accordingly, in 1918 and 1919, the bulk of Jews in East Galicia lent their support to the ZUNR. In Ukraine their coreligionists acted in similar fashion, initially supporting the *Dyrektoriia.* After the *Dyrektoriia* failed to protect Jewish communities from the depredations of Ukrainian nationalist units, however, Jews turned to the Bolsheviks, whose nationality policies offered them better chances of survival amid the horrors of the civil war.[3]

Anti-Jewish violence was an inseparable part of the Russification and Polonization drives. It erupted in stages and was facilitated by two identifiable precipitants—slanderous propaganda campaigns and rumors. Whereas propaganda aimed at specific objectives—for example, the elimination of Jewish economic influence in East Galicia—rumors, on the other hand, expressed collective negative emotions such as the fears and anxieties of the combat zone. In emotionally overloaded wartime societies, however, propaganda and rumors often functioned at cross-purposes and fueled each other, thus validating the necessity of reprisals against the "inner enemy." Correspondingly, the fine line between officially sanctioned and popular violence was blurred. Deportations and expulsions of Jews from strategically sensitive areas paved the way for mob-driven assaults, which unleashed deeply seated societal underpinnings of fear and hate against Jews as the alleged cause of social or political distress. Mob justice also demonstrated the spontaneous and yet focused nature of ethnic violence because Jews were simultaneously targeted as security threats and legitimate targets for personal aggrandizement. Violence also functioned as a means for social status reversal, forcing Jews out of public places such as markets, railroad stations, restaurants, and streets, thus reaffirming the dominant status of the majority groups—Russians and Poles—and the social and psychological downgrading of Jews.

In this context, the role of control agencies in East Galicia was paramount. Although the perpetrators of "unauthorized" violence acted not only against the prescribed conduct of the war but also against societal norms of conduct—the Russian and the Polish militaries publicly disavowed the culprits—official anti-Jewish policies and the frequent inactivity of local officials facilitated popular convictions that attacks were approved or encouraged by higher authorities. Nevertheless, neither the Russian nor the Polish militaries espoused the ideology of extermination. Even during the Great Retreat of 1915, when anti-Jewish violence reached its zenith, it never escalated into genocidal massacres. The Russian army did not seek the physical destruction of Jews, and the Russian government provided a crucial counterbalance to its military institutions. Such a fact is worth mentioning considering that at the time of mass deportations on the eastern front the Young Turks carried out a genocidal campaign against the Armenians.

Although many Polish military and state officials shared anti-Semitic convictions, both tried—at times halfheartedly—to mitigate violence by issuing public appeals and punishing offenders. In addition, the Allied recognition of Poland as an independent and sovereign state, along with the country's multiparty system and relative freedom of the press, allowed Jewish political activists to voice their grievances and protests. Therefore, during the Polish-Soviet war, anti-Jewish assaults never reached the scope of the White Terror in Hungary, where officer squads murdered several thousands Jews purportedly associated with the Communist regime of Bela Kun. The Polish government, in comparison, rejected terror as a structural component of state policy. Perhaps a crucial determinant that spared Polish Jews the fate of their Hungarian coreligionists was the fact that Poland did not endure the vicissitudes of the Soviet regime because the Bolshevik occupation of the borderlands was short lived.

The militant anti-Semitism of World War I and its aftermath proved to be extremely contagious and left lasting imprints on the popular memories of Russian and Polish societies. After the Bolshevik revolution many Russian soldiers and officers wound up in various anti-Bolshevik and insurgent formations. Judeophobia and spy mania, which raged during the anti-Jewish campaigns on the eastern front, were now magnified by the deadly image of "Judeo-Bolshevism." As the old order collapsed, and the restraining influence of the government was no more, these individuals organized and participated in the most brutal massacres of Jews on the by now habitual charges of sabotage, resistance, and economic subversion.[4]

In Poland, the impact of the Polish-Jewish conflict was as profound. Throughout the period between the world wars, distrust and suspicions of ethnic minorities, especially Jews, dominated the country's ethnic policies, and the Endeks and the military remained at the spearhead of anti-Jewish propaganda. In May 1921, acting on a request by the Polish General Staff, Lieutenant Colonel Stanisław Laudański compiled a treatise titled "Genesis of the Jewish Soul" (*Genesis duszy żydowskiej*), in which he conjured up an image of the deadly Jewish threat to the Polish nation. Citing selected passages from the Old Testament and various "scholarly sources," Laudański warned his conationals of an international conspiracy concocted by Jews, who were poised at "dominating international finances, causing economic destabilization by workers' unrest, supporting the communist ideology and anti-Christian organizations, and protecting the rights of man and citizen since [Jews will] be the first to reap benefits." Laudański pointed to the intrinsic weaknesses of the "Christian character," such as altruism and credulity, which allowed Jews to manipulate world opinion. Jews, on the other hand, were "energetic, stubborn, flexible, and patient" and, if left unopposed, would eventually achieve their objectives.[5]

Such a vision of a worldwide "Jewish peril" was echoed by the Endeks and shared by large segments of Polish society. Consequently, the reluctance of the Polish government to implement the Minority Treaty grew concomitantly with the radicalization of Polish politics and the diminishing influence of the Allies in the late 1920s and early 1930s. Perceived as the hand of international Jewry, the treaty remained a major grievance against the Jews, and its unilateral abrogation in September 1934 was greeted with widespread enthusiasm throughout the country. After the death of Piłsudski in 1935, the Polish government and the military adopted some of the ideological viewpoints of the Endeks to gain wider popular support. Actions such as boycotts of Jewish businesses, vicious anti-Semitic propaganda, and physical assaults on Jews became an integral part of public life and reflected official and popular attitudes that would dominate Polish society for decades to come.

Appendix of Population Statistics

Table 1. Jewish Population in East Galicia

Year	Total Population	Jews	% of the Total
1880	3,844,770	516,912	13.4
1890	4,308,151	585,453	13.6
1900	4,814,171	621,036	12.9
1910	5,380,766	662,412	12.3

Sources: Bohdan Wasiutyński, *Ludność żydowska w Polsce w wiekach XIX i XX* (Warsaw: wydawnictwo Kasy im. Mianowskiego, 1930), 90–91; B. Stopnevich, "Naselenie Galitsii," *Ukrainskaia zhizn'*, 11–12 (1914): 48; S. E., "Galichina v tsyfrakh," *Ukrainskaia zhizn'*, 3–4 (1915): 19.

Table 2. Jewish Population in Urban Centers, 1910

District	Total Population	Jews	% of the Total
Bóbrka	5,628	2,502	44.5
Bohorodczany	4,378	1,930	44.1
Borszczów	4,765	1,263	26.5
Brody	18,055	12,188	67.5
Brzeżany	12,717	4,582	36.0
Brzozów	4,438	1,255	28.3
Buczacz	14,286	7,777	54.4
Cieszanów	3,438	1,898	55.2
Czortków	5,167	2,907	56.2
Dobromil	3,363	2,271	62.5
Dolina	9,852	2,555	25.9
Drohobycz	34,665	15,313	44.2
Grodek Jagielloński	12,973	3,866	29.8
Horodenka	11,223	4,210	37.5
Husiatyn	5,799	3,288	56.7
Jarosław	23,965	6,154	25.7
Jaworów	10,211	2,644	25.9
Kałusz	8,653	4,363	50.4
Kamionka Strumiłowa	8,106	3,549	43.8
Kołomyja	42,676	18,930	44.4
Kosów	5,536	2,950	53.3
Lisko	4,588	2,805	61.1
Lwów	206,113	57,387	27.8
Mościska	4,778	2,574	53.9
Nadwórna	8,080	3,772	46.7
Peczeniżyn	6,667	1,777	26.7
Podhajce	5,576	3,497	62.7
Przemyśl	54,078	16,062	29.7
Przemyślany	4,962	2,838	57.2
Radziechów	4,209	1,814	43.1
Rawa Ruska	10,775	6,112	56.7
Rohatyn	7,664	3,254	42.4
Rudki	3,716	1,968	53.0
Sambor	20,257	5,418	26.7
Sanok	10,711	4,073	38.0
Skałat	6,227	2,838	45.6
Skole	6,425	3,099	48.2

Continued on the next page

Table 2. *Continued*

District	Total Population	Jews	% of the Total
Śniatyń	12,342	4,386	35.5
Sokal	11,609	4,516	38.9
Stanisławów	33,328	15,213	45.6
Stary Sambor	4,931	1,827	37.0
Stryj	30,942	10,718	34.6
Tarnopol	33,871	13,997	41.3
Tłumacz	5,719	2,082	36.4
Trembowla	9,075	2,088	23.0
Turka	10,911	4,887	44.8
Zaleszczyki	5,438	3,382	62.2
Zbaraż	9,983	3,291	33.0
Zborów	5,656	2,265	40.0
Złoczów	13,234	5,243	39.6
Żółkiew	9,463	3,845	40.6
Żydaczów	3,873	892	23.0
Total	815,095	304,315	37.3

Source: Bohdan Wasiutyński, *Ludność żydowska w Polsce w wiekach XIX i XX* (Warsaw: wydawnictwo Kasy im. Mianowskiego, 1930), 114–124.

Table 3. Jewish Population in the Countryside, 1910

District	Total Population	Jews	% of the Total	% of Jews in Countryside
Bóbrka	88,526	10,171	11.5	7.4
Bohorodczany	69,462	7,479	10.8	8.5
Borszczów	109,319	12,740	11.7	11.9
Brody	145,780	22,596	15.5	6.7
Brzeżany	104,810	10,744	10.3	5.4
Brzozów	81,408	5,325	6.5	5.3
Buczacz	138,297	17,481	12.6	5.3
Cieszanów	86,549	10,780	12.5	8.8
Czortków	76,447	7,945	10.4	5.5
Dobromil	72,102	7,575	10.5	7.7
Dolina	113,831	12,812	11.3	5.8
Drohobycz	171,696	29,566	17.2	5.8
Grodek Jagielloński	79,592	6,882	8.6	3.0
Horodenka	92,033	10,114	11.0	7.3
Husiatyn	109,319	11,276	10.3	7.0
Jarosław	150,301	14,982	10.0	4.2
Jaworów	86,719	6,353	7.3	4.1
Kałusz	97,421	8,178	8.4	4.3
Kamionka Strumiłowa	75,569	8,788	11.6	7.1
Kołomyja	124,850	23,880	19.1	5.0
Kosów	85,804	9,701	11.3	4.8
Lisko	98,492	13,884	14.1	9.7
Lwów (city)	206,113	57,387	27.8	0.2
Lwów (district)	161,572	14,038	8.7	7.6
Mościska	87,841	7,230	8.2	4.5
Nadwórna	90,662	11,451	12.6	6.3
Peczeniżyn	46,794	4,201	9.0	6.0
Podhajce	93,546	7,316	7.8	4.3
Przemyśl	159,991	22,540	14.1	5.6
Przemyślany	86,568	9,548	11.0	5.6
Radziechów	72,246	9,578	13.3	3.3
Rawa Ruska	115,668	16,711	14.4	6.7
Rohatyn	124,985	13,548	10.8	5.2
Rudki	77,268	6,392	8.3	2.5
Sambor	107,445	8,829	8.2	3.9
Sanok	108,678	11,249	10.4	5.8
Skałat	96,005	12,621	13.1	4.4

Continued on the next page

Table 3. *Continued*

District	Total Population	Jews	% of the Total	% of Jews in Countryside
Skole	55,355	5,918	10.7	5.8
Śniatyń	88,705	10,239	11.6	5.1
Sokal	109,249	16,304	14.9	8.9
Stanisławów	158,065	29,754	18.8	11.1
Stary Sambor	60,810	6,480	10.7	6.3
Stryj	80,222	12,760	15.9	4.1
Tarnopol	142,138	19,722	13.9	3.4
Tłumacz	116,066	9,649	8.3	5.2
Trembowla	81,048	7,278	9.0	5.5
Turka	85,823	11,668	13.6	9.1
Zaleszczyki	76,957	9,237	12.0	8.3
Zbaraż	71,498	5,337	7.5	3.3
Zborów	60,764	6,198	10.2	5.3
Złoczów	117,364	13,586	11.6	6.1
Żółkiew	99,654	9,520	9.6	3.7
Żydaczów	83,339	6,871	8.2	2.8
Total	5,380,766	662,412	12.3	7.1

Sources: Bohdan Wasiutyński, *Ludność żydowska w Polsce w wiekach XIX i XX* (Warsaw: wydawnictwo Kasy im. Mianowskiego, 1930), 96–101, 107–108; Piotr Wróbel, "The Jews of Galicia under Austrian-Polish Rule, 1869–1918," *Austrian History Yearbook* 25 (1994): 110–111; B. Stopnevich, "Naselenie Galitsii," *Ukrainskaia zhizn'*, 11–12 (1914): 52–53; *Haliczanin: kalendarz powszechny zastosowany do potrzeb wszystkich mieszkańców Galicji na rok pański 1918* (L'viv, Ukraine: nakładem Drukarni i Litografii Piller-Neumanna, 1918), 28.

Notes

Abbreviations

AAN	*Archiwum Akt Nowych*
AGAD	*Archiwum Główny Akt Dawnich*
arkush (ark.)	page
BN	*Biblioteka Narodowa*
BŻIH	*Biuletyn Żydowskiego Instytutu Historycznego*
CAW	*Centralne Archiwum Wojskowe*
DALO	*Derzhavnyi arkhiv L'vivs 'koi oblasti*
delo (d.)	file
dział (dz.)	inventory
fond (f.)	group
GARF	*Gosudarstvennyi arkhiv Rossiiskoi Federatsii*
kartka (k.)	page
kartki (kk.)	pages
l., ll.	list, lists
LNB	*Lvivs'ka naukova biblioteka imeni Vasyla Stefanyka Natsional'noi Akademii Nauk Ukrainy*
ob.	opposite side of page
opis' (o.)	inventory (Russian)
opys (o.)	inventory (Ukrainian)
RGVA	*Rossiiskii gosudarstvennyi voennyi arkhiv*
RGVIA	*Rossiiskii gosudarstvennyi voenno-istoricheskii arkhiv*
RTsKhIDNI	*Rossiiskii tsentr khraneniia i izucheniia dokumentov noveisheii istorii*
sprava (spr.)	file (Ukrainian)
sygnatura (sygn.)	file (Polish)
tom (t.)	volume
TsDAVO	*Tsentral'nyi derzhavnyi arkhiv vyshchykh orhaniv vlady i upravlinnia Ukrainy*
TsDIAUK	*Tsentral'nyi derzhavnyi istorychnyi arkhiv Ukrainy u Kyevi*
TsDIAUL	*Tsentral'nyi derzhavnyi istorychnyi arkhiv Ukrainy u L'vovi*
TsKhIDK	*Tsentral'noe khranilishche istroriko-dokumental'nykh kollektsii*

TsNBU	*Tsentral'na naukova biblioteka Ukrainy im. V. I. Vernads'koho*
VIZh	*Voenno-istoricheskii zhurnal*
zv.	opposite side of page

Preface

1. Eric Lohr, "The Russian Army and the Jews: Mass Deportation, Hostages, and Violence during World War I," *Russian Review* 60 (2001): 406–407.

2. Salo W. Baron, "Jews in Russia: The First World War and the Revolutionary Period," in Herbert A. Strauss, ed., *Hostages of Modernization: Studies on Modern Antisemitism, 1870–1933/39* (Berlin: Walter de Gruyter, 1993), 1291–1311.

3. David Vital, *A People Apart: The Jews in Europe, 1789–1939* (Oxford: Oxford University Press, 1999), 727–728.

4. Mark von Hagen, "The Great War and the Mobilization of Ethnicity in the Russian Empire," in Barnett R. Rubin and Jack Snyder, eds., *Post-Soviet Political Order: Conflict and State Building* (London: Routledge, 1998), 34–57, and Mark von Hagen, "The *Levée en masse* from Russian Empire to Soviet Union, 1874–1938," in Daniel Moran and Arthur Waldron, eds., *The People in Arms: Military Myth and National Mobilization since the French Revolution* (Cambridge: Cambridge University Press, 2003), 160, 170; Rogers Brubaker, "Nationalizing States in the Old 'New Europe'—and the New," *Ethnic and Racial Studies* 19, no. 2 (1996): 411–437.

5. I appropriated the term from the article by Leonard Berkowitz and James A. Green, "The 'Stimulus Qualities' of the Scapegoat," *Journal of Abnormal and Social Psychology* 64, no. 4 (1962): 293–301.

6. Jonathan Frankel, "The Paradoxical Politics of Marginality: Thoughts on the Jewish Situation during the Years 1914–1921," *Studies in Contemporary Jewry* 4 (1988): 3–21.

7. Hannah Arendt, *On Violence* (New York: Harcourt Brace, 1970), 51–52.

8. Donald L. Horowitz, *The Deadly Ethnic Riot* (Berkeley and Los Angeles: University of California Press, 2001), 326; Steven E. Barkan and Lynn L. Snowden, *Collective Violence* (Needham Heights, MA: Allyn & Bacon, 2001), 6; Roger D. Peterson, *Understanding Ethnic Violence: Fear, Hatred, and Resentment in Twentieth-Century Eastern Europe* (Cambridge: Cambridge University Press, 2002), 4.

9. Daniel W. Graf, "The Rule of the Generals: Military Government in Western Russia, 1914–1915" (PhD diss., University of Nebraska, 1972); Daniel W. Graf, "Military Rule behind the Russian Front, 1914–1917: The Political Ramifications," *Jahrbücher für Geschichte Osteuropas* 22, no. 3 (1974): 396–411; Mark Levene, "Frontiers of Genocide: Jews in the Eastern War Zones, 1914–1920 and 1941," in Panikos Panayi, ed., *Minorities in Wartime: National and Racial Groupings in Europe, North America and Australia during the Two World Wars* (Oxford: Berg Publishers, 1993), 83–117; Peter Gatrell, *A Whole Empire Is Walking: Refugees in Russia during World War I* (Bloomington, IN: Indiana University Press, 1999); Vejas Liulevicius, *War Land on the Eastern Front: Culture, National Identity and German Occupation in World War I* (Cambridge: Cambridge University Press, 2000); Eric Lohr, *Nationalizing the Russian Empire: The Campaign against Enemy Aliens during World War I* (Cambridge, MA: Harvard University Press, 2003); A. Iu. Bakhturina, *Politika Rossiiskoi imperii v vostochnoi Galitsii v gody pervoi mirovoi voiny* (Moscow: "AIRO-XX," 2000). I am grateful to Eric Lohr for providing me with this source.

10. Michael Gelber, *History of Polish Jewry during the Revival of Poland* (New York: Shengold Publishers, 1990); Jerzy Tomaszewski, "Polskie formacje zbrojne wobec Żydów, 1918–1919," in Jerzy Tomaszewski, ed., *Żydzi w obronie Rzeczypospolitej: materiały konferencji*

w Warszawie 17 i 18 października 1993 r. (Warsaw: Wydawnictwo Cyklady, 1996), 97–111; Jacek Walicki, "Położenie Żydów polskich podczas kampanii 1920 r.," *Acta Universitatis Lodziensis* 52 (1995): 113–125; Frank Golczewski, *Polnisch-Jüdische Beziehungen, 1881–1922: eine Studie zur Geschichte des Antisemitismus in Osteuropa* (Wiesbaden: Franz Steiner Verlag, 1981).

11. The Gregorian calendar was introduced in Russia in 1918.

Introduction

1. Quoted in Tomasz Gąsowski, "Galicja—żydowski matecznik," in Jerzy Chłopecki and Helena Madurowicz-Urbańska, eds., *Galicja i jej dziedzictwo,* part 2, "Społeczeństwo i gospodarka" (Rzeszów, Poland: Wydawnictwo Szkoły Pedagogicznej, 1995), 128.

2. Leonard Prager, "Galicyjsko-żydowska historia w zwierciadle trzech biografii: Mordechaj Gebirtig, Ignacy Schipper i Dow Sadan," in Jerzy Chłopecki and Helena Madurowicz-Urbańska, eds., *Galicja i jej dziedzictwo,* "Społeczeństwo i gospodarka" (Rzeszów, Poland: Wydawnictwo Szkoły Pedagogicznej, 1995), part 2, 138.

3. Computed on the basis of *Haliczanin: kalendarz powszechny zastosowany do potrzeb wszystkich mieszkańców Galicji na rok pański 1918* (L'viv, Ukraine: nakładem Drukarni i Litografii Piller-Neumanna, 1918), 64–71; *Jedność (Organ Żydów Polskich)* 40, no. 17 (December 1911): 3; *Moriah: miesięcznik młodzierzy żydowskiej,* Rocznik 12 (5677–1916/1917): 105. Also see Teresa Andlauer, *Die judische Bevolkerung im Modernisierungsprozess Galiziens (1867–1914)* (Frankfurt am Main: Peter Lang, 2001), 87.

4. Ya. R. Dashkevych, "Vsayemovidnosyny mizh ukrains'kym ta yevreis'kim nacelenniam u Skhidnii Halychyni /kinets' XIX-pochatok XX st./," *Ukrains'kyi istorychnyi zhurnal* 10 (1990): 66; Sarra Rabinovich, "Obrazovanie yevreev v Galitsii," *Vestnik yevreiskogo prosveshcheniia* 23 (1913): 121.

5. Tadeusz Lutman, *Studja nad dziejami handlu Brodów w latach 1773–1880* (L'viv, Ukraine: Zakład Narodowy im. Ossolińskich, 1937), 134–135, 141, 146, 151; Ignacy Schiper, *Dzieje handlu żydowskiego na ziemiach polskich* (Warsaw: nakładem Centrali Związków Kupców, 1937), 439, 440–441; *Almanach i leksykon żydostwa polskiego* (L'viv, Ukraine: nakładem Hermana Dikera, 1937), 35–37; Klaus Hödl, *Als Bettler im Leopoldstadt: Galizische Juden auf dem Weg nach Wien* (Vienna: Bohlau Verlag, 1994), 26–27, 35.

6. Erwin Schmidle, *Juden in der K.u.K Armee, 1788–1918/Jews in the Habsburg Armed Forces* (Eisenstadt, Austria: Österreichisches-Jüdisches Museum, 1989), 102–103, 107, 120; Wolfgang von Weisl, "Juden in der Österreichischen und Österreichisch-Ungarischen Armee," *Zeitschrift für die Geschichte der Juden* 8, no. 1–2 (1971): 8–9; Wilhelm Feldman, *Stronnictwa i programy polityczne w Galicyi, 1846–1906* (Krakow: Spółka Nakładowa "Książka," 1907), 294; *Tsentral'nyi derzhavnyi istorychnyi arkhiv Ukrainy u L'vovi* (TsDIAUL), fond 458, opys 1, sprava 726, arkush 5; ibid., f. 458, o. 1, spr. 64, ark. 1–2; *Voina i yevrei* (St. Petersburg: n.p., 1912), 192.

7. Anton G. Rabinbach, "The Migration of Galician Jews to Vienna, 1857–1880," *Austrian History Yearbook* 11 (1975): 46, 50; Abraham Korkis, "Die wirtschaftliche Lage der Juden in Galizien," *Der Jude: Eine Monatschrift* 2 (1917–1918): 469, 532; also see Abraham Korkis, "Zur Bewegung der jüdischen Bevölkerung in Galizien," in Alfred Nossig, ed., *Jűdische Statistik* (Berlin: "Verein für Jüdische Statistik," 1903), 315; Raphael Mahler, "The Economic Background of Jewish Emigration from Galicia to the United States," *YIVO Annual of Jewish Social Science* 7 (1952): 260–261; Stanisław Szczepanowski, *Nędza Galicyi w cyfrach: program energicznego rozwoju gospodarstwa krajowego* (L'viv, Ukraine: Gubrynowicz i Schmidt, 1888), 116–118.

8. Jacob Bross, "The Beginning of the Jewish Labor Movement in Galicia," *YIVO* 5 (1959): 59, 66, 69; E. Korotkii, B. Kun, and O. Piatnitskii, *Pervyi kongress Kominterna: mart 1919 g.* (Moscow: Partiinoye izdatel'stvo, 1933), 232; Rick Kuhn, "Organizing Yiddish Speaking Workers in Pre–World War I Galicia: The Jewish Social Democratic Party," in Leonard Greenspoon, ed., *Yiddish Language and Culture: Then and Now* (Omaha: Creighton University Press, 1997), 2, 4, 6–7; M. Lozyns'kyi, "Zhydivs'ka sotsial'na demokratiia v Halychyni," *Literaturno-naukovy visnyk* 8, no. 32 (1905): 8; *Archiwum Główny Akt Dawnich* (AGAD), dział "Ministerstwo Spraw Wewnętrznych," sygnatura F24, kartki 523–525, 634–635, 637, 730, 861–862, 976–977.

9. Józef Buszko, *Galicja 1859–1914: Polski Piemont?* (Warsaw: Krajowa Agencja Wydawnicza, 1989), 10; Paul Robert Magocsi, *A History of Ukraine* (Toronto: University of Toronto Press, 1996), 418–422.

10. Paul Robert Magocsi, *The Roots of Ukrainian Nationalism: Galicia as Ukraine's Piedmont* (Toronto: University of Toronto Press, 2002), 73–82.

11. Schiper, *Dzieje handlu żydowskiego,* 449–451; Piotr Wróbel, "Przed odzyskaniem niepodległości," in Jerzy Tomaszewski, ed., *Najnowsze dzieje Żydów w Polsce w zarysie (do 1950 roku)* (Warsaw: Wydawnictwo Naukowe PWN, 1993), 102–103; Walentyna Najdus, *Szkice z historii Galicji* (Warsaw: Książka i Wiedza, 1958), 1, part 1, 187.

12. Wróbel, "Jews of Galicia under Austrian-Polish Rule, 1869–1918." *Austrian History Yearbook* XXV (1994): 103; Artur Eisenbach, "Emancypacja Żydów w dobie rewolucji 1846–49," *Biuletyn Żydowskiego Istytutu Historycznego* (BŻIH), 1/141 (1987): 20–23; Elżbieta Horn, "Posłowie żydowscy i problem żydowski w galicyjskim sejmie krajowym w 1861 r," *BŻIH,* 1/149, part 1 (1989): 39, and 4/152, part 2 (1989): 57, 44; Max Rosenfeld, "Die jüdischen Gemeinden in Österreich," *Der Jude* 2 (1917–1918): 155; G. Wolf, "Zur Lage der Juden in Galizien," *Monatschrift für Geschichte und Wissenschaft des Judentums* 16 (1867): 202; *Archiwum Akt Nowych* (AAN), dz. "Kolekcja materiałów archiwalnych," sygn. 26, t. 1, kk. 2–4.

13. Leila P. Everett, "The Rise of Jewish National Politics in Galicia, 1905–1907," in Andrei S. Markovits and Frank S. Sysyn, eds., *Nationbuilding and the Politics of Nationalism: Essays on Austrian Galicia* (Cambridge, MA: Harvard University Press, 1982), 156–157, 173–177; Kurt Stillschweig, "Nationalism and Autonomy among Eastern European Jewry: Origins and Historical Development up to 1939," *Historica Judaica: A Journal of Studies in Jewish History, Especially in the Legal and Economic History of the Jews* 6 (1944): 44; Ezra Mendelsohn, "From Assimilation to Zionism in Lvov: The Case of Alfred Nossig," *Slavonic and East European Review* 49, no. 117 (1971): 525–526; Feldman, *Stronnictwa i programy polityczne,* 277–278.

14. Brian Porter, *When Nationalism Began to Hate: Imagining Modern Politics in Nineteenth-Century Poland* (New York: Oxford University Press, 2000), 158.

15. J. Kominkowski, *Parę uwag w sprawie Żydów* (Krakow: nakładem autora, 1868), 11; Teofil Merunowicz, *O metodzie i celach rozpraw nad kwestią żydowską* (L'viv, Ukraine: nakładem autora, 1879), 15–16, 21, 22; see also Teofil Merunowicz, *Żydowscy radykaliści* (L'viv, Ukraine: nakładem wydawnictwa "Gazety Narodowej," 1893), 192–193, 196; Kś. M. J., *Tajemnice żydowskie* (Krakow: nakładem autora, 1898), 11–14; Waleryan Kalinka, *Galicya i Kraków pod panowaniem austryackim* (Krakow: Spółka Wydawnicza Polska, 1898), 84–86.

16. *Grzmot,* no. 29, 15 November 1896; no. 33, 25 December 1896; no. 9, 25 March 1897; no. 11, 15 April 1897; no. 12, 25 April 1897; no. 14, 15 May 1897; no. 16, 5 June 1891; no. 18, 25 June 1897; no. 20, 15 July 1897; no. 21, 25 July 1892; no. 23, 15 August 1897; no. 26, 18 September 1897; no. 43, 22 October 1898; no. 51, 17 December 1898; Prawdomowny (Kś. S. Załeski), *Socyalistom naszym na kolęde: "Czerwony Sztandar"* (Krakow: nakładem redakcji "Grzmotu," 1896),

7; Aleksander Czołowski, *Mord rytualny: epizod z przeszłości Lwowa* (L'viv, Ukraine: nakładem autora, 1899), 10; Kś. M., *Skąd się bierze niedowiarstwo między katolikami?* (Nowy Sącz, Poland: nakładem i drukiem J. K. Jakubowskiego, 1900), 10, 16; see also Kś. M., *Pogadanka o socyaliżmie ("Latarnia" oświatlona)* (Krakow: nakładem redakcji "Prawdy," 1903), 36, 48–49.

17. Filip Friedman, "Dzieje Żydów w Galicji (1772–1914)," in Ignacy Schipper, Arieh Tartakower, and Aleks Hafka, *Żydzi w Polsce odrodzonej: działalność społeczna, gospodarcza, oświatowa i kulturalna* (Warsaw: nakładem Wydawnictwa "Żydzi w Polsce Odrodzonej," 1930), 1:394–396; Golczewski, *Polnisch-Jüdische Beziehungen,* 70–84; AGAD, dz. "Ministerstwo Sprawiedliwości," sygn. 310, kk. 1624–1626; ibid., dz. "Ministerstwo Spraw Wewnętrznyckh," sygn. F41, kk. 353–354.

18. Najdus, *Szkice z historii,* 94–95; Czesław Lechicki, "Z dziejów prasy galicyjskiej na przełomie dwoch wieków /'Ruch Katolicki'-'Przedświt'/," *Studia Historyczne* 14, 2/53 (1972): 168; *Jedność,* no. 20, 20 May 1910; Edward Dubanowicz, *Stanowisko ludności żydowskiej w Galicji wobec wyborów do parlamentu wiedeńskiego w r. 1907* (L'viv, Ukraine: Drukarnia "Polonia," 1970), 39–40; AGAD, dz. "Ministerstwo Spraw Wewnętrznych," sygn. F42, k. 833; ibid., sygn. F43, kk. 121–125; Włodzimierz Mich, *Obcy w polskim domu: nacjonalistyczne koncepcje rozwiązania problemu mniejszości narodowych 1918–1939* (Lublin, Poland: Wydawnictwo Uniwersytetu Marii Curie-Składowskiej, 1994), 19, 28, 36.

19. John-Paul Himka, "Ukrainian-Jewish Antagonism in the Galician Countryside during the Late Nineteenth Century," in Peter J. Potichnyj and Howard Aster, eds., *Ukrainian-Jewish Relations in Historical Perspective* (Edmonton: Canadian Institute of Ukrainian Studies, 1988), 121–139; P. G. J. Pulzer, *The Rise of Political Anti-Semitism in Germany and Austria* (New York: John Wiley & Sons, 1964), 215; Andlauer, *Die jüdische Bevölkerung im Modernisierungsprozess,* 139–140.

20. AGAD, dz. "Ministerstwo Sprawiedliwości," sygn. 310, kk. 2625–2632; ibid., dz. "Ministerstwo Spraw Wewnętrznych," sygn. F41, kk. 368–369, 531; *American Jewish Year Book* (New York: American Jewish Committee and Jewish Publication Society of America, 5672), 200; Himka, "Ukrainian-Jewish Antagonism," 111–149; Joachim Schoenfeld, *Jewish Life in Galicia under the Austro-Hungarian Empire and in the Reborn Poland, 1898–1939* (Hoboken, NJ: Ktav Publishing House, 1985), 11–13.

21. Everett, "Rise of Jewish National Politics," 160–162; Jan Kozik, *The Ukrainian National Movement in Galicia: 1815–1847* (Edmonton: Canadian Institute of Ukrainian Studies of Alberta, 1986), 123; Ivan Franko, *Opovidannia ta povisti* (Kiev: derzhavne vydavnytsvo khudozhnioi literatury, 1963); Les' Martovych, *Za mezhu: opovidannia* (Kiev: vydavnytstvo khudozhnioi literatury "Dnipro," 1968), 88–93; AGAD, dz. "Ministerstwo Spraw Wewnętrznych," sygn. 189, n.p.

Chapter 1. Russia Goes to War

1. Maurice Paleologue, "Rosja carów w czasie wielkiej wojny," in Michał Sokolnicki, ed., *Polska w pamiętnikach wielkiej wojny, 1914–1918* (Warsaw: Instytut Wydawniczy "Biblioteka Polska," 1925), 301.

2. Vladimir Stepankovsky, *The Russian Plot to Seize Galicia /Austrian Ruthenia/* (Jersey City, NJ: Ukrainian National Council, 1915), 15; Stephan Tomashivs'kyi, *Die weltpolitische Bedeutung Galiziens* (Munich: F. Brückmann A. G., 1915), 34–41.

3. Jan Leszczyński, *Rządy rosyjskie w kraju tarnopolskim, 1809–1815* (Krakow: Druk W. L. Anczyca i Spółki, 1903), 137; Czesław Blicharski, *Tarnopol w latach 1809–1945 /od pe-*

riodu epopei napoleońskiej do wypędzenia (Biskupice, Poland: n.p., 1993), 30; Ivan Krevets'kyi, "Ostgalizien und Russland," *Ukrainische Rundschau* 8, no. 1 (1910): 7; *Rossiiskii tsentr khraneniia i izucheniia dokumentov noveisheii istorii* (RTsKhIDNI), fond 70, opis' 2, delo 644, tom II, list 26.

4. On the origins and evolution of the Russophiles, see Paul R. Magocsi, "Old Ruthenianism and Russophilism: A New Conceptual Framework for Analysing National Ideologies in Late 19th Century Galicia," in Paul Debreczeny, ed., *American Contribution to the Ninth International Congress of Slavists, Kiev, September 1983* (Columbus, OH: Slavica Publishers, 1983), 2:305–324.

5. P. N. Yefremov, *Vneshniaia politika Rossii, 1907–1914* (Moscow: izdatel'stvo Instituta Mezhdunarodnykh Otnoshenii, 1961), 236–238; "Russische Wählarbeit in Galizien und der Bukowina," *Ukrainische Rundschau* 8, no. 1 (1910): 15–27; Roman Smal'-Stotskyi, "Graf Bobrinskii und die österreichischen Ruthenen," *Ukrainische Rundschau* 10, no. 2–3 (1912): 38–48; Bakhturina, *Politika Rossiiskoi imperii*, 47–50, 54; *Khto pomahaye v Halychyni moskovs'komu ministrovi Stolypinovu? promova posla D-ra Kyryla Tryl'ovoho vyholoshena v Derzhavnii Radi dnia 16 chervnia 1910 roku* (Kolomyja, Ukraine: drukarnia A. B. Kysilevs'koho, 1910), 1–21.

6. Stefan Arski, "Rozmowy z wywiadem austriackim przed pierwszą wojną światową," *Sprawy Międzynarodowe* 12, 11–12/92–93 (1959): 68–77, and 13, 3/96 (1960): 68, 78–86, 92; also see Stefan Arski, "Działalność polskich organizacji w Galicji w świetle korespondencji dyplomatychnej z okresu 1906–1912," *Sprawy Międzynarodowe* 13, 10/103 (1960): 53–66; Armin Müller, "Galizien-Krisenherd in den Beziehungen zwischen Österreich-Ungarn und Russland, 1910–1914," *Jahrbuch für Geschichte der sozialistischen Länder Europas* 28 (1984): 208–210, 231–216; Krevets'kyi, "Ostgalizien und Russland," 9, 12; H. Lemke, "Die Regierung Stürgkh und die Pläne zur Teilung Galiziens," in *Österreich-Ungarn in der Weltpolitik, 1900 bis 1918* (Berlin: Akademie-Verlag, 1965), 267–268, 271; Klaus Bachmann, "Kriegsgrund Galizien: Der ostgalizische Nationalkonflikt und seine aussenpolitischen Auswirkungen vor dem Ersten Weltkrieg," *Österreichische Osthefte* 32 (1990): 59.

7. Wolfdieter Bihl, "Die Beziehungen zwischen Österreich-Ungarn und Russland in Bezug auf die galizische Frage, 1908–1914," in Karlheinz Mack, ed., *Galizien um die Jahrhundertwende: politische, soziale und kulturelle Verbindungen mit Österreich* (Vienna: Verlag für Geschichte und Politik, 1990), 46; Theofil Hornykiewicz, ed., *Ereignisse in der Ukraine, 1914–1922: deren Bedeutung und historische Hitegrunde* (Horn, Austria: Verlag Ferdinand Berger, Philadelphia: 1966), 1:1–4; Müller, "Galizien-Krisenherd," 228. On the impact of the Bosnian crisis on Austro-Russian relations, see Yefremov, *Vneshniaia politika Rossii*, 79–93, and I. V. Bestuzhev, *Bor'ba Rossii po voprosam vneshnei politiki, 1906–1910* (Moscow: izdatel'stvo Akademii Nauk SSSR, 1961), 199–294. For its part, the Russian counterintelligence service kept close surveillance over Polish and Ukrainian national movements in Galicia. A. Yu. Shelukhin, "Razvedovatel'nye organy v strukture vysshego voennogo upravleniia Rossiiskoi Imperii nachala XX veka, 1906–1914," *Vestnik Moskovskogo universiteta*, series 8 (1996): 29.

8. Myroslav Grabets, *K istorii Marmaroshskogo protsessa (delo 94-kh: 29/XII 1913–3/III 1914)* (Uzhhorod, Ukraine: izdanie Karpatorusskoi Trudovoii Partii, 1934); Bachmann, "Kriegsgrund Galizien," 49–50, 57; Müller, "Galizien-Krisenherd," 213; *Die Internationalen Beziehungen im Zeitalter des Imperialismus: Dokumente aus den Archiv der Zaristischen und Prowizorischen Regierung* (Berlin: Verlag der Reimar Hobbing, 1931–1936), I. 1, 235–237, and I. 3, 232–233. Unfortunately, I was unable to gain access to the Archive of Foreign Affairs of

Imperial Russia in Moscow to examine whether Russian officials held any plans in regard to Galician Jews.

9. For example, Salo W. Baron, *The Russian Jew under the Tsars and Soviets* (New York: Schocken Books, 1987); John D. Klier, *Russia Gathers Her Jews: The Origins of the "Jewish Question" in Russia, 1772–1825* (DeKalb: Northern Illinois University Press, 1986).

10. Hans Rogger, "Reforming Jews–Reforming Russians: Gradualism and Pessimism in the Empire of the Tsars," in Strauss, *Hostages of Modernization,* 1208–1229.

11. Vasilii Kiselev, *Galichina i Moldaviia: putevye pis'ma* (Bridgeport, CT: Carpatho-Russian Literary Association, 1976), 202–240; Johannes Rogala von Bieberstein, *Die These von der Verschwörung, 1776–1945: Philosophen, Freimaurer, Juden, Liberale und Sozialisten als Verschwörer gegen die Sozialordnung* (Frankfurt am Main: Peter Lang, 1976), 161; A. Achiezer, "Antisemitism v Rossii: vzgliad kulturologa," *Vestnik yevreiskogo universiteta v Moskve* 1 (1992): 105.

12. Heinz-Dietrich Löwe, *Antisemitismus und reaktionäre Utopie: Russischer Konservatismus im Kampf gegen den Wandel von Staat und Geselschaft, 1890–1917* (Hamburg: Hoffman und Campe Verlag, 1978); also see Heinz-Dietrich Löwe, "Anti-Semitism at the Close of the Tsarist Era," in Strauss, *Hostages of Modernization,* 1188–1207; John Doyle Klier, *Imperial Russia's Jewish Question, 1855–1881* (Cambridge: Cambridge University Press, 1995), 290–291, 389. Also see Erich Haberer, *Jews and Revolution in Nineteenth-century Russia* (Cambridge: Cambridge University Press, 1995).

13. Albert S. Lindemann, *The Jew Accused: Three Anti-Semitic Affairs (Dreyfus, Beilis, Frank), 1894–1915* (New York: Cambridge University Press, 1991), 129–193.

14. Iochanan Petrovskii-Shtern, *Yevrei v russkoi armii, 1827–1914* (Moscow: Novoye Literaturnoye Obozrenie, 2003), 179; A. I. Denikin, *Put' russkogo ofitsera* (New York: izdatel'stvo imeni Chekhova, 1953), 283–285.

15. Mary Neuberger, "The Russo-Turkish War and the 'Eastern Jewish Question': Encounter between Victims and Victors in Ottoman Bulgaria, 1877–8," *East European Jewish Affairs* 26, no. 2 (1996): 51–66; Dietrich Beyrau, *Militär und Gesellschaft im vorrevolutionären Russland* (Cologne: Böhlau Verlag, 1984), 423–429.

16. Bieberstein, *Die These von der Verschwörung,* 200.

17. Hans-Peter Stein, "Der Offizer des russischen Heeres im Zeitabschnitt zwischen Reform und Revolution, 1861–1905," *Forschungen zur osteuropäischen Geschichte* 13 (1967): 460; M. Grulev, *Zapiski generala-yevreia* (Paris: n.p., 1930); Peter Kenez, "A Profile of the Prerevolutionary Officer Corps," *California Slavic Studies* 7 (1973): 148; Joshua A. Sanborn, "Drafting the Nation: Military Conscription and the Formation of a Modern Polity in Tsarist and Soviet Russia, 1905–1925" (PhD diss., University of Chicago, 1998), 203–204, 288; Eli Weinerman, "Racism, Racial Prejudice, and the Jews in Late Imperial Russia," *Ethnic and Racial Studies* 17, no. 3 (1994): 474; *Handbook of the Russian Army* (London: Imperial War Museum, 1996), 12.

18. *Voina i yevrei,* 2, 77, 146–148, 152, 158–160; Petrovskii-Shtern, *Yevrei v russkoi armii,* 355–356.

19. *Voina i yevrei,* 119–120; Petrovskii-Shtern, *Yevrei v russkoi armii,* 297.

20. Shelukhin, "Razvedovatel'nye organy," 22.

21. *Rossiiskii gosudarstvennyi voenno-istoricheskii archiv* (RGVIA), f. 2122, o. 7, d. 15, l. 1.

22. Graf, "Rule of the Generals," 35–37; I. I. Rostunov, *Russkii front pervoii mirovoii voiny* (Moscow: izdatel'stvo "Nauka," 1976), 113–114; N. P. Yeroshkin, *Istoriia gosudarstvennykh uchrezhdenii dorevolutsionnoi Rossii* (Moscow: "Vysshaia shkola," 1983), 292; Mikhail

Lemke, *250 dnei v tsarskoi stavke /25 sent. 1915—2 iula 1916/* (St. Petersburg: Gosudarstvennoe izdatel'stvo, 1920), 42; Bakhturina, *Politika Rossiiskoi Imperii,* 72.

23. Graf, "Rule of the Generals," 42; Richard A. Pierce, *Russian Central Asia, 1867–1917: A Study in Colonial Rule* (Berkeley and Los Angeles: University of California Press, 1960); Theodore R. Weeks, *Nation and State in Late Imperial Russia: Nationalism and Russification on the Western Frontier, 1863–1914* (DeKalb: Northern Illinois University Press, 1996), 174.

24. *Tsentral'nyi derzhavnyi istorychnyi arkhiv Ukrainy u Kyevi* (TsDIAUK), f. 274, o. 5, spr. 11, ark. 69; S. G. Nelipovich, "Repressii protiv poddanykh 'Tsentral'nykh Derzhav': deportatsii v Rossii, 1914–1918 gg," *Voenno-istoricheskii zhurnal (*cited as *VIZh),* 6 (1996): 32–35. After Turkey entered the war in October of 1914, a new circular stipulated the deportations of Turkish subjects.

25. A German term for the Jews who resided in Poland and Russia.

26. A. I. Spiridovich, *Velikaia voina i fevral'skaia revolutsia, 1914–1917 gg.* (New York: Vseslavianskoe izdatel'stvo, 1960–1962), 1:15, 28; A. Bubnov, *V tsarskoi stavke: vospominaniia admirala Bubnova* (New York: izdatel'stvo imeni Chekhova, 1955), 35–41, 45–47; Lemke, *250 dnei,* 81; A. A. Brusilov, *Moi vospominaniia* (Moscow: voyennoye izdatel'stvo Ministerstva Oborony, 1963), 109; Georgii Shavel'skii, *Vospominaniia poslednego protopresvitera russkoi armii i flota* (New York: izdatel'stvo imeni Chekhova, 1954), 1:113–114, 132–133; Alfred Knox, *With the Russian Army, 1914–1917* (London: Hutchinson & Co., 1921), 1:42; Juri Daniloff (Danilov), *Russland im Weltkriege, 1914–1915* (Jena, Germany: Frommanische Buchhandlung Walter Biedermann, 1925), 179–180; and Juri Daniloff (Danilov), *Na puti k krusheniiu: ocherki iz poslednego perioda russkoi monarkhii* (Moscow: voyennoye izdatel'stvo, 1992), 12.

27. Graf, "Rule of the Generals," 19; Lohr, *Nationalizing the Russian Empire,* 137; Simon Dubnov, *Kniga zhizni: vospominaniia i razmyshleniia, materialy dla istorii moego vremeni* (Riga, Latvia: Jaunatnes Gramata, 1934–1951), 2:180.

28. A number of ethnic groups of the central Asia, Ural, and Siberian regions were exempted from service; the people of the Caucasus region served under special status. *Handbook of the Russian Army,* 7–8; Rostunov, *Russkii front pervoi mirovoi voiny,* 48; N. N. Golovin, *Voennye usiliia Rossii v mirovoi voine* (Paris: Tovarishchestvo obyedinennykh izdatelei, 1939), 1:11–12, 86.

29. M. D. Bonch-Bruevich, *Vsia vlast' Sovetam* (Moscow: voyennoye izdatel'stvo Ministerstva Oborony, 1964), 13. For some Russian soldiers and Cossacks, "Jews" and "kikes" represented two different, but equally malicious groups.

30. M. Altshuler, "Russia and Her Jews—The Impact of the 1914 War," *Wiener Library Bulletin* 27, no. 30–31 (1973–1974): 12; "Iz 'chernoi knigi' rossiiskogo yevreistva: materialy dlia istorii voiny 1914–1915," *Yevreiskaia starina* 10 (1918): 199.

31. Altshuler, "Russia and Her Jews," 198; Gregor Alexinski, *Russia and the Great War* (London: T. Fischer Unwin, 1915), 196; TsDIAUK, f. 365, o. 2, spr. 45, ark. 71; Bernard Pares, *Day by Day with the Russian Army* (London: Constable & Company, 1915), 17; Abraham G. Duker, "Jews in the World War: A Brief Historical Sketch," *Contemporary Jewish Record: A Review of Events and a Digest of Opinion* 2, no. 5 (1939): 9–10; John Reed, *The War in Eastern Europe* (New York: Charles Scribner's Sons, 1916), 234.

32. From the recollections of my grandfather, Yeina Raskin, who before World War I had resided in the Poltava province of the Pale.

33. "Is 'chernoi knigi' rossiiskogo yevreistva," 203f–204f.

34. See V. Klembovskii, "Organizatsiia voennogo shpionstva a Avstrii vo vremia voiny 1914–1918," *Voenno-istoricheskii sbornik: trudy voenno-istoricheskoi komissii* 4 (1920): 97; P. G. Kruglov, *Gibel' Imperatorskoi Rossii* (Moscow: "Sovremennik," 1992), 215–216; *Der russischer*

Nachrichtendienst an der Front Ob. Ost: nach der Erfahrungen der Geheimen Feldpolizei (n.p.: Oberbefehlshaber Ost, 1917), 57, 70.

35. *Tsentral'na naukova biblioteka Ukrainy im. V. I. Vernads'koho* (TsNBU), Institute of the Oriental Studies, f. 21, untitled paper, ark. 2–3; "Is 'chernoi knigi' rossiiskogo yevreistva," 220–221; American Jewish Committee, *The Jews in the Eastern War Zone* (New York: American Jewish Committee, 1916), 53.

36. Nelipovich, "Repressii protiv poddannykh 'Tsentral'nykh Derzhav'," 32–42, and S. G. Nelipovich, "General ot infanterii N. N. Yanushkevich: 'nemetskuiu pakost' uvolit' i bez nezhnostei'," *VIZh* 1 (1997): 42–53; Friedrich Rink and J. M. Richey, "Expulsion of the German Colonists from Wolhynia, 1915–1916," *Heritage Review* 25, no. 1 (1995): 19–22; Lawrence J. Flockerzie, "Poland's Louvain: Documents of the Destruction of Kalisz, August 1914," *Polish Review* 38, no. 4 (1983): 73–87; Lohr, *Nationalizing of the Russian Empire,* 150–152; *Voennye prestupleniia Gabsburgskoi monarkhii: Galitskaia Golgofa* (Trumbull, CT: Peter S. Hardy, 1964); Dimitri S. Markoff, *Belgium of the East* (Wilkes-Barre, PA: Peter G. Kohaniuk, 1920); A. S. Riasanov, "Nemetskaia armiia mozhet konkurirovat' s voinami kannibalov," *VIZh* 4 (1998): 40–45; Yu. A. Pisarev, *Serbiia i Chernogoriia v pervoi mirovoi voine* (Moscow: izdatel'stvo "Nauka," 1968), 182–198; Stojan Kiselinovski, *Grchkata kolonizatsija vo egeiska Makedonja, 1913–1940* (Skopje, Macedonia: Institut za natsionalna istoria, 1981), 41–47.

Chapter 2. "Leveling" Jews: Ethnic Policies in Occupied Galicia

1. Holger H. Herwig, *The First World War: Germany and Austria-Hungary, 1914–1918* (London: Arnold, 1997), 89–93.

2. Jerzy Bandrowski, *W płomieniach: Lwów w lecie 1914* (Kiev: nakładem autora, 1917), 16, 18–19.

3. *Słowo Polskie,* no. 366, 19 August 1914; Piotr Wróbel, "Barucha Milcha galicyjskie wspomnienia wojenne, 1914–1920," *BŻIH* 2/158 (1991): 91; TsDIAUK, f. 365, o. 1, spr. 235, ark. 8; *Voennye prestupleniia Gabsburgskoi monarkhii,* 17–21; Orest Mazur and Ivan Pater, "L'viv u roky pershoi svitovoi viiny," in Yarosalv Isaevych, Feodosii Steblii, and Mykola Lytvyn, eds., *L'viv: istorychni narysy* (L'viv, Ukraine: Instytut Ukrainoznavstva im I. Krypyakevycha NAN Ukrainy, 1996), 307.

4. TsNBU, f. 339, spr. 89, ark. 1–2; Octavian C. Tăslăuanu, *With the Austrian Army in Galicia* (London: Skeffington & Son, n.d.), 85; AAN, dz. "Centralna Agencja Polska w Lozannie," box 61 (*Kurjer Poznański,* 28 June 1917; *Dziennik Poznański,* 1914 [no date]); *Nowa reforma,* 25 September 1917).

5. *Słowo Polskie,* no. 337, 4 August 1914; TsDIAUK, f. 361, o. 1, spr. 156, ark. 33–34; AAN, dz. "Centralna Agencja Polska w Lozannie," box 62 (*Głos Narodu,* 10 January 1916), J. Kreppel, *Juden und Judentum von Heute* (Zürich: Amalthea-Verlag, 1925), 67; AGAD, dz. "Ministerstwo Spraw Wewnętrznych," sygn. F34, n.p.; Schipper, "Żydzi galicyjscy w dobie wojny światowej," in *Żydzi w Polsce odrodzonej,* 1:4; Marsha L. Rozenblit, "For Fatherland and Jewish People: Jewish Women in Austria during the First World War," in Franz Coetzee and Marylin Shevin-Coetzee, eds., *Authority, Identity and the Social History of the Great War* (Providence: Berg, 1995), 200–202; Jiri Kudela, "Die Emigration galizischer und osteuropäischen Juden nach Bochmen und Prag zwischen 1914–1916/17," *Studia Rosenthaliana* 23, no. 2 (1989): 122–124.

6. *Jüdische Rundschau: Allgemeine Jüdische Zeitung,* no. 5, 12 February 1915; no. 9, 19 Feb-

ruary 1915; AAN, dz. "Centralna Agencja Polska w Lozannie," box 62 (*Głos Narodu*, 14 October 1916).

7. Arieh Tartakower and Kurt R. Grossman, *The Jewish Refugee* (New York: Institute of Jewish Affairs of the American Jewish Congress and World Jewish Congress, 1944), 14–17; Rozenblit, "For Fatherland and Jewish People," 200–202, 205–206; *Jüdische Rundschau*, no. 1, 1 January 1915; no. 3, 15 January 1915.

8. AGAD, dz. "Ministerstwo Spraw Wewnętrznych," sygn. F34, n.p.; TsDIAUK, f. 365, o. 1, spr. 235, ark. 4, 7; Golczewski, *Polnisch-Jüdische Beziehungen*, 121–122; *Prikarpatskaia Rus'*, no. 1427, 10 October 1914; *Ukrainische Nachrichten: Mitteilungen des Bundes zur Befreiung der Ukraina*, no. 133, 18 December 1914; Jacob Schall, *Żydostwo galicyjskie w czasie inwazji rosyjskiej w latach 1914–1916* (L'viv, Ukraine: nakładem Księgarni I. Madfesa, 1936), 6–7.

9. Ernst Müller-Meinungen, *"Who Are the Huns?": The Law of Nations and Its Breakers* (Berlin: Georg Reimer Publisher, 1915), 163–165, 167–168; Stefan Kestler, *Die deutsche Auslandsaufklärung und das Bild der Ententemächte im Spiegel zeitgenossischer Propagandaveröffentlichungen während des Ersten Weltkrieges* (Frankfurt am Main: Peter Lang, 1994), 199; TsDIAUK, f. 385, o. 7, spr. 102, ark. 50–51; ibid., f. 361, o. 1, spr. 132, ark. 20b.; ibid., f. 365, o. 1, spr. 235, ark. 8; *Prikarpatskaia Rus'*, no. 1415, 26 September 1914; no. 1416, 28 September 1914; no. 1417, 29 September 1914; Spiridovich, *Velikaia voina*, 31–32; Wróbel, "Barucha Milcha galicyjskie wspomnienia," 92; TsNBU, f. 339, spr. 89, ark. 3–4.

10. TsNBU, f. 339, spr. 89, ark. 1–2; *Ukrainische Nachrichten*, no. 40, 19 June 1915; AAN, dz. "Centralna Agencja Polska w Lozannie," box 61 (*Wiedeński Kurjer Polski*, 2 October 1915); Henryka Kramarz, *Samorząd Lwowa w czasie pierwszej wojny światowej i jego rola w życiu miasta* (Krakow: Wydawnictwo Naukowe WSP, 1994), 40; *Lwów po inwazji rosyjskiej, wrzesień-grudzień 1914: opowiadanie naocznego świadka* (Vienna: nakładem Z. Machnowskiego, 1915), 5; "Die Juden Lembergs unter der Russenherrschaft," *Jüdisches Archiv: Mitteilungen des Komitees "Jüdisches Kriegsarchiv,"* 8–9 (1917): 6; Schall, *Żydostwo galicyjskie*, 4–6; Bohdan Janusz, *293 dni rządów rosyjskich we Lwowie (3.IX.1914–22.VI.1915)* (L'viv, Ukraine: Księgarnia Polska Bernarda Połonieckiego, 1915), 44.

11. Igor Slepcov, "K problematike l. svetovoi vojny na východnom Slovensku v rokoch, 1914–1915," *Historie a vojenstvi* 42, no. 3 (1993): 60.

12. Knox, *With the Russian Army*, 1:145–146; David G. Roskies, ed., *The Dybbuk and Other Writings: S. Ansky* (New York: Schocken Books, 1992), 183–185; Reed, *War in Eastern Europe*, 235; Levene, "Frontiers of Genocide," 95–96; "Iz 'chernoi knigi' rossiiskogo yevreistva," 210; Volodymyr Serhiichuk, ed., *Pohromy v Ukraini, 1914–1920: vid shtuchnykh stereotypiv do hirkoi pravdy prykhovuvanoi v radians'kykh arkhivakh* (Kiev: vydavnytstvo imeni Oleny Telihy, 1998), 62–63, 57–58.

13. Bonch-Bruevich, *Vsia vlast' Sovetam*, 24–25.

14. Horowitz, *Deadly Ethnic Riot*, 548; Petersen, *Understanding Ethnic Violence*, 75.

15. Horowitz, *Deadly Ethnic Riot*, 79, 87.

16. John D. Klier and Shlomo Lambroza, eds., *Pogroms: Anti-Jewish Violence in Modern Russian History* (Cambridge: Cambridge University Press, 1992), 33, 164, 292, 323.

17. TsNBU, f. 339, spr. 89, ark. 2; TsDIAUK, f. 361, o. 2, spr. 134, ark. 180b; ibid., f. 361, o. 1, spr. 221, ark. 245; *Derzhavnyi arkhiv L'vivs 'koi oblasti* (DALO), f. 907, o. 1, spr. 28, ark. 7–8; ibid., f. 907, o. 1, spr. 27, ark. 65; ibid., f. 905, o. 1, spr. 5, ark. 7; Kreppel, *Juden und Judentum*, 76.

18. AGAD, dz. "Ministerstwo Spraw Wewnętrznych," sygn. F34, n.p.; Juliusz Starkel, "Diariusz wydarzeń wojennych we Lwowie od 25.VIII.1914–22.IX.1914," *Biblioteka*

Narodowa (BN), Department of Microfilms, dz. "Biblioteka Ossolińskich," microfilm 35577, k. 29; Józef Białynia-Chołodecki, *Lwów w czasie okupacji rosyjskiej/3 września 1914–22 czerwca 1915: z własnych przerzyć i spostrzerzeń* (L'viv, Ukraine: nakładem redakcji, 1930), 47–48, 72; TsNBU, f. 339, spr. 89, ark. 1–2.

19. Lemke, *250 dnei*, 199, 202; Bohdan Janusz, *Dokumenty urzędowe okupacji rosyjskiej Lwowa* (L'viv, Ukraine: nakładem wydawcy, 1916), 25–26; Brusilov, *Moi vospominaniia*, 137. In his memoirs, while admitting the heavy-handed Russian rule in Galicia, Brusilov brushed off pogroms merely as "Cossack excesses" (ibid., 100).

20. Merrit Abrash, "War Arms toward Austria-Hungary: The Czechoslovak Pivot," in Alexander Dallin et al., eds., *Russian Diplomacy and Eastern Europe, 1914–1917* (New York: King's Crown Press, 1963), 80; *Razgrom avstriiskoi armii i vziatie L'vova* (Moscow: Tipografia I. D. Sytina, 1915), 5–6; *Armeiskii vestnik*, no. 14, 9 September 1914.

21. Lemke, *250 dnei*, 202–203; Bohdan Ostap'iuk, *Davnii Ternopil': istorychni narysy, postati, kartyny khliborobs'koi pratsi, tradytsiini sviatkuvannia, spohady* (Miami: Zemliats'ke Ob'yednannia 'Ternopil'shchyna', 1984), 179; Ivan Martyniuk, *Moye ridne selo Tseniv v Berezhanshchini—Ceniv, My Native Village in the Country of Berezhany* (New York: drukarnia Dzh. A. Press, 1976), 470–471; Simon Spund, *Die Schreckenherrschaft der Russen in Stanislau: selbsterlebte Schilderungen* (Budweis, Czech Republic: Selbverlag, 1915), 6–8, 14–15, 19, 22, 24, 35; TsDIAUK, f. 385, o. 7, spr. 102, ark. 51ob.–52; TsDIAUL, f. 146, o. 4, spr. 3560, ark. 96.

22. Fritz Seefeldt, *Der Deutsche in Galizien* (Berlin: Verlag von Julius Belz, 1937), 70.

23. Lev Aba, "Razgrom galitsiiskikh yevreiev v krovavye gody voiny: otryvok iz dnevnika," *Yevreiskaia letopis'* 3 (1924): 169; Tăslăuanu, *With the Austrian Army*, 65; TsNBU, f. 339, spr. 89, ark. 7; Roskies, *Dybbuk and Other Writings*, 171–172; Krepel, *Juden und Judentum*, 77; TsDIAUK, f. 385, o. 7, spr. 102, ark. 51ob.; *Lwów po inwazji rosyjskiej*, 5; Schall, *Żydostwo galicyjskie*, 6; TsDIAUL, f. 694, o. 1, spr. 6, ark. 30; ibid., f. 146, o. 4, spr. 3560, ark. 98–99, 113ob.

24. AGAD, dz. "Ministerstwo Spraw Wewnętrznych," sygn. F34, n.p.; TsDIAUL, f. 694, o. 1, spr. 10, ark. 5; AAN, dz. "Centralna Agencja Polska w Lozannie," box 61 (*Wiedeński Kurjer Polski*, 11 June 1915); *Ukrainische Nachrichten*, no. 22, 19 February 1915; Janusz, *293 dni*, 160–164; Ivan Petrovych, *Halychyna pid chas rosiis'koi okupatsii, serpen' 1914–cherven' 1915* (L'viv, Ukraine: nakladom vydavnytsva "Politychna Biblioteka," 1915), 18–20; *Lwów po inwazji rosyjskiej*, 2–3; Stanisław Maciszewski, *Rosjanie we Lwowie: szkic z niedawnej przeszłości* (L'viv, Ukraine: drukarnia krajowa Szczęsnego Bednarskiego, 1926), 3, 5–6; "Die Juden Lembergs," *Jüdisches Archiv* 8–9 (1917): 4–5; Białynia-Chołodecki, *Lwów w czasie okupacji rosyjskiej*, 91; Schall, *Żydostwo galicyjskie*, 11–12.

25. Schall, *Żydostwo galicyjskie*, 12; Janusz, *293 dni*, 160–164; "Die Juden Lembergs," 8–10; TsDIAUK, f. 361, o. 1, spr. 648, ark. 16.

26. Bronisław Dębiński, "Wspomnienia z lat 1914–1918," BN, microfilm 45109, k. 47; *Prikarpatskaia Rus'*, no. 1416, 28 September 1914; no. 1420, 2 October 1914; *Ukrainische Nachrichten*, no. 22, 19 February 1915; Kreppel, *Juden und Judentum*, 77–78; *Lwów po inwazji*, 13; S. Ansky, *The Enemy at His Pleasure: A Journey through the Jewish Pale of Settlement during World War I* (New York: Metropolitan Books, 2002), 78.

27. "Die Juden Lembergs," 8–10; Schall, *Żydostwo galicyjskie*, 12–13; Maciszewski, *Rosjanie we Lwowie*, 19; TsNBU, f. 339, spr. 31, ark. 3; Janusz, *293 dni*, 164–165; *Odezwy i rozporządzenia z czasów okupacji rosyjskiej Lwowa 1914–1915* (L'viv, Ukraine: Księgarnia H. Altenberg, G. Seyfarth, E. Wende i Spółka, 1916), 24.

28. *Prikarpatskaia Rus'*, no. 1417, 29 September 1914; Janusz, *Dokumenty urzędowe*, 31.

29. TsDIAUK, f. 361, o. 1, spr. 229, ark. 1, 7a; ibid., f. 361, o. 1, spr. 221, ark. 41, 43, 45–46; Schall, *Żydostwo galicyjskie*, 14.

30. Schall, *Żydostwo galicyjskie*, 13–14; Janusz, *293 dni*, 166, 171.

31. AAN, dz. "Centralna Agencja Polska w Lozannie," box 61 (*Wiedeński Kurjer Polski*, 2 October 1915); TsDIAUK, f. 363, o. 1, spr. 70, ark. 3; ibid., f. 361, o. 1, spr. 959, ark. 1–5; ibid., f. 361, o. 1, spr. 960, ark. 27.

32. *Niva: illustrirovannyj zhurnal literatury, politiki i sovremennoi zhizni* 33, no. 16 (August 1914): 1; *Pravitel'stvennyi vestnik*," no. 238, 10 October 1914; no. 258, 12 November 1914; *Armeiskii vestnik*, no. 4, 17 August 1914; no. 7, 24 August 1914; RGVIA, f. 2005, o. 1, d. 13, l. 407; *Ukrainische Nachrichten*, no. 40, 19 June 1915; *Galitsiia i Rossiia* (Moscow: Moskovskoe pechatnoe proizvodstvo, 1914); *Galitsiia, eya proshloe i nastoiashchee* (Moscow: knigoizdatel'stvo "Chitatel'," 1914); A. V. Belgorodskii, *Galitsiia—iskonnoe dostoianie Rossii* (n.p.: izdatel'stvo tovarishchestva I. D. Syrins, 1914); *Zavoevanie vostochnoi Galitsii* (Moscow: izdatel'stvo Sytina, 1914); A. Burchak, *Zavoevanie vostochnoi Galitsii* (Moscow: izdatel'stvo Sytina, 1914).

33. Bakhturina, *Politika Rossiiskoi imperii*, 57–61, 74–75; V. N. Savchenko, "Vostochnaia Galitsiia v 1914–1915 godakh (etnosotsial'nye osobennosti i problema prisoyedineniia k Rossii)," *Voprosy istorii* 11–12 (1996): 99.

34. The reference was derived from the name of the Ukrainian *Het'man* (military leader) Ivan Mazepa, who sided with the Swedes during the Russo-Swedish war of 1700–1721.

35. RGVIA, f. 2005, o. 1, d. 13 (12), l. 635; TsDIAUL, f. 694, o. 1, spr. 10, ark. 7; Starkel, "Diariusz wydarzeń," 17; Isydor Nahayevs'kyi, *Istoriia ryms'kykh vselens'kykh arkhyyereiv*, (Munich: vydannia Ukrains'koho katolyts'koho universytetu im. Sv. Klymenta Papy, 1964–1979), 3: 486–487; Daniloff, *Russland im Weltkriege*, 246; "Perepiska V. A. Sukhomlinova s N. N. Yanushkevichem," *Krasnyi Arkhiv* 2 (1922): 248; *Ukrainische Nachrichten*, no. 133, 18 December 1914; Knox, *With the Russian Army*, 1: 290; Brusilov, *Moi vospominaniia*, 100; "Die Juden Lembergs," 6.

36. RGVIA, f. 2003, o. 2, d. 539 (1), l. 55; ibid., f. 2003, o. 2, d. 539 (7), no list number; *Prikarpatskaia Rus'*, no. 1421, 3 October 1914; no. 1423, 6 October 1914; *Lwów po inwazji*, 6; Janusz, *Dokumenty urzędowe*, 32–34.

37. TsDIAUK, f. 363, o. 2, spr. 2, ark. 2; Janusz, *293 dni*, 147; "Perepiska V. A. Sukhomlinova s N. N. Yanushkevichem," 268; Brusilov, *Moi vospominaniia*, 108–109; Graf, "Rule of the Generals," 109–110; Iurii Daniloff, *Velikii Kniaz' Nikolai Nikolayevich* (Paris: Imprimerie de Navarre, 1930), 217–218; Metropolitan Evlogii, *Put' moyei zhizni: vospominaniia Mitropolita Evlogiia* (Paris: YMCA-Press, 1947), 253–254; *The Letters and Papers of Chaim Weizmann*, series A (London: Oxford University Press, 1968–1984), 7: 12, 26; *Jews in the Eastern War Zone*, 85; P. N. Miliukov, *Political Memoirs, 1905–1917* (Ann Arbor, MI: University of Michigan Press, 1967), 308f; Ansky, *Enemy at His Pleasure*, 75.

38. TsDIAUK, f. 365, o. 1, spr. 4, ark. 32–34; Graf, "Rule of the Generals," 23–25, 108–109; Petrovych, *Halychyna*, 13–18.

39. RGVIA, f. 2003, o. 2, d. 539 (4), ll. 3, 47; ibid., f. 2003, o. 1, d. 1 (1), l. 27; Graf, "Rule of the Generals," 21–23; "Die Juden Lembergs," 7.

40. RGVIA, f. 2003, o. 2, d. 539, l. 23; ibid., f. 2005, o. 1, d. 12 (1), ll. 16–17, 20; ibid., f. 2005, o. 1, d. 13, ll. 18–19, 34; Janusz, *Dokumenty urzędowe okupacji rosyjskiej*, 25–26; *L'vovskoye voennoye slovo*, no. 23, 23 October 1914; *Prikarpatskaia Rus'*, no. 1449, 5 November 1914; Bakhturina, *Politika Rossiiskoi Imperii*, 96; Ansky, *Enemy at His Pleasure*, 67.

41. RGVIA, f. 2003, o. 2, d. 539 (3), ll. 3–4, 67; ibid., f. 2005, o. 1, d. 12 (1), l. 77; *Armeiskii vestnik,* no. 18, 18 September 1914; *Prikarpatskaia Rus',* no. 1414, 23 September 1914; no. 1416, 28 September 1914; "Die Juden Lembergs," 7.

42. Petrovych, *Halychyna,* 115. The persecution of the Germans continued until the end of Russian occupation. TsDIAUK, f. 361, o. 1, spr. 836, ll. 1, 3–4, 7.

43. Spiridovich, *Velikaia voina,* 117; *Ukrainische Nachrichten,* no. 40, 19 June 1915; RGVIA, f. 2005, o. 1, d. 12 (4), ll. 207–208; S. A. Makarchuk, *Ukrains'ka Respublika Halychan: narysy pro ZUNR* (L'viv, Ukraine: Svit, 1997), 34–39; TsNBU, f. 21, spr. 1173, ark. 1–2; Bedwin Sands, *The Russians in Galicia* (New York: "Ukrainian National Council," 1916), 12–13; Petrovych, *Halychyna,* 52–58, 66.

44. Sands, *Russians in Galicia,* 14, 18; Petrovych, *Halychyna,* 71–83, 104; Dmytro Doroshenko, *Moi spohady pro nedavne-mynule (1914–1920)* (Munich: Ukrains'ke vydavnytstvo, 1969), 2:24–28; *Ukrainische Nachrichten,* no. 40, 19 June 1915; Białynia-Chołodecki, *Lwów,* 88; Przysiecki, *Rządy rosyjskie,* 19–20, 65; *L'vovskoye voennoye slovo,* no. 33, 4 November 1914.

45. Bakhturina, *Politika Rossiiskoi imperii,* 66–67; Białynia-Chołodecki, *Lwów,* 88, 93, 102; Przysiecki, *Rządy rosyjskie,* 25–27, 30–31; Janusz, *Rządy rosyjskie,* 120–122; Sands, *Russians in Galicia,* 11.

46. RGVIA, f. 2003, o. 2, d. 539, l. 64; ibid., f. 2003, o. 2, d. 539 (1), l. 24; ibid., f. 2003, o. 2, d. 539 (3), l. 23; ibid., f. 2005, o. 1, d. 12 (1), l. 110; ibid., f. 2005, o. 1, d. 12 (3), ll. 114–115; ibid., f. 2005, o. 1, d. 13 (1), l. 2; TsDIAUK, f. 361, o. 1, spr. 156, ark. 15, 30, 31–32, 33–34; ibid., f. 361, o. 1, spr. 1632, ark. 3; *L'vovskoye voennoye slovo,* no. 32, 2 November 1914; *Pravitel'stvennyi vestnik,* no. 255, 9 November 1914; no. 257, 11 November 1914; Janusz, *Dokumenty urzędowe,* 35; Bakhturina, *Politika Rossiiskoi Imperii,* 64–66; Lohr, *Nationalizing the Russian Empire,* 62–77, 96–97.

47. Lohr, *Nationalizing the Russian Empire,* 62–77; Schiper, "Żydzi galicyjscy," 414–415; Schall, *Żydostwo galicyjskie,* 10; *Gosudarstvennaia Duma,* 1915, 4th convocation, 4th session, 1133; Spiridovich, *Velikaia voina,* 174; Ansky, *Enemy at His Pleasure,* 72; *Internationale Beziehungen im Zeitalter des Imperialismus,* 2, 6.1, 259–261. Bazili, besides reporting on the Jewish issue, also criticized the Russification policy pursued by the administration and the Russian Orthodox clergy. His indiscretion caused the indignation of the front commander, General Ivanov, who ordered Bazili to leave Galicia. Daniloff, *Russland im Weltkriege,* 246–247; also see Daniloff, *Velikii Kniaz',* 220.

48. RGVIA, f. 2005, o. 1, d. 13, ll. 6–7, 34.

49. *Internationale Beziehungen im Zeitalter Imperialismus,* 2, 6.1, 271–272; RGVIA, f. 2005, o. 1, d. 13, l. 11.

50. RGVIA, f. 2005, o. 1, d. 13 (1), ll. 4, 18; ibid., f. 2005, o. 1, d. 13 (12), l. 568; Lohr, *Nationalizing the Russian Empire,* 86–87; Savchenko, "Vostochnaia Galitsiia," 103–104; David G. Rempel, "The Expropriation of the German Colonists in South Russia during the Great War," *Journal of Modern History* 4, no. 1 (1932): 53–54; S. G. Nelipovich, "Rol' voennogo rukovodstva Rossii v 'nemetskom voprose' v gody pervoi mirovoii voiny," in *Rossiiskie nemtsy: problemy istorii, yazyka i sovremennogo polozheniia: materialy mezhdunarodnoi konferentsii, Anapa, 20–25 sentiabria 1995* (Moscow: "Gotika," 1996), 265–266.

51. Anna Veronika Wendland, *Die Russophilen in Galizien: Ukrainische Konservative zwischen Österreich und Russland, 1848–1915* (Vienna: Verlag der Österreichischen Akademie der Wissenschaften, 2001), 554; *Prikarpatskaia Rus',* no. 1454, 29 October (11 November), 1914; TsDIAUK, f. 385, o. 7, spr. 102, ark. 7zv.

52. TsDIAUK, f. 361, o. 1, spr. 94, ark. 9–10; Wendland, *Die Russophilen in Galizien,* 553–554; Sands, *Russians in Galicia,* 17.

53. Hagen, "*Levée en masse,*" 168; Janusz, *Dokumenty urzędowe,* 55; RGVIA, f. 2005, o. 1, d. 13, ll. 34–36, 39–40.

54. RGVIA, f. 2005, o. 1, d. 12, ll. 131–131ob.; ibid., f. 2005, o. 1, d. 12 (4), ll. 274, 287; ibid., f. 2005, o. 1, d. 13 (1), ll. 29–30.

55. DALO, f. 907, o. 1, spr. 28, ark. 41; TsDIAUK, f. 361, o. 1, spr. 221, ark. 224–227; ibid., f. 363, o. 1, spr. 8, ark. 1–2, 4–5, 7, 9; ibid., f. 361, o. 1, spr. 94, ark. 9–10; Wendland, *Die Russophilen in Galizien,* 556.

56. RGVIA, f. 2005, o. 1, d. 12 (3), l. 115; TsDIAUK, f. 361, o. 1, spr. 325, ark. 2–3, 9, 11, 17, 23, 26, 29; ibid., f. 361, o. 1, spr. 109, n.p.

57. TsDIAUK, f. 361, o. 1, spr. 239, ark. 1–5.

58. Ibid., f. 361, o. 1, spr. 239, ark. 6–7; "Dokumenty o presledovaniakh yevreyev," in I. V. Gessen, ed., *Arkhiv russkoi revolutsii* (Berlin: Slovo-Verlag, 1928), 19:248.

59. RGVIA, f. 2005, o. 1, d. 12 (1), l. 9; TsDIAUL, f. 146, o. 8, spr. 1892, ark. 4; *Prikarpatskaia Rus',* no. 1430, 14 October 1914; TsDIAUK, f. 361, o. 1, spr. 231, ark. 30–31.

60. TsDIAUK, f. 361, o. 1, spr. 230, ark. 1, 8, 10, 13–14; TsDIAUL, f. 146, o. 4, spr. 5335, n.p.; Schall, *Żydostwo galicyjskie,* 9–10; Spund, *Die Schreckenherrschaft,* 48; *Jüdische Rundschau,* no. 29, 16 July 1915; *Prikarpatskaia Rus',* no. 1433, 17 October 1914; Sigmund Cybichowski, *Die Besetzung Lembergs im Kriege, 1914–1915: zugleich ein Beiträg zur Prinzipienlehre des internationalen Rechtes* (Munich: Verlag von Duncker & Humblot, 1916), 440–441; Ansky, *Enemy at His Pleasure,* 122–123.

61. *Prilozheniia k stenographicheskim otchetam Gosudarstvennoi Dumy, 1915–1916* (St. Petersburg: Gosudarstvennaia Tipographiia, 1915–1916), 1; Schall, *Żydostwo galicyjskie,* 10.

62. TsDIAUK, f. 361, o. 1, spr. 674, ark. 23; ibid., f. 361, o. 1, spr. 676, ark. 5; Spund, *Die Schreckenherrschaft,* 51–53, 66–68.

63. RGVIA, f. 2003, o. 2, d. 539, ll. 25, 33; ibid., f. 2005, o. 1, d. 13 (10), l. 568; ibid., f. 2005, o. 1, d. 12 (1), ll. 89–90; TsDIAUK, f. 361, o. 1, spr. 677, ark. 2–3; ibid., f. 385, o. 7, spr. 102, ark. 60b.; TsDIAUL, f. 694, o. 1, spr. 1, ark. 14; *Prikarpatskaia Rus',* no. 1528, 28 January 1915; no. 1529, 29 January 1915; Lohr, *Nationalizing the Russian Empire,* 100; Rempel, "Expropriation of the German Colonists," 55; Johannes Schleuning, *Im Kampf und Todesnot: Die Tragödie des Russlanddeutschen* (Berlin: Bernard & Graefe, 1930), 22; TsDIAUK, f. 363, o. 1, spr. 8, ark. 14.

64. RGVIA, f. 13142, o. 1, d. 61, l. 94; ibid., f. 2003, o. 2, d. 539, ll. 23, 52–53, 59–60; "Iz 'chernoi knigi' rossiiskogo evreistva," 264; "Dokumenty o presledovaniakh yevreyev," 250–251; *Prikarpatskaia Rus',* no. 1563, 4 March 1915; TsNBU, f. 339, spr. 89, ark. 16; Schiper, "Żydzi galicyjscy," 415; Janusz, *Dokumenty urzędowe,* 41–42, 58.

65. TsDIAUK, f. 361, o. 1, spr. 553, ark. 1–12, 13–14, 18–23; ibid., f. 365, o. 1, spr. 30, ark. 30; RGVIA, f. 2005, o. 1, d. 13 (10), ll. 407, 430, 436, 438, 440–442; *Prikarpatskaia Rus',* no. 1665, 3 June 1915; AAN, dz. "Centralna Agencja Polska w Lozannie," box 61 (*Kurjer Lwowski,* 4 August 1917); Bakhturina, *Politika Rossiiskoi Imperii,* 83–88; Ansky, *Enemy at His Pleasure,* 149–150.

66. William M. Gliksman, *In the Mirror of Literature: The Economic Life of the Jews in Poland as Reflected in Yiddish Literature, 1914–1939* (New York: Living Books, 1966), 94; TsNBU, f. 339, spr. 89, ark. 17–20; TsDIAUK, f. 385, o. 7, spr. 102, ark. 49–50; Aba, "Razgrom galitsiiskikh yevreiev," 171.

67. TsDIAUK, f. 361, o. 2, spr. 10, ark. 1; Schall, *Żydostwo galicyjskie,* 15–16.

68. Janusz, *293 dni,* 66; Maciszewski, *Rosjanie we Lwowie,* 18; Petrovych, *Halychyna,* 116.

69. RGVIA, f. 2005, o. 1, d. 12 (4), ll. 193–194; TsDIAUK, f. 365, o. 2, spr. 45, ark. 4; Spiridovich, *Velikaia voina,* 37–38.

70. TsDIAUK, f. 361, o. 1, spr. 648, ark. 16; ibid., f. 363, o. 1, spr. 35, ark. 77; Shall, *Żydostwo galicyjskie,* 20–21; *Lwów po inwazji,* 33–34; Janusz, *Dokumenty urzędowe,* 40.

71. TsDIAUK, f. 361, o. 1, spr. 174, ark. 1; ibid., f. 361, o. 1, spr. 847, ark. 1; ibid., f. 361, o. 1, spr. 1920, ark. 5; *Russkoe voennoe slovo,* no. 4, 30 September 1914; no. 5, 2 October 1914; ibid., no. 8, 5 October 1914.

Chapter 3. Russia's Internal Front: Explusions and Deportations

1. Nelipovich, "Rol' voennogo rukovodstva Rossii v 'nemetskom voprose' v gody pervoi mirovoii voiny," 265–266; also see Nelipovich, "Repressii protiv poddannych 'Tsentral'nykh Derzhav'," 32–33, and Nelipovich, "General ot Infanterii N. N. Yanushkevich," 42–43; TsDIAUK, f. 365, o. 2, spr. 45, ark. 4. The Germans issued several proclamations inciting Russian Jews to armed uprising. Egmont Zechlin, *Die Deutsche Politik und die Juden im Ersten Weltkrieg* (Göttingen, Germany: Vandenhoeck & Ruprecht, 1969), 120, 141–143.

2. RGVIA, f. 2005, o. 1, d. 12 (4), ll. 193–194, 196; Spiridovich, *Velikaia voina,* 37–38: Lohr, "Russian Army and the Jews," 406.

3. *Internationale Beziehungen im Zeitalter Imperialismus,* 2, 6.1, 328–329; RGVIA, f. 2003, o. 2, d. 539, l. 33; "Dokumenty o presledovaniiakh yevreev," 247.

4. "Iz chernoi knigi rossiiskogo yevreistva," 251; TsDIAUK, f. 361, o. 1, spr. 221, ark. 46; ibid., f. 363, o. 2, spr. 2, ark. 16; ibid., f. 363, o. 1, spr. 35, ark. 76; ibid., f. 361, o. 1, spr. 674, ark. 18; *Gosudarstvennyi arkhiv Rossiiskoi Federatsii* (GARF), f. D2, o. 1915, d. 391, l. 43.

5. GARF, f. D2, o. 1915, d. 391, ll. 5–104; DALO, f. 907, o. 1, spr. 28, ark. 66; TsDIAUK, f. 361, o. 1, spr. 221, ark. 162–165, 167, 175–176; ibid., f. 361, o. 1, spr. 220, ark. 17–19.

6. TsDIAUK, f. 363, o. 2, spr. 89, ark. 7zv, 10zv.–11zv.; ibid., f. 363, o. 2, spr. 5, ark. 60zv.

7. M. Bonch-Bruevich, *Poteria nami Galitsii v 1915,* part 2, "Katastrofa v 3i armii" (St. Petersburg: izdanie voennoi tipografii GURKKA, 1926), 230–231; also see Bonch-Bruevich, *Vsia vlast' Sovetam,* 56–57; RGVIA, f. 2003, o. 2, d. 539 (3), l. 21.

8. TsDIAUK, f. 361, o. 1, spr. 647, ark. 130; ibid., f. 361, o. 1, spr. 895, ark. 17–18, 21–22; ibid., f. 361, o. 1, spr. 960, ark. 130, 149; ibid., f. 363, o. 1, spr. 35, ark. 73–75; ibid., f. 365, o. 2, spr. 61, ark. 1; RGVIA, f. 2005, o. 1, o. 12 (4), l. 302; Mykola Halagan, *Z moikh spomyniv* (L'viv, Ukraine: vydavnytstvo kooperatyva "Chervona Kalyna," 1930), 2:24–32.

9. *Prikarpatskaia Rus',* no. 1551, 20 February 1915.

10. *Gosudarstvennaia Duma: stenographicheskie otchety,* 4th convocation, sessions 1–3, 27–29 January 1915, 15; *L'vovskoe voennoe slovo,* no. 112, 30 January 1915; AAN, dz. "Centralna Agencja Polska w Lozannie," box 61 (*Wiedeński Kurjer Polski,* 8 April 1915); *Russkoe znamia,* no. 13, 17 January 1915; TsDIAUK, f. 385, o. 7, spr. 102, ark. 70b.

11. RGVIA, f. 2003, o. 2, d. 539 (2), l. 105; TsDIAUK, f. 361, o. 1, spr. 685, ark. 3, 7, 10, 22, 26; ibid., f. 361, o. 1, spr. 857, ark. 1, 4–6, 7, 9; ibid., f. 361, o. 1, spr. 924, ark. 1, 5, 6, 17, 19, 27; TsNBU, f. 339, spr. 89, ark. 10, 12; Bakhturina, *Politika Rossiiskoi Imperii,* 193–194.

12. GARF, f. D2, o. 1915, d. 391, ll. 5–104; TsDIAUK, f. 361, o. 1, spr. 672, ark. 1, 4, 6–8, 10, 13, 19, 22, 27, 28; ibid., f. 361, o. 1, spr. 679, ark. 11; ibid., f. 361, o. 1, spr. 221, ark. 53–55,57–60.

13. Nelipovich, "Rol' voennogo rukovodstva," 266–270; also Nelipovich, "Repressii protiv poddannykh 'Tsentral'nykh Derzhav'," 38, and Nelipovich, "General ot infanterii N. N. Yanushkevich," 44; "Iz chernoi knigi rossiiskogo yevreistva," 220–221; Graf, "Rule of the of Generals," 125–126.

14. RGVIA, f. 2003, o. 2, d. 539 (1), ll. 30, 120–121; ibid., f. 2003, o. 2, d. 539 (2), ll. 122–123; ibid., f. 2003, o. 2, d. 539 (3), l. 15; *Prikarpatskaia Rus',* no. 1552, 21 February 1915; TsDIAUK, f. 361, o. 1, spr. 674, ark. 4.

15. TsDIAUK, f. 361, o. 1, spr. 674, ark. 13–16, 45.

16. Ibid., f. 361, o. 1, spr. 651, ark. 1, 6; ibid., f. 361, o. 1, spr. 180, ark. 2; ibid., f. 361, o. 1, spr. 679, ark. 20, 39–40, 57, 59–61; ibid., f. 361, o. 1, spr. 896, ark. 11–12; ibid., f. 361, o. 1, spr. 674, ark. 4–5, 46; ibid., f. 361, o. 1, spr. 906, ark. 3; DALO, f. 907, o. 1, spr. 94, ark. 13–16, 28, 45; RGVIA, f. 2003, o. 2, d. 539 (1), ll. 32, 34; ibid., f. 2003, o. 2, d. 539 (2), ll. 33–35, 43–44, 47, 48; GARF, f. D2, o. 1915, d. 391, ll. 5–104; 10, 12, 15, 19, 43, 48; *Jüdische Rundschau,* no. 22, 28 May 1915.

17. TsDIAUK, f. 361, o. 1, spr. 827, ark. 1–2, 16, 24, 28, 33; TsNBU, f. 339, spr. 89, ark. 10, 12, 14, 15–16, 24, 28, 33; RGVIA, f. 2005, o. 1, d. 51 (1), ll. 2–3; *Ukrainische Nachrichten,* no. 40, 19 June 1915; Ansky, *Enemy at His Pleasure,* 90.

18. TsDIAUK, f. 361, o. 1, spr. 132, ark. 2zv.; Wróbel, "Barucha Milcha galicyjskie wspomnienia," 92; TsNBU, f. 339, spr. 89, ark. 2–3; Shall, *Żydostwo galicyjskie,* 6–8; Schiper, "Żydzi galicyjscy," 414; Białynia-Chołodecki, *Lwów w czasie okupacji,* 114–115; Przysiecki, *Rządy rosyjskie,* 15; *L'vovskoe voennoe slovo,* no. 170, 7 May 1915; no. 174, 12 May 1915; no. 175, 13 May 1915.

19. TsDIAUK, f. 361, o. 1, spr. 838, ark. 2, 9, 60; ibid., f. 361, o. 1, spr. 780, ark. 166–167, 170, 175, 180, 193–194, 265; ibid., f. 361, o. 1, spr. 647, ark. 115; ibid., f. 361, o. 1, spr. 570, ark. 1, 3; ibid., f. 361, o. 1, spr. 571, ark. 13, 15, 24, 25; ibid., f. 361, o. 1, spr. 648, ark. 22–24; ibid., f. 361, o. 1, spr. 833, ark. 1, 2, 4–5; RGVIA, f. 2005, o. 1, d. 12 (3), ll. 114–115, 118; ibid., f. 2003, o. 2, d. 539 (2), ll. 107–120.

20. TsDIAUK, f. 361, o. 1, spr. 674, ark. 77–78; ibid., f. 361, o. 1, spr. 674, ark. 77–80; ibid., f. 361, o. 1, spr. 780, ark. 53, 86, 95, 137, 161, 185; ibid., f. 361, o. 1, spr. 554, ark. 1–2; ibid., f. 361, o. 2, spr. 134, ark. 21–21zv; ibid., f. 361, o. 1, spr. 571, ark. 37; ibid., f. 365, o. 2, spr. 10, ark. 153–154, 181zv.; ibid., f. 363, o. 1, spr. 32, ark. 51, 57; ibid., f. 363, o. 1, spr. 67, ark. 212; ibid., f. 365, o. 1, spr. 1, ark. 123; RGVIA, f. 2005, o. 1, o. 102 (1), ll. 18–78; ibid., f. 2005, o. 1, o. 12 (4), ll. 293–296, 298; AGAD, dz. "Ministerstwo Spraw Wewnętrznych," sygn. F35, n.p.

21. RGVIA, f. 2003, o. 2, d. 539 (1), l. 33; ibid., f. 13142, o. 1, d. 19, l. 5; ibid., f. 13142, o. 1, d. 61, l. 43, ibid., f. 13142, o. 1, d. 72, l. 3; TsDIAUL, f. 146, o. 4, spr. 3560, ark. 46; Aba, "Razgrom galitsiiskikh yevreiev," 169; AGAD, dz. "Ministerstwo Spraw Wewnętrznych," sygn. F34, n.p.; DALO, f. 907, o. 1, spr. 94, ark. 10, 12, 15; TsDIAUK, f. 363, o. 1, spr. 35, ark. 49; ibid., f. 361, o. 1, spr. 674, ark. 53–60; Janusz, *293 dni,* 250–251; Schiper, "Żydzi galicyjscy w dobie wojny światowej," 414; Stanisław Rossowski, *Lwów podczas inwazyi* (L'viv, Ukraine: H. Altenberg, 1917), 193; Ansky, *Enemy at His Pleasure,* 124.

22. RGVIA, f. 2003, o. 2, d. 539, l. 64; ibid., f. 2003, o. 2, d. 539 (1), ll. 38–40; *Pravitel'stvennyi vestnik,* no. 255, 9 November 1914; no. 257, 11 November 1914; *L'vovskoe voennoe slovo,* no. 32, 2 November 1914; Schall, *Żydostwo galicyjskie,* 7–8; Spund, *Die Schreckenherrschaft,* 39–49; TsDIAUL, f. 146, op. 4, spr. 3560, ark. 39, 59–60, 96, 115–115zv; ibid., f. 146, op. 8, spr. 1895, ark. 44; TsDIAUK, f. 363, o. 1, spr. 86, ark. 11, 20, 22–26, 30, 46; ibid., f. 363, o. 1, spr. 101, ark. 3–4; ibid., f. 361, o. 1, spr. 674, ark. 23; ibid., f. 361, o. 1, spr. 676, ark. 5; ibid., f. 363, o. 1, spr. 26, ark. 2, 5; "Zur Lage der Juden in Ősterreich," *Jüdisches Archiv* 1 (1915): 5; "Die Kozaken in Mikulczyn (Galizien)," *Jüdisches Archiv* 1 (1915): 9; *Jüdische Rundschau,* no. 5, 29 January 1915; Spund, *Die Schreckenherrschaft,* 51–53, 66–68; Müller-Meiningen, *"Who Are the Huns?"* 158; *Ukrainische Nachrichten,* no. 30, 17 May 1915; Schall, *Żydostwo galicyjskie,* 23; Reed, *War in Eastern Europe,* 141.

23. Graf, "Rule of the Generals," 126–127; TsDIAUK, f. 361, o. 1, spr. 674, ark. 29–30; RGVIA, f. 2003, o. 2, d. 539 (1), l. 32.

24. RGVIA, f. 2003, o. 2, d. 539 (2), ll. 105–106; TsDIAUK, f. 361, o. 1, spr. 674, ark. 41.

25. RGVIA, f. 2003, o. 2, d. 539 (1), l. 32; ibid., f. 2003, o. 2, d. 539 (2), l. 106; ibid., f. 2005,

o. 1, d. 12 (1), ll. 110–112, 114; ibid., f. 2005, o. 1, d. 12 (3), ll. 114–115; ibid., f. 2005, o. 1, d. 12 (3), l. 115; ibid., f. 2005, o. 1, d. 13 (11), l. 635; ibid., f. 2003, o. 2, d. 539 (4), ll. 44–45; ibid., f. 13142, o. 1, d. 81, ll. 11, 19, 21, 43, 55, 59, 61–62, 98, 102–103, 108–109; ibid., f. 13142, o. 1, d. 72, ll. 12, 15, 17, 18, 21–22, 23, 77, 79–80, 98–99, 102–103, 108, 121; *L'vovskii vestnik,* no. 5, 5 March 1915; no. 8, 8 March 1915; TsDIAUK, f. 361, o. 1, spr. 553, ark. 24; ibid., f. 363, o. 1, spr. 70, ark. 49; ibid., f. 361, o. 1, spr. 674, ark. 33–35; "Dokumenty o presledovaniakh yevreiev," 252–253; Przysiecki, *Rządy rosyjskie,* 50; *Novyi krai,* no. 28, 12 April 1915.

26. RGVIA, f. 2005, o. 1, d. 12 (3), l. 120; Rostunov, *Russkii front,* 246; *Ukrainische Nachrichten,* no. 41, 26 June 1915; Schall, *Żydostwo galicyjskie,* 25–26.

27. *L'vovskoe voennoe slovo,* no. 170, 7 May 1915; no. 174, 12 May 1915; no. 176, 14 May 1915; Nelipovich, "Rol' voennogo rukovodstva," 275; Graf, "Rule of the Generals," 130–132.

28. Graf, "Rule of the Generals," 136–138; Denikin, *Put' russkogo ofitsera,* 324–325; *Russkoe znamia,* no. 84, 15 April 1915; TsDIAUK, f. 385, o. 7, spr. 102, ark. 70b.; ibid., f. 361, o. 1, spr. 674, ark. 61, 63–64; RGVIA, f. 2003, o. 2, d. 539 (4), l. 29.

29. Schall, *Żydostwo galicyjskie,* 23; Reed, *War in Eastern Europe,* 141; *Die Wahrheit: unabhängige Zeitschrift für jüdische Interessen,* no. 15, 16 April 1915; TsDIAUK, f. 361, o. 1, spr. 674, ark. 122, 125; TsDIAUL, f. 146, o. 4, spr. 3560, ark. 114; ibid. f. 146, o. 8, spr. 1886, ark. 9; ibid., f. 146, o. 4, spr. 3560, ark. 98–99, 113ob., 114, 115; f. 146, o. 8, spr. 1892, ark. 4; ibid., f. 361, o. 1, spr. 674, ark. 118–119; ibid., f. 365, o. 1, spr. 163, ark. 2, 4, 8–9, 33, 48–50, 71; ibid., f. 365, o. 1, spr. 186, ark. 2, 8; ibid., f. 365, o. 1, spr. 142, ark. 16–17, 26; ibid., f. 361, o. 1, spr. 870, ark. 1; ibid., f. 363, o. 1, spr. 8, ark. 30, 38, 57; *Dziennik Polski,* no. 169, 22 June 1915; Leszek Podhorodecki, *Dzieje Lwowa* (Warsaw: Oficyna Wydawnicza Volumen, 1993), 159; AAN, dz. "Centralna Agencja Polska w Lozannie," box 61 (*Głos Narodu,* 22 August 1917); *Prikarpatskaia Rus',* no. 1690, 6 August 1915; no. 1693, 9 August 1915; no. 1709, 25 August 1915; Iryna Pohrebyns'ka i Maksym Gon, *Yevrei v Zakhidnoukrains'kii Narodnii Respublitsi: do problemy ukrains'ko-yevreis'kykh vzayemyn* (Kiev: Instytut natsional'nykh vidnosyn ta politolohii NAN Ukrainy, 1997), 28; Ansky, *Enemy at His Pleasure,* 155.

30. RGVIA, f. 2005, o. 1, d. 12 (4), l. 296; Rempel, "Expropriation of the German Colonists," 61; Schleuning, *In Kampf und Todesnot,* 23; Heinz Ingenhorst, *Die Russlanddeutschen: Aussiedler zwischen Tradition und Moderne* (Frankfurt: Campus Verlag, 1997), 32–33; Detlef Brandes, "Von der Verfolgungen im Ersten Weltkrieg biz zur Deportation," in Gerd von Stricker, ed., *Deutsche Geschichte im Osten Europas: Russland* (Berlin: Siedler, 1997), 131–133.

31. Quoted in Sanborn, "Drafting the Nation," 294.

32. Danilov, *Velikii Kniaz',* 202–203; Rostunov, *Russkii front,* 246; Evlogii, *Put' moyei zhizni,* 273; Norman Stone, *The Eastern Front 1914–1917* (London: Hodder and Stoughton, 1975), 165–166; *Gosudarstvennaia Duma: stenographicheskie otchety,* 1915, 4th convocation, 4th session, 1133; Spiridovich, *Velikaia voina,* 174; Graf, "Rule of the Generals," 129–132; TsDIAUK, f. 361, o. 1, spr. 552, n.p.; ibid., f. 361, o. 1, spr. 481, ark. 9–10; ibid., f. 361, o. 1, spr. 674, ark. 65–68, 70, 73–76, 84, 101, 108–110; ibid., f. 361, o. 1, spr. 680, ark. 20–22, 43.

33. AAN, dz. "Centralna Agencja Polska w Lozannie," box 61 (*Czas,* 7 February 1918).

34. Ibid., box 61 (*Wiedeński Kurjer Polski,* 8 July 1915); TsDIAUK, f. 361, o. 1, spr. 552, n.p.; ibid., f. 361, o. 1, spr. 674, ark. 85, 100; ibid., f. 363, o. 1, spr. 73b, ark. 11–12; *Prikarpatskaia Rus',* no. 1666, 4 June 1915; Janusz, *293 dni,* 256, 259; GARF, f. D2, o. 1915, d. 391, ll. 5–104.

35. For the situation created by refugees and deportees in Russia proper, see Paul P. Gronsky, *The War and the Russian Government* (New Haven, CT: Yale University Press, 1929), 231–252; American Jewish Committee, *Jews in the Eastern War Zone,* 21–22, 24–25, 72–83; Gatrell, *Whole Empire Walking,* 28–29. See debates in the State Council in A. N.

Yakhontov, "Tiazhelye dni (sekretnye zasedaniia Soveta Ministrov 16 iulia—2 sentiabria 1915 goda," *Arkhiv russkoi revolutsii* 18:42–45, 47–50, 57.

36. *Gosudarstvennaia Duma: stenographicheskie otchety,* 1915, 4th convocation, 4th session, 58, 125, 162–163, 1067; *Prilozhenie k stenographicheskim* otchetam, 4th convocation, 4th session, 1–2; A. A. Polivanov, *Iz dnevnikov i vospominanii po dolzhnosti voennogo ministra i yego pomoshchnika 1907–1916 gg: memuary* (Moscow: Vyzshyi Voennyi Redaktsionnyi Sovet, 1924), 220; DALO, f. 907, o. 1, spr. 94, ark. 60; TsDIAUK, f. 361, o. 1, spr. 780, ark. 142, 146–147, 166–167, 170, 175, 180, 193–194, 265; ibid., f. 361, o. 1, spr. 896, ark. 50.

37. "Dopros kniazia N. B. Shcherbatova, 27 sentiabria 1917 g.," in P. E. Shchegolev, ed., *Padenie tsarskogo regima: stenographicheskie otchety doprosov i pokazanii, dannykh v 1917 g. v Chrezvychainoi Sledstvennoi Komissii Vremennogo Pravitel'stva* (Leningrad: Gosudarstvennoe izdatel'stvo, 1925), 7:228; TsDIAUK, f. 361, o. 1, spr. 316, n.p.

38. TsNBU, f. 339, spr. 89, ark. 9–10; TsDIAUK, f. 361, o. 1, spr. 674, ark. 99; ibid., f. 365, o. 1, spr. 1, ark. 93–94; ibid., f. 361, o. 1, spr. 751, ark. 1–3; ibid., f. 361, o. 1, spr. 847, ark. 1; *Gosudarstvennaia Duma: stenograficheskie otchety,* 4th convocation, 4th session, 19 (31) July 1915, 1067; AAN, dz. "Centralna Agencja Polska w Lozannie," box 61 (*Kurjer Poranny,* 20 April 1915; *Rech',* 18 April 1915); RGVIA, f. 2003, o. 2, d. 539 (3), l. 3, 15; Danilov, *Velikii Kniaz',* 200–201; *Prikarpatskaia Rus',* no. 1608, 7 April 1915; GARF, f. D2, o. 1915, d. 391, ll. 5–104; TsDIAUL, f. 146, o. 4, spr. 3560, ark. 115zv. Also see Bobrinskii's letter to the chief of staff of the southwestern front, General Alekseev, in which the governor-general stressed the futility of the army's anti-Jewish measures. TsDIAUK, f. 361, o. 1, spr. 674, ark. 86–88, 90–91, 93; ibid., f. 361, o. 1, spr. 754, ark. 2, 5.

39. TsDIAUK, f. 361, o. 1, spr. 839, ark. 10–26; AAN, dz. "Centralna Agencja Polska w Lozannie," box 61 (*Nowa reforma,* 27 September 1915; 19, 21, 25, 26, 27 April 1916; 1, 4, 6 May 1916; *Wiedeński Kurjer Polski,* 10 October 1916, 17 October 1915; *Głos Narodu,* 10 November 1915; *Die Zeit,* 25 April 1916; *Dziennik Petrogradski,* 18 January 1916).

40. A. I. Denikin, *Ocherki russkoi smuty: krushenie vlasti i armii, fevral'-sentiabr' 1917g* (Moscow: "Nauka," 1991), 24; Golovin, *Voennye usiliia,* 2, 139.

41. *Ukrainische Nachrichten,* no. 65, 11 December 1915; TsDIAUK, f. 361, o. 1, spr. 1920, ark. 5, 14–15, 17; ibid., f. 363, o. 1, spr. 35, ark. 40–41; AAN, dz. "Centralna Agencja Polska w Lozannie," box 61 (*Rech',* 16 [29] August 1916; *Kurjer Nowy,* 18 August 1916; *Dziennik Petrogradski,* 16 May 1917; *Wiedeński Kurjer Polski,* 2 July 1916); RGVIA, f. 2005, o. 1, d. 12 (4), l. 301; ibid., f. 2003, o. 2, d. 539, ll. 16, 31, 107–120; ibid., f. 2005, o. 1, d. 12 (3), ll. 131–132; *Prilozhenie k stenographicheskim otchetam,* 4th convocation, 4th session, 1–5; "Dopros kniazia N. B. Shcherbatova," 241; M. Bonch-Bruevich, *Poteria nami Galitsyi,* part 1, "Cherez Karpaty v Vengriiu zimoiu 1915 goda" (Moscow: 20-ya Gosudarstvennaia tipografiia, 1920), 230–231; Lemke, *250 dnei,* 110–111; V. V. Chernavin, "Gibel' kadrovykh russkikh ofitserov," *VIZh* 5 (1999): 85–93; Ansky, *Enemy at His Pleasure,* 129–130.

42. The first survey of this kind was done in April 1915. RGVIA, f. 2005, o. 1, d. 12 (3), ll. 115–116; ibid., f. 2005, o. 1, d. 13 (1), no list number; ibid., f. 13142, o. 1, d. 81, ll. 11, 19, 21, 43, 55, 59, 61–62, 98, 102–103, 108–109; ibid., f. 13142, o. 1, d. 72, ll. 12, 15, 17–18, 21–23, 77, 79–80, 98–99, 102–103, 108, 121; ibid., f. 2005, o. 1, d. 155, ll. 8–11, 13, 33–34; ibid., f. 2003, o. 2, d. 539 (4), ll. 44–45; TsDIAUK, f. 363, o. 1, spr. 70, ark. 109–110, 113–116.

43. "Dopros K. D. Kafarova, 14 aprelia 1917 g.," *Padenie tsarskogo rezhima* 2:135–136; *Prilozhenie k stenographicheskim otchetam,* 4th convocation, 4th session, 1; *Armeiskii vestnik,* no. 218, 10 January 1916; no number, 22 March 1916; *Gosudarstvennaia Duma: stenographicheskie otchety,* 4th convocation, 4th session, 11, 12 February 1916, 1456.

44. RGVIA, f. 2005, o. 1, d. 12 (3), l. 116; ibid., f. 2005, o. 1, d. 51 (1), ll. 2–3; TsDIAUK,

f. 361, o. 1, spr. 1698, ark. 2, 6; ibid., f. 363, o. 1, spr. 73b, ark. 11–12; GARF, f. D2, o. 1915, d. 391, ll. 2, 5, 12, 25, 66; Aba," Razgrom galitsiiskikh yevreiev," 171; Florence Farmborough, *Nurse at the Russian Front: A Diary, 1914–1918* (London: Constable and Company, 1974), 180–182; AAN, dz. "Centralna Agencja Polska w Lozannie," box 61 (*Głos Narodu,* 19 August 1917).

45. Schiper, "Żydzi galicyjscy w dobie wojny," 416–417.

46. *Armeiskii vestnik,* 22 March 1916; Rostunov, *Russkii front,* 311–325.

47. Nicholas N. Golovine, *The Russian Army in the World War* (New Haven, CT: Yale University Press, 1981), 242; Aba, "Razgrom galitsiiskikh yevreiev," 174–176; Martyniuk, *Tseniv,* 478; AAN, dz. "Centralna Agencja Polska w Lozannie," box 61 (*Dziennik Kijowski,* 25 September 1916, 9 October 1916, 23 October 1916; *Naprzód,* 30 December 1916); TsDIAUK, f. 361, o. 1, spr. 1681, ark. 3–4. The June 1916 offensive also hit German-Galician settlements with particular fury. Fritz Seefeldt, *So war es in Galizien: Personliche Erzählungen* (Eutin, Germany: Struve's Buchdruckerei und Verlag OHG, 1933), 1:14–28.

48. TsDIAUK, f. 363, o. 1, spr. 32, ark. 212; ibid., f. 361, o. 1, spr. 1144, ark. 7, 11; ibid., f. 361, o. 1, spr. 1259, ark. 6, 8; RGVIA, f. 2003, o. 2, d. 539 (3), l. 273; AAN, dz. "Centralna Agencja Polska w Lozannie," box 61 (*Kurjer Lwowski,* 23 July 1916; *Deutsche Warschauer Zeitung,* 23 July 1916; *Dziennik Berliński,* 4 August 1916; *Kurjer Codzienny,* 12 August 1916; *Vremia,* 2 September 1916; *Głos Polski,* 18 October 1916; *Novoe vremia,* 29 November 1916; *Kurjer Poznański,* 12 January 1917); Schiper, "Żydzi galicyjscy w dobie wojny," 417–418; Ansky, *Enemy at His Pleasure,* 226.

49. TsDIAUK, f. 363, o. 1, spr. 8, ark. 2, 4–7, 9–10, 13, 24; ibid., f. 361, o. 1, spr. 1640, ark. 1, 3, 5–15, 19, 24, 28, 35, 41; *Jüdische Rundschau,* no. 33, 18 August 1916.

50. *Jüdische Rundschau,* no. 18, 4 May 1917; *Gosudarstvennaia Duma: stenographicheskie otchety,* 1916–1917, 4th convocation, 5th session, 1612; AAN, dz. "Centralna Agencja Polska w Lozannie," box 61 (*Nowa Reforma,* 25 September 1917), GARF, f. 1800, o. 1, d. 43, ll. 5–6.

51. Allan K. Wildman, *The End of the Russian Imperial Army: The Old Army and the Soldiers' Revolt (March–April 1917)* (Princeton, NJ: Princeton University Press, 1980), 336; *Nova Rada,* no. 116, 19 August 1917; TsNBU, f. 152, spr. 15, ark. 1; AAN, dz. "Centralna Agencja Polska w Lozannie," box 61 (*Kurjer Lwowski,* 28 August 1917); TsDIAUK, f. 361, o. 1, spr. 1706, ark. 28; A. Kavtaradze, "Iiun'skoe nastuplenie russkoi armii v 1917," *VIZh* 5 (1967): 112–113.

52. GARF, f. 1800, o. 1, d. 43, ll. 11–13, 15; ibid., f. 1800, o. 1, d. 174, ll. 16–17; ibid., f. 6281, o. 1, d. 26, ll. 1–2; TsDIAUK, f. 361, o. 1, spr. 1689, ark. 57; ibid., f. 361, o. 1, spr. 1640, ark. 58–59, 61; *Nova Rada,* no. 3, 29 March 1917; no. 7, 6 April 1917; no. 53, 4 June 1917; no. 77, 1 July 1917; no. 116, 19 August 1917; TsNBU, f. 29, spr. 1836, ark. 1; AAN, dz. "Centralna Agencja Polska w Lozannie," box 61 (*Kurjer Lwowski,* 16 January 1917; *Kurjer Codzienny,* 30 April 1917; *Dziennik Berliński,* 23 May 1917).

53. N. M. Yakupov, *Revolutsiia i mir: soldatskie massy protiv imperialisticheskoi voiny, 1917–mart 1918 gg.* (Moscow: "Mysl'," 1980), 91; Wildman, *End of the Russian Imperial Army,* 337, 339, 346; Denikin, *Ocherki russkoi smuty,* 104, 168; *Nova Rada,* no. 84, 9 July 1917; no. 86, 12 July 1917; no. 85, 11 July 1917; no. 116, 19 August 1917; no. 126, 31 August 1917; *Kurjer Stanisławowski,* no. 1573, 17 March 1918; Farmborough, *Nurse at the Russian Front,* 287; Golovin, *Voennye usiliia,* 2:208; Knox, *With the Russian Army,* 666–668; AAN, dz. "Centralna Agencja Polska w Lozannie," box 61 (*Nowa Reforma,* 28 July 1917, 25 September 1917, 21 December 1917; *Czas,* 27 July 1917, 28 July 1917, 1 August 1917, 12 December 1917; *Wiedeński Kurjer Polski,* 30 June 1917, 31 June 1917, 28 July 1917; *Głos Narodu,* 25 July 1917, 28 July 1917, 31 July 1917, 5 August 1917, 23 August 1917; *Norddeutsche Allgemeine Zeitung,* 29 July 1917; *Dziennik*

Petrogradski, 9 August 1917; *Neue Freie Presse,* 4 August 1917; *Kraj,* 5 August 1917; *Gazeta Narodowa,* 26 July 1917, 5 August 1917; *Dziennik Kijowski,* 24 July 1917, 9 August 1917; *Naprzód,* 11 August 1917; *Dilo,* 24 July 1917; *Kurjer Lwowski,* 18 August 1917; *Frankfurter Zeitung,* 31 August 1917; *Basler Nachrichten,* 5 September 1917); Blicharski, *Tarnopol,* 221.

54. *Nova Rada,* no. 160, 12 October 1917; AAN, dz. "Centralna Agencja Polska w Lozannie," box 61 (*Neue Freie Presse,*" 25 December 1917; *Naprzód,* 30 December 1917).

55. RGVIA, f. 2003, o. 2, d. 539 (3), ll. 16–17; TsDIAUK, f. 361, o. 1, spr. 896, ark. 24, 27, 33, 37, 47, 52, 64, 67, 82–83, 118–119, 128, 130, 172, 174–175, 245–248, 324, 516–517, 583, 622; ibid., f. 361, o. 1, spr. 897, ark. 2–6, 11–12, 13–14, 34–35; ibid., f. 361, o. 1, spr. 839, ark. 10–26; ibid., f. 363, o. 1, spr. 73b, ark. 6; ibid., f. 365, o. 1, spr. 142, ark. 16–17, 26; ibid., f. 365, o. 1, spr. 163, ark. 2, 4, 5, 8, 48–50, 71; ibid., f. 363, o. 1, spr. 8, ark. 30, 38, 57; AAN, dz. "Centralna Agencja Polska w Lozannie," box 61 (*Nowa Reforma,* 27 September 1915; *Głos Narodu,* 10 November 1915; *Dilo,* 17 March 1916; *Wiedeński Kurjer Polski,* 10 October 1916, 17 October 1916; *Die Zeit,* 25 April 1916; *Dziennik Petrogradski,* 18 January 1916; *Nowa Reforma,* 19, 21, 25, 26, 27 April 1916, 1, 4, 6 May 1916); *Jüdische Rundschau,* no. 2, 14 January 1916; no. 3, 21 January 1916; no. 6, 11 February 1916; no. 7, 18 February 1916; no. 13, 31 March 1916; no. 14. 7 April 1916; no. 18, 5 May 1916; *Ukrainische Nachrichten,* no. 56, 9 October 1915; Aba," Razgrom galitsiiskikh yevreiev," 170; *Die Wahrheit: unabhängige Zeitschrift für jüdische Interessen,* no. 15, 16 April 1915; Ansky, *Enemy at His Pleasure, 136;* Golczewski, *Polnisch-Jüdische Beziehungen,* 123f; A. N. Yakhontov, "Tiazhelye dni," 42–45, 47–50.

Chapter 4. Polish-Jewish Relations during World War I

1. *Słowo Polskie,* no. 375, 25 August 1914; Henryka Kramarz, "Lwów i jego samorząd w chwili wybuchu wielkiej wojny," *Studia Historyczne* 35 no. 2/137 (1992): 92; Jan Hupka, *Z czasów wielkiej wojny: pamiętnik niekombatanta* (L'viv, Ukraine: Księgarnia Gubrynowicz i Syn, 1937), 133; Alojzy Zielecki, "Żydzi w Polskim ruchu niepodległościowym w Galicji przed pierwszą wojną światową i w czasie jej trwania," in Feliks Kiryk, ed., *Żydzi w Małopolsce: studia z dziejów osadnictwa i życia społecznego* (Przemyśl, Poland: Południowo-Wschodni Instytut Naukowy w Przemyślu, 1991), 292–294; Dashkevych, "Vzayemovidnosyny mizh ukrains'kym ta yevreis'kym naselenniam," 71.

2. *Niva,* no. 33, 16 August 1914, 2.

3. Edward Chwalewik and Stanisława Waroczewska, eds., *Księga tęczowa Polaków: zbiór dokumentów niedyplomatycznych od 8 sierpnia 1914 do 4 kwietnia 1915 r.* (Warsaw: drukarnia naukowa, 1915), 13, 19–20, 41, 45, 55, 89; RTsKhIDNI, f. 70, o. 2, d. 644, ll. 164, 167–168, 184.

4. S. Hirszhorn, "Dzieje Żydów w Królestwie Polskim od 1864 do 1918 r.," in *Żydzi w Polsce odrodzonej,* 1:486–487; Golczewski, *Polnisch-Jüdische Beziehungen,* 123–125; AAN, dz. "Centralna Agencja Polska w Lozannie," box 61 (*Nowa reforma,* 16 March 1916).

5. "Pokazaniia A. R. Lednitskogo, 27 sentiabria 1917," *Padenie tsarskogo rezhima* 7:240; *Gosudarstvennaia Duma: stenographicheskie otchety,* 4th convocation, 4th session, 1133; Spund, *Die Schreckenherrschaft der Russen in Stanislau,* 6–8, 14–15, 19, 22, 24, 35; Marzell Chłamtacz, *Lembergs politische physionognomie während der russischen Invasion /3.IX 1914–22.VI. 1915/: Erinnerungen und Betrachtungen* (Vienna: Verlag von Rudolf Lechner & Sohn, 1916), 28; *Die Juden im Kriege: Denkschrift des Jüdischen Sozialistischen Arbeiterverbandes Poale-Zion an das Internationale Sozialistische Bureau* (The Hague: Zweite Erweiterte Auflage, 1917), 71–72; AGAD, dz. "Ministerstwo Spraw Wewnętrznych," sygn. F35, n.p.; *Die Wahrheit: unab-*

hängige Zeitschrift für jüdische Interessen, no. 15, 16 April 1915; TsDIAUL, f. 146, o. 8, spr. 1884, ark. 22, 27–29.

6. Piotr Wróbel, "Żydzi polscy w czasie I wojny światowej," *Przegląd Historyczny* 83, no. 4 (1992), 645; Hirszhorn, "Dzieje Żydów w Królestwie Polskim," 487–488; Ansky, *Enemy at His Pleasure,* 13; I. Kanan, *Polsko-yevreiskie otnoshenia (34-aia voina): sbornik statei* (St. Petersburg: izdatel'stvo "Vostok," 1915), 24, 144–145, 147, 149–150; *Zjednoczenie,* no. 1, 2 February 1915; *Die Juden im Kriege,* 76–78.

7. *Die Militärverwaltung in den von Österreich-Ungarischen Truppen besetzten Gebieten* (New Haven, CT: Yale University Press, 1928), 13–14, 33–40; Kestler, *Die deutsche Auslandsaufklärung,* 208–209, 212–213.

8. W. Kaplun-Kogan, *Der Krieg: Eine Schicksalsstunde des jüdischen Volkes* (Bonn: A. Marcus & E. Webers Verlag, 1915), 19. The quotation in Ezra Mendelsohn, *Zionism in Poland: The Formative Years, 1915–1926* (New Haven, CT: Yale University Press, 1981), 39.

9. Wróbel, "Żydzi polscy," 636; Felix A. Theilhaber, *Die Juden im Weltkriege: mit besonderer Berüchsichtigung der Verhältnisse für Deutschland* (Berlin: Welt-Verlag, 1916), 56; Kaplun-Kogan, *Der Krieg,* 7–12; Zechlin, *Die deutsche Politik,* 110.

10. Kanan, *Polsko-yevreiskie otnosheniia,* 134–135; *Die Juden im Kriege,* 73.

11. Golczewski, *Polnisch-Jüdische Beziehungen,* 134–137; Mendelsohn, *Zionism in Poland,* 41–42; Michał Bobrzyński, *Wskrzeszenie Państwa Polskiego: szkic historyczny* (Krakow: Krakowska Spółka Wydawnicza, 1920), 1:77; Hupka, *Z czasów wielkiej wojny,* 75, 103–104, 126–127; Zielecki, "Żydzi w polskim ruchu niepodległościowym," 295; TsDIAUL, f. 146, o. 8, spr. 1884, ark. 34.

12. Leon Grossfeld, *Polityka państw centralnych wobec sprawy polskiej w latach pierwszej wojny światowej, 1914–1918* (Warsaw: Państwowe Wydawnictwo Naukowe, 1962), 27–28, 105–106; Eldon Ray Burke, "Polish Policy of the Central Powers during the World War" (PhD diss., University of Chicago, 1936), 94–103; Stanisław Dzierzbicki, *Pamiętnik z lat wojny 1915–1918* (Warsaw: Państwowy Instytut Wydawniczy, 1983), 63; Hirszhorn, "Dzieje Żydów w Królewstwie Polskiem," 493–494; Jerzy Holzer and Jan Molenda, *Polska w pierwszej wojnie światowej* (Warsaw: Wiedza Powszechna, 1963), 55–59, 118–133, 141; Mendelsohn, *Zionism in Poland,* 41; Bohdan Skaradziński, *Polskie lata, 1919–1920* (Warsaw: Oficyna Wydawnicza Volumen, 1993), 1:32.

13. AAN, dz. "Centralna Agencja Polska w Lozannie," box 61 (*Głos Narodu,* 3 March 1916; *Dziennik Kijowski,* 23 October 1916; *Kurjer Lwowski,* 16 January 1917); AGAD, dz. "Ministerstwo Spraw Wewnętrznych," sygn. F34, n.p.; ibid., sygn. F35, n.p.; *Ukrainische Nachrichten,* no. 44, 11 July 1915; TsDIAUL, f. 146, o. 4, spr. 3560, ark. 113zv, 98–99; ibid., f. 146, o. 4, spr. 5135, ark. 18, 44, 56–57, 71–72; Golczewski, *Polnisch-Jüdische Beziehungen,* 131f; Kreppel, *Juden und Judentum,* 158; Jan Dąbski, *Wojna i ludzie: wspomnienia z lat 1914–1915 /fragmenty/* (Warsaw: Ludowa Spółdzielnia Wydawnicza, 1969), 57, 61, 73; Hupka, *Z czasów wielkiej wojny,* 182; Kanan, *Polsko-yevreiskie otnosheniia,* 40; *Jüdische Rundschau,* no. 33, 13 August 1915; Zechlin, *Die deutsche Politik und die Juden,* 126–138, 144–154; Wróbel, "Przed odzyskaniem niepodleglości," 122; Mendelsohn, *Zionism in Poland,* 40–41.

14. AGAD, dz. "Ministerstwo Spraw Wewnętrznych," sygn. F35, n.p.; AAN, dz. "Centralna Agencja Polska w Lozannie," box 61 (*Dziennik Kijowski,* 23 October 1916); *Ukrainische Nachrichten,* no. 44, 11 July 1915; TsDIAUL, f. 146, o. 8, spr. 1898, ark. 6; ibid., f. 146, o. 8, spr. 1884, ark. 1, 20–21; RGVIA, f. 2005, o. 1, d. 13 (11), n.p.; Bandrowski, *W płomienich,* 9–10, 28, 41, 65, 78, 101–104, 107; *Jüdische Rundschau,* no. 33, 13 August 1915; Chimen Abramsky, "Lucien Wolf's Efforts for the Jewish Communities in Central and Eastern Europe," *Jewish Historical Studies: Transactions of the Jewish Historical Society of England* 29 (1982–1986): 290.

15. Wróbel, "Przed odzyskaniem niepodleglości," 131.

16. Grossfeld, *Polityka państw centralnych*, 187; Burke, "Polish Policy," 32–33; Hupka, *Z czasów wielkiej wojny*, 286; Zielecki, "Żydzi w polskim ruchu niepodległościowym," 294–295; Zechlin, *Die Deutsche Politik*, 198–209, 211–214; AAN, dz. "Centralna Agencja Polska w Lozannie," box 61 (*Kurjer Poznański*, 28 April 1917; *Głos Narodu*, 16 August 1917, 6 September 1917; *Kurjer Lwowski*, 31 August 1917; *Nowa Reforma*, 7 September 1917); *Nova Rada*, no. 28, 2 May 1917; Wróbel, "Przed odzyskaniem niepodleglości," 133.

17. Roman Dmowski, *Polityka polska i odbudowanie państwa* (Warsaw: Instytut Wydawniczy Pax, 1988), 2:175, 279, 301–302.

18. *Tsentral'noe khranilishche istroriko-dokumental'nykh kollektsii* (TsKhIDK), f. 461, o. 1, d. 533, l. 126.

19. *Rossiiskii gosudarstvennyi voennyi arkhiv* (RGVA), f. 1, o. 3, d. 81c, ll. 2, 41; TsDIAUL, f. 146, o. 8, spr. 2684, ark. 35; DALO, f. 350, o. 1, spr. 4552, ark. 8–10, 23ob., 27–30; Christoph Mick, "Nationalisierung in einer multiethnischen Stadt: interethnische Konflikte in Lemberg, 1890–1920," *Archiv für Sozialgeschichte* 40 (2000): 135–136; R. W., "Austriacki wywiad wojskowy we Lwowie w przededniu wypadków listopadowych," in Jarosław Waniorek, ed., *Obrona Lwowa, 1–22 listopada 1918* (Warsaw: Oficyna Wydawnicza Volumen, 1991–1993), 2:662; Kreppel, *Juden und Judentum*, 159; *Zjednoczenie: pismo poświęcone idei zespolenia Żydów z narodem polskim*, 3 March 1918, 45–47. In a secret provision to the treaty, the dual monarchy promised to integrate East Galicia and Bukovina into a new crown land. Grossfeld, *Polityka państw centralnych*, 267, 271–273; Burke, "Polish Policy," 66–67; Dzierzbicki, *Pamiętnik*, 275.

20. Richard Georg Plaschka, Horst Haselsteiner, and Arnold Suppan, *Innere Front: Militärassistenz, Widerstand und Umsturz in der Donaumonarchie 1918* (Munich: R. Oldenbourg Verlag, 1974), 1:92–93, 101–106, 301–302 2:89; DALO, f. 350, o. 1, spr. 4552, ark. 48–48ob., 60–60ob.; ibid., f. 256, o. 1, spr. 76, ark. 22, 31; Mendelsohn, *Zionism in Poland*, 88–89; Bobrzyński, *Wskrzeszenie państwa polskiego* 2:27–28; "Aneksy," in *Obrona Lwowa* 2:699, 705–707; Wróbel, "Jews of Galicia," 135–136.

21. Petersen, *Understanding Ethnic Violence*, 3.

22. Ivan Lysiak-Rudnyts'kyi, *Istorychni ese* (Kiev: "Osnovy," 1994), 1:413–450; Mychailo Lozyns'kyi, *Halychyna v rr. 1918–1920* (New York: vydavnytstvo "Chervona Kalyna," 1970), 12–40; Osyp Dumin, *Istoriia Lehionu Ukrains'kykh Sichovykh Stril'tsiv* (L'viv, Ukraine: Chervona Kalyna, 1936); Makarchuk, *Ukrains'ka Respublika Halychan*, 26–40; Holzer and Molenda, *Polska w pierwszej wojnie światowej*, 199; Tadeusz Dąbkowski, *Ukraiński ruch narodowy w Galicji Wschodniej, 1912–1923* (Warsaw: Instytut Krajów Socyalistycznych PAN, 1985), 77, 79–80.

23. M. P. Lytvyn and K. E. Naumenko, *Istoria ZUNR* (L'viv, Ukraine: Instytut ukrainoznavstva NAN Ukrainy, 1995), 29; Roman Matejko and Bohdan Kravchuk, *Za ridnyi krai, za narid svii: Ukrains'ka Halyts'ka Armiia na Ternopil'shchyni* (Ternopil', Ukraine: n.p., 1993), 4.

24. AAN, dz. "Centralna Agencja Polska w Lozannie," box 61, (*Dilo*, 27 October 1918, and 29 October 1918); Witold Stankiewicz, *Konflikty społeczne na wsi polskiej, 1918–1920* (Warsaw: Państwowe Wydawnictwo Naukowe, 1963), 156; M. Gon, "Yevreis'ki politychni partii na Zakhidnii Ukraiini, 1918–1929" (Kiev State University, diss. of Candidate of Historical Sciences, 1998), 42, 62; Pogrebyns'ka i Gon, *Yevrei v Zakhidnoukrains'kii Respublitsi*, 35; "Aneksy," in *Obrona Lwowa* 2:719.

25. Marian Fuks, "Żydzi w zaraniu niepodległości Polski," BŻIH 2/150 (1989): 38; Gaisbauer, *Davidstern und Doppeladler*, 540; *Nowy Dziennik*, no. 122, 10 November 1918; "Pog-

romen in Polen und Galizien," *Neue Jüdische Monatshefte,* Heft 3/5, 10 December 1918, 56–58.

Chapter 5. The Lwów Pogrom, November 22–24, 1918

1. Michael A. Meyer, ed., *German-Jewish History in Modern Times* (New York: Columbia University Press, 1997), 3:384.

2. *Chwila,* no. 110, 5 May 1919; no. 116, 11 May 1919; R. W., "Austriacki wywiad wojskowy we Lwowie," in *Obrona Lwowa* 2:677–678.

3. Lemki or Rusins, an ethnocultural group that inhabited southern districts of West Galicia.

4. TsDIAUL, f. 359, o. 1, spr. 370, ark. 96–97; *Nova Rada,* no. 203, 2 November 1918; Hornykiewicz, *Ereignisse,* 4:44f; Zygmunt Lasocki, *Wspomnienia szefa administrcji P. K. L. i K. Rz.* (Krakow: nakładem autora, 1931), 7; Lytvyn and Naumenko, *Istoria ZUNR,* 29; Matejko and Kravchuk, *Za ridnyi krai, za narid svii,* 4; Mykhailo Hutsulak, *Pershyi lystopad 1918 rok: zi spohadamy i zhyttiepysamy chleniv Komitetu vykonavtsiv lystopadovoho chynu* (New York: nakladom Komitetu vykonavtsiv lystopadovoho chynu, 1973), 16.

5. Lasocki, *Wspomnienia,* 24; *Listopad 1.-22.XI.1918 we Lwowie* (L'viv, Ukraine: Zakład Narodowy imienia Ossolińskich, 1919), 2–4, 23; Białynia-Chołodecki, *Lwów w listopadzie,* 17–18.

6. W. Kutschabsky, *Die Westukraine im Kampfe mit Polen und dem Bolschewismus in den Jahren 1918–1923* (Berlin: Junker und Dünnhaupt Verlag, 1934), 39; Lozyns'kyi, *Halychyna,* 41–43; Hornykiewicz, *Ereignisse,* 4:47f; Zdzisław Konieczny, *Walki polsko-ukraińskie w Przemyślu i okolicy: listopad-grudzień 1918* (Przemyśl, Poland: Spółdzielnia Inwalidów "Praca" w Przemyślu, 1993), 29; Plaschka, Haselsteiner, and Suppan, *Innere Front* 2:309, 311, 312–313, 316; Białynia-Chołodecki, *Lwów w listopadzie,* 10.

7. Wacław Lipiński, *Wśród lwowskich orląt* (Warsaw: Wojskowy Instytut Naukowo-Wydawniczy, 1931), 79; Adam Ciołkosz, "Dzielnica żydowska obozu w Jabłonnie," *Zeszyty Historyczne* 15 (1969): 190; Marian E. Wagner, *Lwowski chłopaka na wojnach: strzępy wspomnień z walecznych lat 1918–1921* (n.p., n.d.), 25; *Pobudka: Organ Komitetu Obywatelskiego VI-go Okręgu m. Lwowa,* no. 2, 7 November 1918; no. 18, 23 November 1918; Jan Gella, *Ruski miesiąc 1/XI-22/XI 1918: ilustrowany opis walk listopadowych we Lwowie* (L'viv, Ukraine: Instytut Literacki "Lektor," 1918), 214; Białynia-Chołodecki, *Lwów w listopadzie,* 10, 17–18; *Gazeta Poranna,* no. 4441, 2 November 1918; Lasocki, *Wspomnienia,* 39; Artur W. Hausner, *Listopad 1918 r.* (L'viv, Ukraine: nakładem zarządu okręgowego związku pracowników kolejowych Polskiej Z. Z. K. we Lwowie, 1929), 14.

8. Rosa Bailly, *A City Fights for Freedom: The Rising of Lwów in 1918–1919* (London: Publishing Committee Leopolis, 1956), 235–236; Białynia-Chołodecki, *Lwów w listopadzie,* 26–27; Gon, "Yevreis'ki politychni partii," 42–43; AAN, dz. "Kancelaria cywilna Naczelnika Państwa," sygn. 179, part 1, kk. 9–10; *Tsentral'nyi derzhavnyi arkhiv vyshchykh orhaniv vlady i upravlinnia Ukrainy* (TsDAVO), f. 2188, o. 1, spr. 1, ark. 13; ibid., f. 2188, o. 2, spr. 8, ark. 12; *Chwila,* no. 1, 10 January 1919; *Nowy Dziennik,* no. 145, 3 December 1918; Abraham Inster, *Dokumenty fałszu: prawda o tragedii żydostwa lwowskiego w listopadzie 1918* (L'viv, Ukraine: nakładem drukarni Ignacego Jaegera, 1933), 31, 84–86; Ozjasz Wasser, "Rola Żydow w listopadowej obronie Lwowa w 1918 r," in *Obrona Lwowa* 2:837–838; Jozef Bendow, *Der Lemberger Judenpogrom /November 1918–Jänner 1919* (Vienna: M. Hickl-Verlag, 1919), 15, 18.

9. Franciszek Salezy Krysiak, *Z dni grozy we Lwowie /od 1–22 listopada 1918 r./* (Krakow:

G. Gebethner i Spółka, 1919), 29–30; *Gazeta Poranna,* no. 4442, 3 November 1918; Witold Hupert, *Walki o Lwów /od 1 listopada 1918 do 1 maja 1919/* (Warsaw: Księgarnia Wojskowa, 1933), 41; AAN, dz. "Ambasada RP w Londynie," sygn. 1380, k. 18; *Pobudka,* no. 4, 9 November 1918.

10. *Nova Rada,* no. 229, 21 November (4 December) 1918; no. 234, 28 November (11 December) 1918; *Gazeta Poranna,* no. 4465, 8 December 1918; TsDAVO, f. 2188, o. 1, spr. 278, ark. 45; Białynia-Chołodecki, *Lwów w listopadzie,* 39; Gella, *Ruski miesiąc,* 36; Jerzy Tomaszewski, "Lwów, 22 listopada 1918 roku," *Przegląd Historyczny* 75, no. 2 (1984): 281; Grzegorz Łukomski, Czesław Partacz, and Bogusław Polak, *Wojna polsko-ukraińska, 1918–1919: działania bojowe-aspekty polityczne-kalendarium* (Koszalin, Poland: Wydawnictwo Uczelniane Wyższej Szkoły Inżynierskiej w Koszalinie, 1994), 81; Maciej Kozłowski, *Zapomniana wojna: walki o Lwów i Galicję Wschodnią* (Bydgoszcz, Poland: Instytut Wydawniczy "Świadectwo," 1999), 215.

11. Bailly, *City Fights for Freedom,* 102; Wasser, "Rola Żydów," 839; Józef Grabowski, "Listopadowe boje o szkołę kadecką," in *Obrona Lwowa* 2:146; Bendow, *Der Lemberger Judenpogrom,* 16; Hausner, *Listopad 1918 r.,* 56–57.

12. TsDAVO, f. 2188, o. 2, spr. 143, ark. 14; Tomaszewski, "Lwów, 22 listopada," 281; Pogrebyns'ka i Gon, *Yevrei v Zakhidnoukrains'kii Narodnii Respublitsi,* 41; *Neue Lemberger Zeitung,* no. 601, 17 November 1918; Kozłowski, *Zapomniana wojna,* 142, 149.

13. Lasocki, *Wspomnienia,* 39; Makarchuk, *Ukrains'ka Respublika Halychan,* 92; Bailly, *City Fights for Freedom,* 102; Gella, *Ruski miesiąc,* 28.

14. TsDAVO, f. 2188, o. 1, spr. 1, ark. 11, 15; ibid., f. 2188, o. 4, spr. 27, ark. 2, 15.

15. Ibid., f. 2188, o. 2, spr. 107, ark. 15; ibid., f. 2188, o. 2, spr. 8, ark. 8; Tomaszewski, "Lwów, 22 listopada," 282; Karol Baczyński, "Wspomnienia z czasu obrony Lwowa," in *Obrona Lwowa* 1:29; Franciszek Jarzębiński, "Prawy pododcinek sektora Bema," in *Obrona Lwowa* 2:203; Wit Sulimirski, "Grupa 'Sokół'-Macierz," in *Obrona Lwowa* 2:468; Tadeusz Kotik, "Walki w dzielnicy Żółkiewskiej," in *Obrona Lwowa* 2:222; Antoni Jakubski, "Walki listopadowe we Lwowie w świetle krytyk," in *Obrona Lwowa* 2:179.

16. TsDAVO, f. 2188, o. 2, spr. 143, ark. 46; ibid., f. 2188, o. 1, spr. 1, ark. 13; ibid., f. 2188, o. 2, spr. 8, ark. 12; Bailly, *City Fights for Freedom,* 103, 235–236; *Chwila,* no. 1, 10 January 1919; ibid., no. 18, 31 January 1919; *Nowy Dziennik,* no. 145, 3 December 1918; Inster, *Dokumenty fałszu,* 31, 84–86.

17. TsDAVO, f. 2188, o. 2, spr. 8, ark. 5; ibid., f. 2188, o. 1, spr. 1, ark. 15; ibid., f. 2188, o. 4, spr. 27, ark. 2; ibid., f. 2188, o. 2, spr. 143, ark. 14; *Centralne Archiwum Wojskowe* (CAW), dz. "Inwentarze kolekcji materiałów drukowanych i archiwaliów prywatnych," sygn. 444.1.1, n.p.; *Chwila,* no. 1, 10 January 1919; *Pobudka,* no. 5, 10 November 1918; Oleksa Kuz'ma, *Lystopadowe dni 1918* (L'viv, Ukraine: nakladem avtora, 1931), 192–193; Gella, *Ruski miesiąc,* 19; Krysiak, *Z dni grozy,* 37, 45; Bailly, *City Fights for Freedom,* 258; *Neue Lemberger Zeitung,* no. 602, 18 November 1918; Hausner, *Listopad 1918 r.,* 59.

18. Piotr Wróbel, "The Seeds of Violence: The Brutalization of an East European Region, 1917–1921," *Journal of Modern European History* 1 (2002): 137–138; TsDAVO, f. 2188, o. 2, spr. 106, ark. 2, 24; ibid., f. 2188, o. 1, spr. 278, ark. 15; ibid., f. 2188, o. 2, spr. 8, ark. 2; ibid., f. 2188, o. 2, spr. 143, ark. 35; Volodymyr Kalyna, "Z lystopadovykh boiiv na Pidzamchi," in *Nash L'viv: yuvileinyi zbirnyk 1252–1952* (New York: vydavnytstvo "Chervona Kalyna," 1953), 152; Kozłowski, *Zapomniana wojna,* 198; Białynia-Chołodecki, *Lwów w listopadzie,* 35–36; Krysiak, *Z dni grozy,* 80–81; *Pobudka,* no. 3, 8 November 1918; *Gazeta Poranna,* no. 4442, 4 November 1918; Kuz'ma, *Lystopadowe dni,* 177.

19. TsDAVO, f. 2188, o. 2, spr. 143, ark. 14; *Chwila,* no. 1, 10 January 1919; no. 8, 19 January

1919; no. 276, 21 October 1919; *Nowy Dziennik,* no. 140, 28 November 1918; Gon, "Yevreis'ki politychni partii," 48; Gella, *Ruski miesiąc,* 50; Kuz'ma, *Lystopadowe dni,* 354.

20. Krysiak, *Z dni grozy,* 103–105, 135–136; Gella, *Ruski miesiąc,* 82–106; AAN, dz. "Kancelaria cywilna Naczelnika Państwa," sygn. 179, part 1, kk. 42–43; Antoni Jakubski, "W obronie prawdy," in *Obrona Lwowa* 2:812; Białynia-Chołodecki, *Lwów w listopadzie,* 26–27; Gella, *Ruski miesiąc,* 50; Krysiak, *Z dni grozy,* 65; *Chwila,* no. 276, 21 October 1919; *Pobudka,* no. 12, 17 November 1918; Czesław Mączyński, *Boje Lwowskie* (Warsaw: nakładem spółki wydawnictwa Rzeczpospolita, 1921), 9–10.

21. Gon, "Yevreis'ki politychni partii," 43; Lasocki, *Wspomnienia,* 40; *Neue Lemberger Zeitung,* no. 605, 21 November 1918.

22. Kozłowski, *Zapomniana wojna,* 213.

23. AAN, dz. "Kancelaria cywilna Naczelnika Państwa," sygn. 179, part 1, k. 12; *Chwila,* no. 507, 14 June 1920.

24. *Listopad 1.-22.XI.1918 Lwowie,* 27; Mączyński, *Boje Lwowskie,* 19–21; Hupert, *Walki o Lwów,* 92–96.

25. AAN, dz. "Kancelaria cywilna Naczelnika Państwa," part 1, sygn. 57, k. 6; Bolesław Roja, *Legendy i fakty* (Warsaw: nakładem księgarni F. Hoesicka, 1931), 206–207; Mączyński, "O stanowisku Żydów," in *Obrona Lwowa* 2:819; Roman Abraham, "Pododcinek Góra Stracenia," in *Obrona Lwowa* 2:618–635.

26. DALO, f. 271, o. 1, spr. 446, ark. 81–81ob.; *Gazeta Poranna,* no. 4465, 8 December 1918; Kenneth Bourne and D. Cameron Watt, eds., *British Documents on Foreign Affairs: Reports and Papers from the Foreign Office, Confidential Print,* part 2, series A (n.p.: University Publication of America, 1984–1997), 4:208–209; Bendow, *Der Lemberger Judenpogrom,* 141–159.

27. Kuz'ma, *Lystopadowe dni,* 377; Inster, *Dokumenty fałszu,* 27, 50, 55, 86; Hausner, *Listopad 1918 r.,* 70; Tadeusz Kotik, "Walki w dzielnicy Żółkiewskiej," in *Obrona Lwowa* 2:226; Stanisław Łapiński-Nilski and Aleksander Kron, *Listopad we Lwowie /1918 r./* (Warsaw: nakładem wydawnictwa "Rząd i Wojsko," 1920), 53; *Chwila,* no. 1, 10 January 1919; AAN, dz. "Kancelaria cywilna Naczelnika Państwa," sygn. 179, part 1, kk. 14, 16–17, 21–22; Baczyński, "Wspomnienia z czasu obrony Lwowa," in *Obrona Lwowa* 2:30.

28. Inster, *Dokumenty fałszu,* 94–95; Mączyński, *Boje Lwowskie,* 22; Tomaszewski, "Lwów, 22 listopada," 284; Roja, *Legeny i fakty,* 325; *Gazeta Poranna,* no. 4447, 23 November 1918; Wasser, "Rola Żydów," 840–841.

29. Łapiński and Kron, *Listopad we Lwowie,* 10, 72; Makarchuk, *Ukrains'ka Respublika Halychan,* 81; Roja, *Legendy i fakty,* 190, 203, 207, 324; *Pobudka,* no. 19, 24 November 1918; CAW, dz. "Inwentarze kolekcji materiałów drukowanych i archiwaliów prywatnych," sygn. 444.1.1, n.p.; ibid., dz. "Dowództwo WP na Galicję Wshodnią," sygn. I.304.1.63, n.p.; TsDIAUL, f. 212, o. 1, spr. 111, ark. 6–9.

30. TSDIAUL, f. 212, o. 1, spr. 111, ark. 6–9; *Gazeta Poranna,* no. 4447, 23 November 1918.

31. Roja, *Legendy i fakty,* 205–206, 214, 236; Tomaszewski, "Lwów, 22 listopada," 284–285; AAN, dz. "Kancelaria cywilna Naczelnika Państwa," sygn. 179, part 1, k. 24; Inster, *Dokumenty fałszu,* 27; Baczyński, "Wspomnienia z czasu obrony Lwowa," 30.

32. Konieczny, *Walki polsko-ukraińskie w Przemyślu,* 29.

33. *Vpered,* no. 51, 31 January 1919; CAW, dz. "Inwentarz wycinków prasowych," sygn. 410.9.2, press clips from *Republika,* 15 February 1919, part 12, and 20 February 1919, part 16; Ludwik Mroczka, *Galicji rozstanie z Austrią: zarys monograficzny* (Krakow: Wydawnictwo Naukowe WSP, 1990), 249–250; Konieczny, *Walki polsko-ukraińskie w Przemyślu,* 69, 71.

34. Ivan Kryp'yakevych, *Istorychni prokhody po L'vovi* (L'viv, Ukraine: nakladem Tovarystva "Prosvita" u L'vovi, 1932), 163; DALO, f. 1, o. 58, spr. 95, ark. 23; *Chwila,* no. 16,

29 January 1919; CAW, dz. "Inwentarze kolekcji materiałów drukowanych i archiwaliów prywatnych," sygn. 410.9.2, press clips from *Republika,* 15 February 1919, part 12, and 5 March 1919, part 27; AAN, dz. "Kancelaria cywilna Naczelnika Państwa," sygn. 179, part 3, kk. 38–39; Lasocki, *Wspomnienia,* 42; *Nowy Dziennik,* no. 146, 4 December 1918; Tomaszewski, "Lwów, 22 listopada," 284; Mączyński, *Boje Lwowskie,* 168.

35. CAW, dz. "Dowództwo WP na Galicję Wshodnią," sygn. I.304.1.68, n.p.; TsDIAUL, f. 212, o. 1, spr. 33, ark. 10. According to various sources, the total casualties for the three weeks of the fighting ranged between 210 killed and 760 wounded for the Poles and 48 killed and 192 wounded for Ukrainians. These numbers seem plausible. Białynia-Chołodecki, *Lwów w listopadzie,* 43–44; Łapiński and Kron, *Listopad we Lwowie,* 82; *Chwila,* no. 276, 21 October 1919; no. 277, 22 October 1919.

36. Tomaszewski, "Lwów, 22 listopada," 283. See an allegation that the commission's findings were influenced by the Jewish-Masonic leanings of its members in Leszek Tomaszewski, "Lwów—listopad 1918—niezwykłe losy pewnego dokumentu," *Dzieje Najnowsze* 25, no. 4 (1993): 163–173.

37. Ciołkosz, "Dzielnica żydowska obozu w Jabłonnie," 190–191; AAN, "Centralna Agencja Polska w Lozannie," box 246 (*Kölnische Zeitung,* 5 December 1918; *Volksrecht,* 2 December 1918); RTsKhIDNI, f. 70, o. 5, d. 434, l. 203; *Nowy Dziennik,* no. 142, 30 November 1918; Lasocki, *Wspomnienia,* 41, 48, 109–110; "Pogromen in Polen und Galizien," *Neue Jüdische Monatsheft* 3, no. 5 (10 December 1918): 51–56; Krysiak, *Z dni grozy,* 130–131; *Chwila,* no. 332, 16 December 1919; Bendow, *Der Lemberger Judenpogrom,* 12, 33, 38, 43; *British Documents on Foreign Affairs,* 208; *Borot'ba,* no. 1(58), 26 January 1919; Pogrebyns'ka i Gon, *Yevrei v Zakhidnoukrains'kii Narodnii Respublitsi,* 41–42; *Kievskaia mysl',* no. 227, 16 November 1918.

38. Norman Davies, "Great Britain and the Polish Jews, 1918–1920," *Journal of Contemporary History* 8, no. 2 (1973): 121, 126–127, 138; Antoni Chołoniewski, *My, Żydzi i Kongres wobec zaburzeń galicyjskich* (Krakow: nakład Tow. Im. Stefana Buszczyńskiego, 1919), 33–35; Janusz Pajewski, *Budowa Drugiej Rzeczypospolitej, 1918–1926* (Krakow: nakładem Polskiej Akademii Umiejętności, 1995), 178.

39. Mieczysław Sobczak, *Stosunek Narodowej Demokracji do kwestii żydowskiej w Polsce w latach 1918–1939* (Wrocław, Poland: Wydawnictwo Akademii Ekonomicznej im. Oskara Langego, 1998), 45; AAN, dz. "Kancelaria cywilna Naczelnika Państwa," sygn. 179, part 1, kk. 33, 38, part 3, k. 33; *Nowy Dziennik,* no. 142, 30 November 1918; Mroczka, *Galicji rozstanie z Austrią,* 187; *Kievskaia mysl',* no. 228, 17 November 1918.

40. Sobczak, *Stosunek Narodowej Demokracji,* 45; AAN, dz. "Kancelaria cywilna Naczelnika Państwa," sygn. 179, part 1, kk. 33, 38, part 3, k. 33; *Pobudka,* no. 21, 26 November 1918; *Nowy Dziennik,* no. 142, 30 November 1918; *Kievskaia mysl',* no. 228, 17 November 1918; no. 235, 27 November 1918; Mroczka, *Galicji rozstanie z Austrią,* 187.

41. Hupka, *Z czasów wielkiej wojny,* 390; Hupert, *Walki o Lwów,* 97; Krysiak, *Z dni grozy,* 139–142; Ludwik Baar, "Milicja wojskowa w obronie Lwowa," in *Obrona Lwowa* 2:63; Andrzej Sas-Matkowski, "Służba artylerii," in *Obrona Lwowa* 2:237; Mączyński, *Boje Lwowskie,* 28–29, 31; *Pobudka,* no. 23, 28 November 1918; no. 27, 2 December 1918; no. 30, 5 December 1918; *Nowy Dziennik,* no. 146, 4 December 1918; no. 157, 15 December 1918.

42. *Lvivs'ka naukova biblioteka imeni Vasyla Stefanyka Natsional'noi Akademii Nauk Ukrainy* (LNB), Department of Manuscripts, f. "Komitet natsional'noi oborony," spr. 9(OH), ark. 1–3; AAN, dz. "Centralna Agencja Polska w Lozannie," box 246 (*Głos Narodu,* 8 December 1918); Krysiak, *Z dni grozy,* 28–29, 132–135; Inster, *Dokumenty fałszu,* 70–75.

43. Bobrzyński, *Wskrzeszenie Państwa Polskiego* 2:31–32.

44. Hupert, *Walki o Lwów,* 12, 26–27; LNB, f. "Komitet natsional'noi oborony," spr. 9 (OH), ark. 3; AAN, dz. "Kancelaria cywilna Naczelnika Państwa," sygn. 179, part 3, 36–37; Jakubski, "Wypadki listopadowe," 180–184.

45. Stefan Mękarski, "Czesław Mączyński," in *Obrona Lwowa* 2:27–28; Jakubski, "Walki listopadowe," 180–181.

46. AAN, dz. "Amabassada RP w Paryżu," sygn. 301, kk. 33–34, 40, 43; Bendow, *Der Lemberger Judenpogrom,* 56, 59; Ciołkosz, "Dzielnica żydowska," 190–191.

47. Israel Cohen, "My Mission to Poland (1918–1919)," *Jewish Social Studies* 13 (1951): 162; GARF, f. 130, o. 4, d. 400 (2), l. 75.

48. Morgenthau also asserted that 164 individuals, including 10 Jews, were sentenced by Polish courts for participating in the pogrom. These numbers are not corroborated by other sources. *Chwila,* no. 394, 18 February 1920. Also see DALO, f. 1, o. 58, spr. 95, ark. 16.

49. DALO, f. 271, o. 1, spr. 445, ark. 3; ibid., f. 271, o. 1, spr. 453, ark. 1–20b.; ibid., f. 1, o. 58, spr. 95, ark. 3; RTsKhIDNI, f. 70, o. 5, d. 434, l. 203; AAN, dz. "Kancelaria cywilna Naczelnika Państwa," sygn. 179, part 2, k. 6; part 1, kk. 1, 3–6; Roja, *Legendy i fakty,* 204, 221; Hupka, *Z czasów wielkiej wojny,* 390; Hupert, *Walki o Lwów,* 97; Krysiak, *Z dni grozy,* 139–142; Baar, "Milicja wojskowa," 63; Sas-Matkowski, "Służba artylerii," in *Obrona Lwowa,* 2:237; Mączyński, *Boje Lwowskie,* 28–29, 31; *Pobudka,* no. 23, 28 November 1918; no. 27, 2 December 1918; no. 30, 5 December 1918; no. 30, 5 December 1918; no. 34, 9 December 1918; *Nowy Dziennik,* no. 142, 30 November 1918; no. 146, 4 December 1918; no. 157, 15 December 1918, *Kievskaia mysl',* no. 235, 27 November (10 December) 1918; Mroczka, *Galicji rozstanie z Austrią,* 187; AAN, dz. "Agencja Polska w Lozannie," box 246 (*St. Galler Tagblatt,* n.d.); Lasocki, *Wspomnienia,* 110.

50. Mendelsohn, *Zionism in Poland,* 89–90.

51. Inster, *Dokumenty fałszu,* 89–90; AAN, dz. "Kancelaria cywilna Naczelnika Państwa," sygn. 179, part 1, k. 33; *Nowy Dziennik,* no. 143, 1 December 1918; no. 154, 12 December 1918.

52. Inster, *Dokumenty fałszu,* 87–88; Wasser, "Rola Żydów," 833–835ff.

53. *Chwila,* no. 276, 21 October 1919; ibid., no. 277, 22 October 1919; CAW, dz. "Inwentarze kolekcji materiałów drukowanych," sygn. 410.9.2, press clip from *Republika,* 11 March 1919, part 32.

54. *Lwów po inwazji rosyjskiej,* 9; Kozłowski, *Zapomniana wojna,* 215.

55. TsDAVO, f. 2188, o. 2, spr. 143, ark. 35; Łukomski, Partacz, and Polak, *Wojna polsko-ukraińska,* 82–83; *Nowy Dziennik,* no. 140, 28 November 1918; Makarchuk, *Ukrains'ka Respublika Halyczan,* 104; Krysiak, *Z dni grozy,* 129–130; Sulimirski, "Grupa 'Sokół'-Macierz," 469; Mączyński, *Boje Lwowskie,* 23, 181; see also Mączyński, "O stanowisku Żydów w czasie walk listopadowych," 817–821; Roja, *Legendy i fakty,* 207, 325; Tomaszewski, "Lwów, 22 listopada," 284; Hupert, *Walki o Lwów,* 92–96; AAN, dz. "Kancelaria cywilna Naczelnika Państwa," part 1, sygn. 179, k. 30; Ciołkosz, "Dzielnica żydowska," 190–191; Lipiński, *Wśród Lwowskich orląt,* 79; *Pobudka,* no. 18, 23 November 1918; Gella, *Ruski miesiąc,* 214; Jakubski, "Walki listopadowe," 179–180.

56. Łukomski, Partacz, and Polak, *Wojna polsko-ukraińska,* 81; TsDAVO, f. 2188, o. 2, spr. 143, ark. 14.

57. DALO, f. 271, o. 1, spr. 446, ark. 58, 81–81ob., 111–111ob.; AAN, dz. "Centralna Agencja Polska w Lozannie," box 246 (*Goniec Krakowski,* 28 December 1918); ibid., dz. "Ambasada RP w Paryżu," sygn. 301, k. 44; *Chwila,* no. 163, 27 June 1919; no. 240, 12 September 1919; ibid., no. 244, 16 September 1919; no. 798, 8 April 1921.

58. TsDIAUL, f. 212, o. 1, spr. 111, ark. 6–9; CAW, dz. "Dowództwo WP na Galicję Wshodnią," sygn. I.304.1.63, n.p.; *Pobudka,* no. 20, 25 November 1918; Mroczka, *Galicji rozstanie z Austrią,* 187; AAN, dz. "Centralna Agencja Polska w Lozannie," box 246 (*St. Galler Tagblatt,* n.d.); Lasocki, *Wspomnienia,* 110.

Chapter 6. The Polish Frontier Wars, 1919–1920

1. Leopold Halpern, "Polityka żydowska w Sejmie i Senacie Rzeczypospolitej Polskiej, 1919–1933," *Sprawy Narodowościowe* 7, no. 1 (1933): 4.

2. Paweł Korzec, "Polish-Jewish Relations during World War I," in Strauss, *Hostages of Modernization,* 1028; *Chwila,* no. 1, 10 January 1919.

3. Pajewski, *Budowa Drugiej Rzeczypospolitej,* 178; Dariusz Jeziorny, "Sprawa ochrony praw mniejszosci żydowskiej w Polsce w dobie konferencji pokojowej w Paryżu w 1919 roku," in Pawel Samuś, ed., *Z dziejów Drugiej Rzeczypospolitej,* series *Acta Universitatis Lodziensis* 54 (1995): 46–47; Mark Levene, *Wars, Jews, and the New Europe: The Diplomacy of Lucien Wolf, 1914–1919* (Oxford: Oxford University Press, 1992), 220; *Chwila,* no. 1, 10 January 1919; no. 4, 15 January 1919; *Gazeta Żydowska,* no. 4, 12 January 1919; Gelber, *National Autonomy of Eastern Galician Jewry,* 247.

4. Sobczak, *Stosunek Narodowej Demokracji do kwestii żydowskiej,* 40; Pajewski, *Budowa Drugiej Rzeczypospolitej,* 175–177; *Chwila,* no. 61, 15 March 1919.

5. RTsKhIDNI, f. 70, o. 5, d. 434, ll. 202–203; AAN, dz. "Kancelaria cywilna Naczelnika Państwa," sygn. 179, part 2, kk. 6, 26–27; ibid., part 3, kk. 17–21; *Gazeta Żydowska,* no. 2, 10 January 1919; Bobrzyński, *Wskrzeszenie Państwa Polskiego* 2:64; *Chwila,* no. 10, 22 January 1919; CAW, dz. "Dowództwo WP na Galicję Wshodnią," sygn. I.304.1.11, kk. 274, 313; ibid., sygn. I.304.1/12, k. 10; ibid., sygn. I.304.1.67, n.p.; ibid., sygn. I.304.1.64, kk. 14, 18, 21, 27; ibid., sygn. I.304.1.63, n.p.; LNB, f. "Komitet natsional'noi oborony," spr. KNO-1, ark. 32, 37; Mączyński, "O stanowisku żydów," 820; *Żołnierz Polski,* no. 5, 26 January 1919; Jeziorny, "Sprawa ochrony praw mniejszosci żydowskiej," 42–43.

6. Ludwik Mroczka, "Przyczynek do kwestii żydowskiej w Galicji u progu Drugiej Rzeczypospolitej," in *Żydzi w Małopolsce,* 302–303.

7. LNB, f. "Komitet natsional'noi oborony," spr. KNO-1, ark. 32; Levene, *Wars, Jews, and the New Europe,* 211–212; Przemysław Piotr Żurawski vel Grajewski, *Sprawa ukraińska na konferencji pokojowej w Paryżu w roku 1919* (Warsaw: Wydawnictwo Naukowe *Semper,* 1995), 19–20; Jeziorny, "Sprawa ochrony praw mniejszości żydowskiej," 44–45, 49, 58–59; K. Lundgreen-Nielsen, *The Polish Problem at the Paris Peace Conference: A Study of Politics of the Great Powers and the Poles, 1918–1919* (Odense, Denmark: Odense University Press, 1979), 190; Mroczka, *Galicji rozstanie z Austrią,* 216–217; CAW, dz. "Dowództwo Frontu Galicyjskiego," sygn. I.310.1.66, n.p.; ibid., dz. "Dowództwo Frontu Galicyjsko-Wołyńskiego," sygn. I.310.2.11, kk. 64, 217; Antoni Deblessem, *Wspomnienia z prac i walk o polskość Stanisławowa: ze specjalnym podkreśleniem akcji P. O. W. z czasów 1918–1920 r.* (Zolochiv, Ukraine: nakładem autora, 1934), 71; Mieczysław Wojciechowski, "Niemcy, Polacy i Żydzi w Prusach Zachodnich w latach 1877–1920," in B. Breysach et al., eds., *Ze sobą, obok siebie, przeciwko siebie: Polacy, Żydzi, Austriacy i Niemcy w XIX i na początku XX wieku* (Krakow: Wydawnictwo Znak, 1995), 185.

8. *Sprawozdania stenograficzne Sejmu Ustawodawczego* (cited as SsSU) (Warsaw: Druk Bogusławskiego, 1919), 3rd session, 20 February 1919, 67–68; ibid., 5th session, 24 February 1919, 183–191; ibid., 6th session, 25 February 1919, 209–212; ibid., 7th session, 26 February 1919, 281–285; ibid., 15th session, 18 March 1919, 794–795, 800; AAN, dz. "Kancelaria cywilna

Naczelnika Państwa," sygn. 179, part 3, kk. 28–29; CAW, dz. "Dowództwo WP na Galicję Wschodnią," sygn. I.304.1.67, k. 256; *Chwila,* no. 23, 6 February 1919; no. 103, 27 April 1919; no. 104, 28 April 1919; no. 152, 16 June 1919; Halpern, *Polityka żydowska w Sejmie i Senacie,* 11; TsKhIDK, f. 461, o. 1, d. 533, ll. 131, 134–135.

9. *Chwila,* no. 154, 18 June 1919; no. 183, 17 July 1919.

10. Ibid., no. 197, 31 July 1919; Pajewski, *Budowa Drugiej Rzeczypospolitej,* 179–180.

11. Pajewski, *Budowa Drugiej Rzeczypospolitej,* 178–179; Jeziorny, "Ochrona praw mniejszości," 59.

12. *Chwila,* no. 196, 30 July 1919; Bobrzyński, *Wskrzeszenie Państwa Polskiego,* 82–83; Jeziorny, "Sprawa ochrony praw mniejszości żydowskiej," 59–60; Gelber, *National Autonomy of Eastern Galician Jewry,* 301.

13. *Chwila,* no. 168, 2 July 1919; TsKhIDK, f. 416, o. 1, d. 533, l. 131, 134–135; SsSU, 33rd session, 6 May 1919, 29; ibid., 48th session, 12 June 1919, 63–67; ibid., 57th session, 27 June 1919, 59–63; ibid., 70th session, 16 July 1919, 61; ibid., 81st session, 30 July 1919, 50, 86; RTsKhIDNI, f. 70, o. 5, d. 434, ll. 202–203; Gelber, *National Autonomy of Eastern Galician Jewry,* 305.

14. *Dzień,* no. 43, 24 November 1919.

15. Ibid., no. 120, 19 February 1920; Aaron M. Margalith, *With Firmness in the Right: American Diplomatic Action Affecting Jews, 1840–1945* (New York: American Jewish Committee, 1946), 160–165.

16. AAN, dz. "Ambasada RP w Londynie," sygn. 1380, kk. 42–43; Levene, *War, Jews and the New Europe,* 292; *British Documents on Foreign Affairs,* part 2, series I, 3:204–205.

17. Mroczka, "Przyczynek do kwestii żydowskiej," 305–306. Also see Mark Levene, "Britain, a British Jew, and Jewish Relations with the New Poland: The Making of the Polish Minorities Treaty of 1919," *Polin: Studies in Polish Jewry* 8 (1994): 16–17.

18. *Ukrains'ke slovo,* no. 253, 3 November 1918; *Chwila,* no. 1, 10 January 1919; no. 4, 15 January 1919; *Gazeta Żydowska,* no. 4, 12 January 1919; Gelber, *National Autonomy of Eastern Galician Jewry,* 245, 247.

19. CAW, dz. "Inwentarz wycinków prasowych," sygn. 410.9.2, k. 2; *Vpered,* no. 51, 31 January 1919; no. 59, 11 February 1919; *Gazeta Żydowska,* no. 9, 17 January 1919; Mykhailo Lozyns'kyi, *Halyczyna w rr. 1918–1920* (Vienna: drukarnia J. N. Vernau, 1922), 90–91; Gelber, *National Autonomy of Eastern Galician Jewry,* 290–291; TsDAVO, f. 2188, o. 4, spr. 1, ark. 13.

20. Pogrebyns'ka i Gon, *Yevrei v Zakhidnoukrains'kii Narodnii Respublitsi,* 47, 50, 51.

21. CAW, dz. "Dowództwo WP na Galicję Wschodnią," sygn. I.304.1/12, k. 10; ibid., dz. "Dowództwo Frontu Galicyjskiego," sygn. I.310.1.31, kk. 28–29; ibid., dz. "Inwentarz wycinkow prasowych," sygn. 410.9.2, press clip from *Republika,* no. 4/39, 19 March 1919; *Gazeta Żydowska,* no. 9, 17 January 1919; no. 10, 18 January 1919; Michał Adamczyk, "Zachodnioukraińska Republika Ludowa, 1918–1919," in Zygmunt Mańkowski, ed., *Niepodległość Polski w 1918 roku a procesy państwowotwórcze w Europie Środkowo-wschodniej* (Lublin, Poland: Wydawnictwo Uniwersytetu Marii Curie-Skłodowskiej, 1966), 193–194; AAN, dz. "Prezydium Rady Ministrów," Rkt 10/t. 2, kk. 83–84, 227; TsDIAUL, f. 146, o. 8, spr. 3029, ark. 22–23, 60–61, 63, 68, 79, 82.

22. TsDAVO, f. 2192, o. 1, spr. 1, ark. 267; ibid., f. 2192, o. 1, spr. 2, ark. 203–205; ibid., f. 208, o. 1, spr. 46c, ark. 20; Stanisław Wiszniewski, *Brzeżany i kresy w wojnie ukraińsko-polskiej, 1918–1919* (L'viv, Ukraine: Wydawnictwo Biblioteki Kresowej, 1925), 95; *Chwila,* no. 7, 18 January 1919; Viktor Vorobets', "Pershi dni ukrains'koi derzhavnos'ti v Kolomyi," *Ukrains'kyi skytalets'* (February 1921), 10; LNB, f. "Komitet natsional'noi oborony," spr.

KNO-5, ark. 40; CAW, dz. "Dowództwo WP na Galicję Wshodnią," sygn. I.304.1.11, kk. 313, 430, 450, 454, 468; ibid., sygn. I.304.1.12, k. 1; Andrii Chaikovs'kyi, *Chorni riadky: moi spomyny za chas vid 1 listopada 1918 do 13 travnia 1919* (L'viv, Ukraine: vydavnytstvo kooperatyva "Chervona Kalyna, 1930), 20. Also see a list of Jewish casualties in the UHA roster *Zhalibna knyha: poimennyi spys polehlykh chleniv UHA u vyzvol'nii viini* (Zhovkva, Ukraine: n.p., n.d.).

23. Nachman G-r, "Peredistoriia ta istoriia zhydivs'koho proboyovoho kurinia I korpusu UHA," *Ukrains'kyi skytalets'* (February 1921): 18–21; Chaikovs'kyi, *Chorni riadky,* 110–111; Wiszniewski, *Brzeżany i kresy,* 112; Dashkevych, "Vzayemovidnosyny mizh ukrains'kym ta yevreis'kim naselenniam," 71–72; Vasyl' Volyts'kyi, "241 kurin' im. Petra Doroshenka," in *Kolomyja i Kolomyivshchyna,* 799; Stepan Sulyatyts'kyi, "Proboyovyi 'Hutsul'skyi kurin'," in *Kolomyja i Kolomyivshchyna,* 809.

24. CAW, dz. "Dowództwo WP na Galicję Wschodnią," sygn. I.304.1.11, k. 500; ibid., dz. "Dowództwo Frontu Galicyjskiego," sygn. 1.310.1.28, k. 948; Wiszniewski, *Brzeżany i kresy,* 69, 111; TsDIAUL, f. 146, o. 8, spr. 3025, ark. 1, 24–25; Chaikovs'kyi, *Chorni riadky,* 92.

25. CAW, dz. "Dowództwo WP na Galicję Wschodnią," sygn. I.304.1.11, k. 313; ibid., sygn. I.304.1.12, k. 2; ibid., sygn. I.304.1.63, n.p.; Wróbel, "Barucha Milcha wspomnienia wojenne," 96; LNB, f. "Komitet natsional'noi oborony," spr. KNO-5, ark. 43–44; *Chwila,* no. 86, 9 April 1919; no. 94, 17 April 1919; no. 136, 31 May 1919; no. 140, 4 June 1919; no. 148, 12 June 1919; no. 152, 16 June 1919; AAN, dz. "Kolekcja odpisów dokumentów," sygn. 58, k. 37; Wiszniewski, *Brzeżany i kresy,* 63, 86, 107, 110; Gelber, *National Autonomy of Eastern Galician Jewry,* 260–261; TsDAVO, f. 2188, o. 4, spr. 36, ark. 137–138; ibid., f. 2192, o. 1, spr. 1, ark. 184, 222; TsDIAUL, f. 146, o. 8, spr. 3029, ark. 1, 26–28, 72.

26. Gelber, *National Autonomy of Eastern Galician Jewry,* 257; *Vpered,* no. 64, 20 February 1919; CAW, dz. "Inwentarz wycinków prasowych," sygn. 410.9.2 (clip from *Republika,* 15 February 1919, part 12). The quotation in *Gazeta żydowska,* no. 10, 18 January 1919.

27. Joanna Michlic-Coren, "Anti-Jewish Violence in Poland, 1918–1939 and 1945–1947," *Polin: Studies in Polish Jewry* 13 (2000): 44; AAN, dz. "Kancelaria cywilna Naczelnika Państwa," sygn. 179, part 2, kk. 1, 10–23, 29, 37–38, 52–53, 97, 101–102; ibid., part 2, sygn. 181, k. 4; ibid., part 3, sygn. 181, kk. 2–5, 8, 10, 14–16, 37–38, 44–57; CAW, "Dowództwo WP na Galicję Wshodnią," sygn. I.304.1.63, n.p.; sygn. I. 304.1.11, kk. 301, 303, 427; sygn. I.304.1.67, kk. 76, 131, 364, 904; ibid., sygn. I.304.1.34, k. 14; *Pobudka,* no. 37, 12 December 1918; *Chwila,* no. 4, 15 January 1919; no. 5, 16 January 1919; no. 22, 5 February 1919; no. 29, 12 February 1919; *Gazeta Żydowska,* no. 2, 10 January 1919; DALO, f. 256, o. 1, spr. 5, ark. 14, 24–25; ibid., f. 271, o. 1, spr. 451, ark. 3–4.

28. TsDIAUL, f. 146, o. 8, spr. 3024, ark. 10; TsDAVO, f. 2192, o. 2, spr. 19, ark. 34; *Chwila,* no. 437, 1 April 1919; no. 259, 3 October 1919; *Pogromy, uchinennye belopoliakami (ofitsyal'nye dokumenty, obsledovaniia i svidetel'skie pokazaniia),* in *Materialy ob antiyevreiskikh pogromakh,* lst series: *Pogromy v Belorussii,* lst issue (Moscow: yevreiskii obshchestvennyi komitet po okazaniiu pomoshchi postradavshim ot pogromov i stikhiinykh bedstvii, 1922), 5, 52–54, 60–65, 68.

29. *Chwila,* no. 22, 5 February 1919; no. 23, 6 February 1919; TsDIAUL, f. 146, o. 8, spr. 3025, ark. 1–3, 5, 8, 10, 24–26; ibid., f. 212, o. 1, spr. 250, ark. 2–7; CAW, dz. "Dowództwo WP na Galicję Wschodnią" sygn. I.304.1.64, n.p.; ibid., sygn. I.304.1.63, kk. 213–214; ibid., sygn. I.304.1.63, n.p.; ibid., dz. "Front Galicyjski," sygn. I.310.1.28, k. 84; AAN, dz. "Ambasada RP w Paryżu," sygn. 301, kk. 44–48; Wróbel, "Barucha Milcha wspomnienia wojenne," 96–97; Lasocki, *Wspomnienia szefa administracji,* 151; Hupka, *Z czasów wielkiej wojny,* 420–421, 429; *Chwila,* no. 97, 21 April 1919; no. 98, 22 April 1919; no. 116, 11 May 1919; no. 134, 29 May 1919;

no. 136, 31 May 1919; no. 137, 1 June 1919; no. 139, 3 June 1919; no. 142, 6 June 1919; no. 144, 8 June 1919; no. 152, 16 June 1919; no. 169, 3 July 1919; no. 177, 11 July 1919; no. 271, 16 October 1919; Jerzy Tomaszewski, "Pinsk, 5 April 1919," *Polin* 1 (1986): 227–251; also Jerzy Tomaszewski, *Rzeczpospolita wielu narodów* (Warsaw: Czytelnik, 1985), 144–145; Jerzy Lewandowski, "History and Myth: Pinsk, April 1919," *Polin* 2 (1987): 55–56; Wiszniewski, *Brzeżany i kresy,* 69, 73, 75, 80–81; Sarunas Liekis, Lidia Miliakova, and Antony Polonsky, "Three Documents on Anti-Jewish Violence in the Eastern Kresy during the Polish-Soviet Conflict," *Polin: Studies in Polish Jewry* 14 (2001): 118.

30. Holzer and Molenda, *Polska w pierwszej wojnie światowej,* 102; Stankiewicz, *Konflikty społeczne,* 161–163; Zbigniew Landau and Jerzy Tomaszewski, *W dobie inflacji* (Warsaw: Książka i Wiedza, 1967), in *Gospodarka Polski międzywojennej, 1918–1939* (Warsaw: Zakład Najnowszej Historii Gospodarczej Polski), 1:60.

31. Landau and Tomaszewski, *W dobie inflacji,* 122; Wiszniewski, *Brzeżany i kresy w wojnie,* 185; Holzer and Molenda, *Polska w pierwszej wojnie światowej,* 102; CAW, dz. "Dowództwo Frontu Galicyjskiego," sygn. I.310.1.28, n.p.; ibid., sygn. I.310.1.27, kk. 136–141.

32. CAW, dz. "Dowództwo Frontu Galicyjskiego," sygn. I.310.1.26, kk. 76–77; ibid., sygn. I.310.1.31, kk. 26–27, 29; Łukomski, Partacz, and Polak, *Wojna polsko-ukraińska,* 220; TsDIAUL, f. 581, o. 1, spr. 139, ark. 26, 51; Leon Grosfeld, *Polskie reakcyjne formacje wojskowe w Rosji, 1917–1919* (Warsaw: Państwowe Wydawnictwo Naukowe, 1956), 171–175; *Pogromy, uchinennye belopoliakami,* 60–65, 68; Jerzy Tomaszewski, "Społeczność żydowska a Polacy w II Rzeczypospolitej," in *Polska-Polacy-Mniejszośi Narodowe* (Wrocław, Poland: Zakład Narodowy imienia Ossolińskich, 1992), 114.

33. Tomaszewski, "Polskie formacje zbrojne," 103–105; CAW, *Dziennik Rozporządzeń Komisji Wojskowej i Dziennik Rozkazów Wojskowych,* no. 1, 28 October 1918–no. 14, 30 December 1918; Liekis, Miliakova, and Polonsky, "Three Documents on Anti-Jewish Violence," 117.

34. Liekis, Miliakova, and Polonsky, "Three Documents on Anti-Jewish Violence," 121–149; *Chwila,* no. 179, 13 July 1919; no. 183, 17 July 1919; *British Documents on Foreign Affairs,* part 2, series 1, 3:212.

35. "Ekonomicheskoe polozhenie yevreyev v Pol'she," in *Yevreiskii vestnik: nauchno-literaturnyi sbornik* (Leningrad: obshchestvo rasprostraneniia prosveshcheniia miezhdu yevreiami, 1928), 197; TsDIAUL, f. 146, o. 8, spr. 3029, ark. 60–61; ibid., f. 212, o. 1, spr. 250, ark. 2–7; LNB, f. "Materialy viis'kovoi sektsii," spr. KNO-3, ark. 81; ibid., "Komitet natsional'noi oborony," spr. KNO-1, ark. 37; *Dzień,* no. 125, 25 February 1919; *Chwila,* no. 4, 15 January 1919; no. 23, 6 February 1919.

36. TsDIAUL, f. 212, o. 1, spr. 78, ark. 3; LNB, f. "Komitet natsional'noi oborony," spr. KNO-1, ark. 127, 156–158, 289–290; ibid., f. "Materialy viis'kovoi sektsii," spr. KNO-3, ark. 34–35, 81; *Chwila,* no. 83, 6 April 1919; no. 87, 10 April 1919; CAW, dz. "Dowództwo WP na Galicję Wschodnią," sygn. I.304.1.39, n.p.; ibid., sygn. 304.1.67, k. 904; ibid., sygn. I.304.1.12, k. 2; ibid., sygn. I.304.1.63, n.p.; ibid., sygn. I.304.1.34, n.p.

37. AAN, dz. "Prezydium Rady Ministrów," sygn. Rkt. 10/1, kk. 66; TsDIAUL, f. 146, o. 8, spr. 3025, ark. 5, 8; LNB, f. "Korespondentsiia /vhidna i vykhidna/," spr. KNO-2, ark. 26; *Chwila,* no. 151, 15 June 1919.

38. LNB, f. "Korespondentsiia /vhidna i vykhidna/," spr. KNO-2, ark. 19–21, 216, 218–219; TsDAVO, f. 2192, o. 2, spr. 6, ark. 179; ibid., f. 2188, o. 2, spr. 132, ark. 25; AAN, dz. "Prezydium Rady Ministrów," Rkt 10/t. 1, kk. 67, 135–136, 145, 150; ibid., Rkt 10/t. 2, kk. 78–79, 227–229; ibid., dz. "Ambasada RP w Londynie," sygn. 1380, kk. 18–20, 49; TsDIAUL, f. 146, o. 8, spr. 3024, ark. 3–5, 8; ibid., f. 146, o. 8, spr. 3025, ark. 5; ibid., f. 146, o. 8, spr. 3034,

ark. 10, 24; ibid., f. 146, o. 8, spr. 3124, ark. 1–2, 24, 27; ibid., f. 146, o. 8, spr. 4008, ark. 4; *Chwila,* no. 136, 31 May 1919; no. 151, 15 June 1919; no. 403, 27 February 1920; no. 455, 21 April 1920; CAW, dz. "Dowództwo Frontu Galicyjsko-Wołyńskiego," sygn. I.310.1.25, k. 546; *Dzień,* no. 2, 9 October 1919; SsSU, 103rd session, 25 November 1919, 37.

39. LNB, f. "Korespondentsiia /vkhidna i vykhidna/," spr. KON-2, ark. 19–20, 64, 216, 231; *Chwila,* no. 403, 27 February 1920.

40. Landau and Tomaszewski, *W dobie inflacji,* 154, 157, 161–164, 168; LNB, f. "Korespondentsiia /vkhidna i vykhidna/," spr. KON-2, ark. 64, 216, 231.

41. LNB, f. "Komitet natsional'noi oborony," spr. KON-2, ark. 46, 99, 231; TsDIAUL, f. 146, o. 8, spr. 3850, ark. 1–4; ibid., f. 146, o. 8, spr. 3144, ark. 35; ibid., f. 146, o. 8, spr. 3026, ark. 16–18, 23; ibid., f. 146, o. 8, spr. 3027, ark. 22–24, 30, 34, 73; *Chwila,* no. 376, 31 January 1920; no. 384, 8 February 1920; no. 385, 9 February 1920.

42. CAW, dz. "Dowództwo Frontu Galicyjskiego," sygn. I.310.1.30, n.p.; TsDIAUL, f. 146, o. 8, spr. 3851, ark. 1; *Chwila,* no. 365, 20 January 1920; no. 396, 20 February 1920; no. 397, 21 February 1920; no. 430, 25 March 1920; no. 437, 1 April 1920; no. 441, 7 April 1920; no. 484, 21 May 1920; Walicki, "Położenie Żydów polskich," 113–114.

43. TsDIAUL, f. 146, o. 8, spr. 3027, ark. 91; ibid., f. 146, o. 8, spr. 3822, ark. 3, 8; *Chwila,* no. 556, 2 August 1920; no. 573, 19 August 1920; *Inwazja Bolszewicka a Żydzi: zbiór dokumentów* (Warsaw: I. Hendler, 1921), 3–5, 17–54, 105, 107–108, 116–117, 123–127, 132–133, 182; *Pogromy, uchinennye belopoliakami,* 69–70; Norman Davies, *White Eagle, Red Star: The Polish-Soviet War, 1919–1920* (New York: St. Martin's Press, 1972), 151–152; Grzegorz Łukomski, Bogusław Polak, and Mieczysław Wrzosek, *Wojna polsko-bolszewicka, 1919–1920: działania bojowe-kalendarium* (Koszalin, Poland: Wyższa Szkoła Inżynierska w Koszalinie, 1990), 2:39–44; AAN, dz. "Ambasada RP w Paryżu," sygn. 301, kk. 50–51, 61–64; ibid., dz. "Ambasada RP w Berlinie," sygn. 3891, k. 17; Walicki, "Położenie Żydów polskich," 113–115; Tomaszewski, "Polskie formacje zbrojne," 102, 106.

44. André Gerrits, "Antisemitism and Anti-Communism: The Myth of 'Judeo-Communism' in Eastern Europe," *East European Jewish Affairs* 25, no. 1 (1995): 49–72; Jeff Schatz, *The Generation: The Rise and Fall of the Jewish Communists of Poland* (Berkeley and Los Angeles: University of California Press, 1991), 76–77; Jeffrey S. Kopstein and Jason Wittenberg, "Who Voted Communist? Reconsidering the Social Bases of Radicalism in Interwar Poland," *Slavic Review* 62, no. 1 (2003): 87–107.

45. DALO, f. 256, o. 1, spr. 74, ark. 7; Stankiewicz, *Konflikty społeczne,* 305–307; AAN, dz. "Towarzystwo Straży Kresowej, 1918–1927," sygn. 324, kk. 3–5.

46. Janusz Szczepański, *Społeczeństwo Polski w walce z najazdem bolszewickim 1920 roku* (Warsaw: Naczelna Dyrekcja Archiwów Państwowych, 2000), 228; Stankiewicz, *Konflikty społeczne,* 288–291, 303–304, 317–318; Landau and Tomaszewski, *W dobie inflacji,* 157.

47. Nina Zielińska, "Postawy mieszkańców Wołynia w czasie wojny polsko-bolszewickiej (na podstawie raportów Towarzystwa Straży Kresowej)," in Ryszard Kołodziejczyk, ed., *Społeczeństwo polskie w dobie I wojny światowej i wojny polsko-bolszewickiej 1920 roku* (Kielce, Poland: Kieleckie Towarzystwo Naukowe, 2001), 277–278; B. K. Johnpoll, *The Politics of Futility: The Central Jewish Workers Bund of Poland, 1917–1943* (Ithaca, NY: Cornell University Press, 1967), 92–95; Mendelsohn, *Zionism in Poland,* 148–153; Walicki, "Położenie Żydów," 116.

48. TsDIAUL, f. 146, o. 8, spr. 3857, ark. 9; ibid., f. 146, o. 8, spr. 3822, ark. 4; ibid., f. 146, o. 8, spr. 4878, ark. 20–20zv.; *Żydzi-Bolszewicy a Polska* (Warsaw: Włościanski Związek Oświaty, 1920); AAN, dz. "Ambasada RP w Berlinie," sygn. 3891, k. 17; *Chwila,* no. 538,

15 July 1920; no. 539, 16 July 1920; no. 540, 17 July 1920; no. 618, 6 October 1920; *Boj o Lwów,* 25; Tomaszewski, "Polskie formacje zbrojne," 101; *Inwazja bolszewicka a Żydzi,* 114–119; Walicki, "Położenie Żydów," 114–119.

49. DALO, f. 271, o. 1, spr. 451, ark. 7–8; TsDIAUL, f. 146, o. 8, spr. 4138, ark. 1–3; ibid., f. 146, o. 8, spr. 3799, ark. 11, 13–14, 43; ibid., f. 146, o. 8, spr. 3845, ark. 1, 19, 24–25; ibid., f. 146, o. 8, spr. 4001, ark. 1; ibid., f. 146, o. 8, spr. 3027, ark. 91; ibid., f. 146, o. 8, spr. 3144, ark. 1–3, 7; ibid., f. 146, o. 8, spr. 3822, ark. 2–3, 5–9, 11–12; *Kryvava knyha* (Vienna: vydannia Uriadu Zakhidno-Ukrains'koi Narodnoi Republiki, 1921), part 2, "Ukrains'ka Halychyna pid okupatsiyeiu Pol'shchi v rr. 1919–1920," 133; CAW, dz. "Dowództwo Frontu Galicyjskiego," sygn. I.310.1.66, n.p.; ibid., dz. "Dowództwo WP na Galicję Wschodnią," sygn. I.304.1.63, n.p.; Artur Leinwand, "Obrona Lwowa w 1920 roku," *Rocznik Lwowski* (1991), 26–27.

50. M. R. Lytvyn, "Nove pro diial'nis't' Halyts'kogo orhanizatsiinogo komitetu KP(b)U," *Ukrains'kyi istorychnyi zhurnal* 2/347 (1990): 127, 130; L. Nahorna, *Feliks Kon* (Kiev: Derzhavne vydavnytstvo politychnoi literatury, 1963), 83–84; Nykyfor Hirniak, *Ostatnii akt trahedii Ukrains'koi Halyts'koi Armii* (Perth Amboy, NJ: vydannia Ukrains'kogo Viis'kovo-Istorychnogo Instytutu v SShA, 1959), 234, 240–241.

51. DALO, f. 256, o. 1, spr. 37, ark. 21–37, 39–62, 66–83; ibid., f. 271, o. 1, spr. 34, ark. 1–4; TsDIAUL, f. 146, o. 8, spr. 4877, ark. 8, 30, 39, 42–43, 51–52.

52. Kopstein and Wittenberg, "Who Voted Communist?" 89.

53. TsDAVO, f. 2997, o. 1, spr. 106, ark. 1, 4; ibid., f. 2997, o. 1, spr. 143, ark. 1–3; ibid., f. 2997, o. 1, spr. 161, 2–5; ibid., f. 2997, o. 1, spr. 54, ark. 1; Wróbel, "Barucha Milcha wspomnienia," 98; *Chwila,* no. 565, 11 August 1920; no. 587, 2 September 1920; no. 603, 20 September 1920; no. 608, 26 September 1920; no. 621, 9 October 1920; *British Documents on Foreign Affairs,* part 2, series A, 4:104; RGVA, f. 245, o. 2, d. 92 (2,3), ll. 51, 103, 105, 107; ibid., f. 245, o. 1, spr. 29, l. 379; f. 245, o. 9, d. 2, l. 163; ibid., f. 245, o. 1, d. 12, ll. 131, 380. Also see Stephen Brown, "Communists and the Red Cavalry: The Political Education of the Konarmiia in the Russian Civil War, 1918–1920," *Slavonic and East European Review* 73 (1995): 85–86, 88.

54. Stankiewicz, *Konflikty społeczne,* 311.

55. *Chwila,* no. 602, 23 August 1920; no. 587, 2 September 1920; no. 592, 7 September 1920; no. 596, 11 September 1920; no. 599, 16 September 1920; no. 608, 26 September 1920; no. 621, 9 October 1920; no. 656, 13 November 1920; TsDIAUL, f. 146, o. 8, spr. 4129, ark. 1; ibid., f. 146, o. 8, spr. 3822, ark. 7–10; ibid., f. 146, o. 8, spr. 3851, ark. 1, 7, 10, 13–14; CAW, dz. "Dowództwo Frontu Galicyjsko-Wołyńskiego," sygn. I.301.22.2, k. 31; Walicki, "Położenie Żydów polskich," 115; Wróbel, "Barucha Milcha wspomnienia," 97; Deblessem, *Wspomnienia z prac i walk,* 88; Wiktor Dzierżykraj Stokalski, *Dzieje partyzantki z lat 1917–1920* (L'viv, Ukraine: nakładem autora, 1927), 19. Quotation in I. K. Rybalka, ed., *Grazhdanskaia voina na Ukraine, 1918–1920: sbornik dokumentov i materialov v trekh tomakh, chetyrekh knigakh* (Kiev: "Naukova Dumka," 1967), 3:479.

56. Wasiutyński, *Ludność żydowska,* 90–91; *Chwila,* no. 616, 4 October 1920; no. 730, 28 January 1921; no. 765, 4 March 1921; TsDIAUL, f. 146, o. 8, spr. 3822, ark. 3; ibid., f. 146, o. 8, spr. 3857, ark. 4–5, 8, 9; AAN, dz. "Ambasada RP w Paryżu," sygn. 301, k. 54.

57. Stephanie Laudyn, *A World Problem: Jews-Poland-Humanity* (Chicago: American Catalogue Printing Co., 1920).

58. *Chwila,* no. 698, 25 December 1920.

59. Szyja Bronstejn, *Ludność żydowska w Polsce w okresie międzywojennym: studium statystyczne* (Wrocław, Poland: Zakład Narodowy im. Ossolińskich, 1963), 71–73; Ignacy

Schiper, *Dzieje handlu żydowskiego na ziemiach polskich* (Warsaw: nakładem Centrali Związku Kupców, 1937), 593; Landau and Tomaszewski, *W dobie inflacji,* 58.

Conclusion

1. Norman Rufus C. Cohn, *Warrant for Genocide: The Myth of the Jewish World-Conspiracy and the "Protocols of the Elders of Zion"* (New York: Harper & Row, 1967), 16.

2. Panikos Panayi, "Dominant Societies and Minorities in the Two World Wars," in *Minorities in Wartime,* 6–15.

3. Henry Abramson, *A Prayer for the Government: Jews and Ukrainians in Revolutionary Times, 1917–1920* (Cambridge, MA: Harvard University Press, 1999).

4. See, for example, A. A. Goldenveiser, "Iz kievskikh vospominanii, 1917–1920," in S. A. Alekseev, ed., *Revolutsiia na Ukrainie po memuaram belykh* (Moscow: Gosudarstvennoye izdatel'stvo, 1930), 53–58.

5. CAW, dz. "Inwentarz kolekcji prasowych i archiwaliów prywatnych," sygn. I.440.12/8.231, kk. 52, 125.

Glossary of Foreign Words and Terms

cordon sanitaire	sanitary cordon
Dyrektoriia	Ukrainian national government during Russian civil war
Endeks	Polish National Democratic Party
francs-tireurs	enemy irregulars
Galizianer	Galician Jew
Galrevkom	Galician Revolutionary Council
gubernii	provinces
inorodtsy	non-Russians
Koło Polskie	Galician-Polish group in Austrian parliament
narodowść	ethnicity, nationality
numerus clausus	limited quota
odżydzenie	de-Judaization
odżydzić	de-Judaize
Okhrana	Russian secret political police
Ostjuden	German term for Jews who lived in Poland and Russia
ostraska	lesson
rzeczpospolita	commonwealth
Sejm	Polish parliament
shtetlach	Jewish settlement
sobstvenniki	private owners
Stavka	Russian General Headquarters
szlachta	Polish gentry
szumowiny	dregs (of society)
voevody	Russian military commanders

voiska	territory of Cossack troops
zasil'ye	foreign predominance
Żydowska Rada Narodowa(ŻRN)	Jewish National Council

Bibliography

Archival Sources

Archiwum Akt Nowych (AAN), Warsaw
    dział—Ambasada RP w Londynie
    d.—Centralna Agencja Polska w Lozannie
    d.—Kancelaria cywilna Naczelnika Państwa
    d.—Prezydium Rady Ministrów
    d.—Towarzystwo Straży Kresowej, 1918–1927
Archiwum Główny Akt Dawnich (AGAD), Warsaw
    d.—C.i.K: Ministerstwo Spraw Wewnętrznych /Ministerium des Innern/
    d.—Ministerstwo Sprawiedliwości
Biblioteka Narodowa (BN), Warsaw, Department of Microfilms
    d.—Biblioteka Ossolińskich
Centralne Archiwum Wojskowe (CAW), Warsaw
    d.—Dowództwo Frontu Galicyjskiego
    d.—Dowództwo Frontu Galicyjsko-Wołyńskiego
    d.—Dowództwo WP na Galicje Wshodnią
    Dziennik Rozporządzeń Komisji Wojskowej i Dziennik Rozkazów Wojskowych, October 1918–December 1918.
        d.—Front Galicyjski
        d.—Inwentarze kolekcji i materiałów drukowanych i archiwaliów prywatnych, 1918–1939
Derzhavnyi arkhiv L'vivs'koi oblasti (DALO), L'viv, Ukraine
    fond 1—L'vovskoe voevodskoe upravlenie. Presidial'nyi otdel i podotdel obshchestvennoi bezopasnosti
    f. 256—Dokumenty L'vovskogo voevodskogo upravleniia gosudarstvennoi politsii i drugikh vedomstv o bor'be s revolutsionnym dvizheniem
    f. 271—Dyrektsiia politsii u L'vovi
    f. 338—Kraevaia organizatsiia vseobshchikh sionistov vo L'vove, 1895–1902, 1940
    f. 350—Dyrektsiia departamentu politsii u L'vovi
    f. 905—Upravlinnia nacha'lnyka Brodivs'koho povitu
    f. 906—Upravlinnia Brods'kogo povitovoho komisara, m. Brody, 1917–1918

f. 907—Kantselariia L'vovskogo gubernatora

f. 908—Upravlenie nachal'nika Kolbushevskogo uyezda

Gosudarstvennyi arkhiv Rossiiskoi Federatsii (GARF), Moscow

f. 130—Biulleteni obzorov zarubezhnoi pressy

f. D2—O vyselenii iz Galitsii lits zapodozrennykh v zaniatiiakh voennym shpionstvom

f. 1800—Materialy po istorii voiny 1914–1917 gg.

f. 6281—Kollektsiia dokumentov otnosiashchikhsia k pervoi mirovoi voine

L'vivs'ka naukova biblioteka im. Vasyla Stefanyka Natsional'noi Akademii Nauk Ukrainy (LNB), L'viv, Ukraine, Department of Manuscripts

f. Komitet natsional'noi oborony

f. Materialy viis'kovoi sektsii

f. Korespondentsiia /vhidna i vykhidna/

Rossiiskii gosudarstvennyi voennyi arkhiv (RGVA), Moscow

f. 1—Upravlenie delami Narodnogo Komissariata po voennym delam

f. 245—Upravlenie 1-i Konnoi Armii

Rossiiskii gosudarstvennyi voenno-istoricheskii arkhiv (RGVIA), Moscow

f. 2003—Shtab verhovnogo glavnokomanduiushchego (*Stavka*)

f. 2005—Upravlenie grazhdanskoi kantselarii shtaba verkhovnogo glavnokomanduiushchego

f. 2116—Obshchii korpusnoi sud III armii

f. 2122—Stab 5-i armii

f. 13142—Shtab kreposti Peremyshl'

f. 13216—Upravlenie voennogo general-gubernatora oblastei Avstro-Vengrii, zaniatykh po pravu voiny

Rossiiskii tsentr khraneniia i izucheniia dokumentov noveishei istorii (RTsKhIDNI), Moscow

f. 17—Zasedaniia Politburo TsK RKP (Bol'shevikov)

f. 70–Tsentral'nyi Ispolnitel'nyi Komitet Kommunisticheskoi Partii (Bol'shevikov)

Tsentral'na naukova biblioteka Ukrainy im. V. I. Vernads'koho (TsNBU), Kiev, Department of Manuscripts

f. 339—An-Ski, S. A. /Rappoport, S. A/

f. XXI

f. XXIX

Tsentral'noe khranilishche istoriko-dokumental'nykh kollektsii (TsKhIDK), Moscow

f. 461—Ekspozitura II otdela General'nogo Shtaba

f. 476—Verkhovnoe komandovanie Voiska Pol'skogo

f. 1275—Dokumental'nye materialy sobrannye imperskim arkhivom v g. Potsdam (kollektsia): pervaia mirovaia voina

Tsentral'nyi derzhavnyi arkhiv vyshchykh orhaniv vlady i upravlinnia Ukrainy (TsDAVO), Kiev

f. 208—Materialy Nachal'noi Komandy Ukrains'koi Halyts'koi Armii

f. 2188—Nachal'naia komanda Galitskoi armii zapadnoi oblasti Ukrainskoi Narodnoi Respubliki, g. Chortkov

f. 2192—Dyktator Zakhidnoi Oblasti Ukrains'koi Narodnoi Respubliky, m. Chortkiv, m. Kam'yanets'-Podil's'k

f. 2992—Materialy pro Zakhidno-Ukrains'ku Narodnu Respubliku

f. 2997—Halyts'ka Nadzvychaina Komisiya po borot'bi z kontrevolutsiyeiu, spekulatsiyeiu ta zlovzhyvanniamy po sluzhbi, 1920

f. 3300—Moskovskoe yevreiskoe obshchestvo pomoshchi zhertvam voiny

Tsentral'nyi derzhavnyi istorychnyi arkhiv Ukrainy u Kyevi (TsDIAUK), Kiev

f. 361—Kantselariia voennogo general-gubernatora Galitsii

f. 363—Shtab voennogo general-gubernatora Galitsii

f. 365—Vremennoye zhandarmskoye upravlenie voennogo general-gubernatora Galitsii

f. 385—Odesskoye okhrannoye otdelenie

Tsentral'nyi derzhavnyi istorychnyi arkhiv Ukrainy u L'vovi (TsDIAUL), L'viv, Ukraine

f. 141—Dokumenty pro finansovo-mainovi spravy yevreis'koho naselennia na terytorii Rechi Pospolitoi i Halychyny

f. 146—Halyts'ke namisnytstvo, 1772–1921

f. 212—Pravliacha komisiia dla Halychyny, Teshyns'koi Sylezii i gorishnioi spravy ta spyzhu v m. L'vovi

f. 458—Derzhavna prokuratura m. L'viv

f. 581—Kolektsiia dokumentiv pro diial'nis't uriadiv i armii Ukrains'koi Narodnoi Respubliky ta Zakhidnoukrains'koi Narodnoi Respubliky, 1914–1939

f. 694—Materialy pro perebuvannia rosiis'kykh viis'k na terytorii Halychyny v period pershoi svitovoi viiny (kolektsiia), 1914–1919

Primary Sources

Aba, Lev. "Razgrom galitsiiskikh yevreiev v krovavye gody voiny: otryvok iz dnevnika." *Yevreiskaia letopis'* 3 (1924): 169–176.

Alekseev, S. A., ed. *Revolutsiia na Ukrainie po memuaram belykh.* Moscow: Gosudarstvennoye izdatel'stvo, 1930.

Alexinsky, Gregor. *Russia and the Great War.* London: T. Fischer Unwin, 1915.

American Jewish Committee. *American Jewish Year Book.* New York: American Jewish Committee and Jewish Publication Society of America, 1903, 1911.

———. *The Jews in the Eastern War Zone.* New York: American Jewish Committee, 1916.

Ansky, S. *The Enemy at His Pleasure: A Journey through the Jewish Pale of Settlement during World War I.* New York: Metropolitan Books, 2002.

Bandrowski, Jerzy. *W płomieniach: Lwów w lecie 1914.* Kiev: nakładem autora, 1917.

Belgorodskii, A. V. *Galitsiia—iskonnoe dostoyanie Rossii.* N.p.: izdatel'stvo tovarishchestva I. D. Syrins, 1914.

Bendow, Jozef. *Der Lemberger Judenpogrom /November 1918–Jänner 1919.* Vienna: M. Hickl-Verlag, 1919.

Białynia-Chołodecki, Józef. *Lwów w czasie okupacji rosyjskiej /3 września 1914–22 czerwca 1915/: z własnych przerzyć i spostrzezeń.* L'viv, Ukraine: nakładem redakcji, 1930.

———. *Lwów w listopadzie roku 1918.* L'viv, Ukraine: drukarnia Piller—Neumanna, 1919.

Bobrzyński, Michał. *Wskrzeszenie Państwa Polskiego: szkic historyczny.* 2 vols. Krakow: Krakowska Spółka Wydawnicza, 1920.

Bonch-Bruyevich, M. *Poteria Galitsii v 1915.* Part I. Moscow: 20-ya gosudarstvennaia tipografiia, 1920.

———. *Poteria nami Galitsyi.* Part 2. St. Petersburg: Izdanie voennoi tipografii GURKKA, 1926.

———. *Vsia vlast Sovetam!* Moscow: voyennoye izdatel'stvo Ministerstva Oborony, 1964.

Bourne, Kenneth, and D. Cameron Watt, eds. *British Documents on Foreign Affairs: Reports and Papers from the Foreign Office. Confidential Print.* Part 2, Series F. 67 vols. N.p.: University Publications of America, 1984–1997.

Brusilov, A. A. *Moi vospominaniia.* Moscow: voyennoye izdatel'stvo Ministerstva Oborony, 1963.

Bubnov, A. *V tsarskoi stavke: vospominaniia admirala Bubnova.* New York: izdatel'stvo imeni Chekhova, 1955.

Burchak, A. *Zavoevanie vostochnoi Galitsii.* Moscow: izdatel'stvo Sytina, 1914.

Chaikovs'kyi, Andrii. *Chorni riadky: moi spomyny za chas vid 1 listopada 1918 do 13 travnia 1919.* L'viv, Ukraine: vydavnytstvo kooperatyva "Chervona Kalyna," 1930.

Chłamtacz, Marzell. *Lembergs politische physionognomie während der russischen Invasion /3.IX 1914–22.VI. 1915/: Erinnerungen und Betrachtungen.* Vienna: Verlag von Rudolf Lechner & Sohn, 1916.

Chołoniewski, Antoni. *My, Żydzi i Kongres wobec zaburzeń galicyjskich.* Krakow: nakład Tow. im. Stefana Buszczyńskiego, 1919.

Chwalewik, Edward, and Stanisława Waroczewska, eds. *Księga tęczowa Polaków: zbiór dokumentów niedyplomatycznych od 8 sierpnia 1914 do 4 kwietnia 1915 r.* Warsaw: Drukarnia Naukowa, 1915.

Cybichowski, Sigmund. *Die Besetzung Lembergs im Kriege, 1914–1915: zugleich ein Beiträg zur Prinzipienlehre des internationalen Rechtes.* Munich: Verlag von Duncker & Humblot, 1916.

Czołowski, Aleksandr. *Mord rytualny: epizod z przeszłości Lwowa.* L'viv, Ukraine: nakładem autora, 1899.

Dąbski, Jan. *Wojna i ludzie: wspomnienia z lat 1914–1915 /fragmenty/.* Warsaw: Ludowa Spółdzielnia Wydawnicza, 1969.

Daniloff, Jurii. *Na puti k krusheniiu: ocherki iz poslednego perioda russkoi monarkhii.* Moscow: Voennoe izdatel'stvo, 1992.

———. *Russland im Weltkriege 1914–1915.* Jena, Germany: Fromanische Buchandlung "Walter Biedermann," 1925.

———. *Velikii Kniaz' Nikolai Nikolayevich.* Paris: Imprimerie de Navarre, 1930.

Deblessem, Antoni. *Wspomnienia z prac i walk o polskość Stanisławowa: ze specjalnym podkreśleniem akcji P.O.W. z czasów 1918–1920 r.* Zolochiv, Ukraine: nakładem autora, 1934.

Denikin, A. I. *Ocherki russkoi smuty: krushenie vlasti i armii, fevral'-sentiabr' 1917g.* Moscow: "Nauka," 1991.

———. *Put' russkogo ofitsera.* New York: izdatel'stvo imeni Chekhova, 1953.

Dmowski, Roman. *Polityka polska i odbudowanie państwa.* 2 vols. Warsaw: Instytut Wydawniczy Pax, 1988.

Doroshenko, Dmytro. *Moi spomyny pro nedavnie-mynule 1914–1917.* 2nd ed. 2 vols. Munich: Ukrains'ke vydavnytstvo, 1969.

Dubnov, S. M. *Kniga zhizni: vospominaniia i razmyshleniia, materialy dla istorii moego vremeni.* 3 vols. Riga, Latvia: "Jaunatnes Gramata," 1934–1951.

Dzierzbicki, Stanisław. *Pamiętnik z lat wojny 1915–1918.* Warsaw: Państwowy Instytut Wydawniczy, 1983.

Dzierżykraj Stokalski, Wiktor. *Dzieje partyzantki z lat 1917–1920.* L'viv, Ukraine: nakładem autora, 1927.

Dumin, Osyp. *Istoriia Lehionu Ukrains'kykh Sichovykh Stril'tsiv.* L'viv, Ukraine: Chervona Kalyna, 1936.

Farmborough, Florence. *Nurse at the Russian Front: A Diary, 1914–1918.* London: Constable and Company, 1974.

Feldman, Wilhelm. *Stronnictwa i programy polityczne w Galicyi, 1846–1906.* Krakow: Spółka Nakładowa "Książka," 1907.

Galitsiia, eya proshloye i nastoiashchee. Moscow: knigoizdatels'tvo "Chitatel'," 1914.

Galitsiia i Rossiia. Moscow: Moskovskoye pechatnoye proizvodstvo, 1914.

Gella, Jan. *Ruski miesiąc 1/XI-22/XI 1918: ilustrowany opis walk listopadowych we Lwowie.* L'viv, Ukraine: Instytut Literacki "Lektor," 1918.

Gessen, I. V., ed. *Archiv russkoii revolutsii.* 22 vols. Berlin: Slovo-Verlag, 1928.

Golovin, N. N. *Iz istorii kampanii 1914 goda na russkom fronte.* Prague: izdatel'stvo "Plamia," 1926.

Gosudarstvennaia Duma: stenographicheskie otchety, 1915–1916. St. Petersburg: Gosudarstvennaia tipografiia, 1915–1916.

Grulev, M. *Zapiski generala-yevreia.* Paris: n.p., 1930.

Halagan, Mykola. *Z moikh spomyniv.* 4 vols. L'viv, Ukraine: vydavnytstvo kooperatyva "Chervona Kalyna," 1930.

Haliczanin: kalendarz powszechny zastosowany do potrzeb wszystkich mieszkańców Galicji na rok pański 1918. L'viv, Ukraine: nakładem drukarni i litografii Piller-Neumanna, 1918.

Handbook of the Russian Army. London: Imperial War Museum, 1996.

Hausner, Artur W. *Listopad 1918 r.* L'viv, Ukraine: nakładem zarządu okręgowego związku pracowników kolejowych Polskiej Z. Z. K. we Lwowie, 1929.

Hornykiewicz, Theofil, ed. *Ereignisse in der Ukraine 1914–1922: deren Bedeutung und historische Hintergrűnde.* 4 vols. Horn, Austria: Verlag Ferdinand Berger, 1966.

Hupert, Witold. *Walki o Lwów /od 1 listopada 1918 do 1 maja 1919.* Warsaw: Księgarnia Wojskowa, 1933.

Hupka, Jan. *Z czasów wielkiej wojny: pamiętnik nie kombatanta.* L'viv, Ukraine: Księgarnia Gubrynowicz i Syn, 1937.

Hutsulak, Mykhailo. *Pershyi lystopad 1918 rok: zi spohadamy i zhyttiepysamy chleniv Komitetu vykonavtsiv lystopadovoho chynu.* New York: nakladom Komitetu vykonavtsiv lystopadovoho chynu, 1973.

Inster, Abraham. *Dokumenty fałszu: prawda o tragedii żydostwa lwowskiego w listopadzie 1918.* L'viv, Ukraine: nakładem drukarni Ignacego Jaegera, 1933.

Die Internationalen Beziehungen im Zeitalter des Imperialismus: Dokumente aus den Archiven der Zaristischen und Provizorischen Regierung. 11 Vols. Berlin: Verlag der Reimar Hobbing G.M.B.H., 1931–1936.

Inwazja Bolszewicka a Żydzi: zbiór dokumentów. Warsaw: I. Hendler, 1921.

Janusz, Bohdan. *Dokumenty urzędowe okupacji rosyjskiej Lwowa.* L'viv, Ukraine: nakładem wydawcy, 1916.

———. *293 dni rządów rosyjskich we Lwowie (3.IX.1914–22.VI.1915).* L'viv, Ukraine: Księgarnia Polska Bernarda Połonieckiego, 1915.

Die Juden im Kriege: Denkschrift des Jűdischen Sozialistischen Arbeiterverbandes Poale-Zion an das Internationale Sozialistische Bureau. The Hague: Zweite Erweiterte Auflage, 1917.

Kalinka, Waleryan. *Galicya i Kraków pod panowaniem austryackim.* Krakow: Spółka Wydawnicza Polska, 1898.

Kanan, I. *Polsko-yevreiskie otnosheniia (34-aia voina): sbornik statei.* St. Petersburg: izdatel'stvo "Vostok," 1915.

Kaplun-Kogan, W. *Der Krieg: Eine Schicksalsstunde des jűdischen Volkes.* Bonn: A. Marcus & E. Webers Verlag, 1915.

Khto pomahaye v Halychyni moskovs'komu ministrovi Stolypinovu? Promova posla d-ra Kyryla Tryl'ovoho vyholoshena v Derzhavnii Radi dnia 16 chervnia 1910 roku. Kolomyja, Ukraine: drukarnia A. B. Kysilevs'koho, 1910.

Kiselev, Vasilli. *Galichina i Moldaviia: putevye pis'ma.* Bridgeport, CT: Carpatho-Russian Literary Association, 1976.

Knox, Alfred. *With the Russian Army 1914–1917.* 2 vols. London: Hutchinson & Co., 1921.

Kolomyia i Kolomyivshchyna: zbirnyk spomyniv i statei pro nedavne mynule. Philadelphia: vydannia Komitetu Kolomyian, 1988.

Kominkowski, J. *Parę uwag w sprawie żydów.* Krakow: nakładem autora, 1868.

Krasnyi arkhiv. 10 vols. Berlin: Russkoye slovo, 1922.

Krevets'kyi, Ivan. "Ostgalizien und Russland." *Ukrainische Rundschau* 8, no. 1 (1910): 4–11.

Kruglov, P. G. *Gibel' Imperatorskoii Rossii.* Moscow: "Sovremennik," 1992.

Krysiak, Franciszek Salezy. *Z dni grozy we Lwowie /od 1–22 listopada 1918 r./* Krakow: G. Gebethner i Spółka, 1919.

Kryvava knyha. 2 Parts. Vienna: vydannia Uriadu Zakhidno-Ukrains'koi Narodnoi Respubliki, 1921.

Kś. M. *Pogadanka o socyaliźmie ("Latarnia" oświatlona).* Krakow: nakładem redakcji "Prawdy," 1903.

——. *Skąd się bierze niedowiarstwo między katolikami?* Nowy Sącz, Poland: nakładem i drukiem J. K. Jakubowskiego, 1900.

Kś. M. J. *Tajemnice żydowskie.* Krakow: nakładem autora, 1898.

Kuz'ma, Oleksa. *Lystopadowe dni 1918.* L'viv, Ukraine: nakładem autora, 1931.

Łapiński-Nilski, Stanisław and Aleksander Kron. *Listopad we Lwowie /1918 r./* Warsaw: nakładem Wydawnictwa "Rząd i Wojsko," 1920.

Lasocki, Zygmund. *Wspomnienia szefa administracji P. K. L. i K. Rz.* Krakow: nakładem autora, 1931.

Laudyn, Stephanie. *A World Problem: Jews-Poland-Humanity.* Chicago: American Catalogue Printing Co., 1920.

Lemke, Michael. *250 dnei v tsarskoi stavke /25 sent. 1915–2 iula 1916/.* St. Petersburg: Gosudarstvennoe izdatel'stvo, 1920.

Letters and Papers of Chaim Weizmann. 25 vols. London: Oxford University Press, 1968–1984.

Lipiński, Wacław. *Wsród lwowskich orląt.* Warsaw: Wojskowy Instytut Naukowo—Wydawniczy, 1931.

Listopad 1.–22.XI.1918 we Lwowie. L'viv, Ukraine: Zakład Narodowy imienia Ossolińskich we Lwowie, 1919.

Lozyns'kyi, M. "Zhydivs'ka sotsial'na demokratiia v Halychyni." *Literaturno-naukovy visnyk* 8, no. 32 (1905): 1–21.

Lwów po inwazji rosyjskiej, wrzesień-grudzień 1914: opowiadanie naocznego świadka. Vienna: nakładem Z. Machnowskiego, 1915.

Maciszewski, Stanisław. *Rosjanie we Lwowie: szkic z niedawnej przeszłości.* L'viv, Ukraine: Drukarnia Krajowa Szczęsnego Bednarskiego, 1926.

Mączyński, Czesław. *Boje Lwowskie.* Warsaw: nakładem Spółki Wydawnictwa Rzeczpospolita, 1921.

Markoff, Dimitri S. *Belgium of the East.* Wilkes-Barre, PA: Peter G. Kohaniuk, 1920.

Merunowicz, Teofil. *O metodzie i celach rozpraw nad kwestią żydowską.* L'viv, Ukraine: nakładem autora, 1879.

——. *Żydowscy radykaliści.* L'viv, Ukraine: nakładem wydawnictwa "Gazety Narodowej," 1893.

Metropolitan Evlogii. *Put' moyei zhizni: vospominaniia Mitropolita Evlogiia.* Paris: YMCA-Press, 1947.

Die Militärverwaltung in den von Österreich-Ungarischen Truppen besetzten Gebieten. New Haven, CT: Yale University Press, 1928.

Miliukov, P. N. *Political Memoirs, 1905–1917.* Ann Arbor, MI: University of Michigan Press, 1967.

Moriah: miesięcznik młodzierzy żydowskiej. Rocznik 12 (5677–1916/1917).

Müller-Meinungen, Ernst. *"Who are the Huns?" The Law of Nations and Its Breakers.* Berlin: Georg Reimer Publisher, 1915.

Niva: illustrirovannyj zhurnal literatury, politiki i sovremennoi zhizni no. 33, 16 August 1914.

Nossig, Alfred, ed. *Jüdische Statistik.* Berlin: "Verein für Jüdische Statistik," 1903.

Odezwy i rozporządzenia z czasów okupacji rosyjskiej Lwowa 1914–1915. L'viv, Ukraine: Księgarnia H. Altenberg, G. Seyfarth, E. Wende i Spólka, 1916.

Pares, Bernard. *Day by Day with the Russian Army 1914–1915.* London: Constable & Company, 1915.

Petrovych, Ivan. *Halychyna pid chas rosiis'koi okupatsii, serpen' 1914-cherven' 1915.* L'viv, Ukraine: "Politychna Biblioteka," 1915.

Pogromy, uchinennye belopoliakami (Ofitsyal'nye dokumenty, obsledovaniia i svidetel'skie pokazaniia.) In *Materialy ob antiyevreiskikh pogromakh,* 1st Series: *Pogromy v Belorussii,* 1st Issue. Moscow: Yevreiskii obshchestvennyi komitet po okazaniiu pomoshchi postradavshim ot pogromov i stikhiinykh bedstvii, 1922.

Polivanov, A. A. *Iz dnevnikov i vospominanii po dolzhnosti voennogo ministra i yego pomoshchnika 1907–1916 gg: memuary.* Moscow: Vyzshyi Voennyi Redaktsyonnyi Sovet, 1924.

Prawdomowny (Ks. S. Załeski). *Socyalistom naszym na kolęde: "Czerwony Sztandar."* Krakow: nakładem redakcji "Grzmotu," 1896.

Prilozhenie k stenographicheskim otchetam Gosudarstvennoi Dumy, 1915–1916. St. Petersburg: Gosudarstvennaia tipografiia, 1915–1916.

Przysiecki, Felix. *Rządy rosyjskie w Galicji Wschodniej.* Piotrków, Poland: wydawnictwo Wiadomości Polskich, 1915.

Razgrom avstriiskoi armii i vziatie L'vova. Moscow: tipografiia I. D. Sytina, 1915.

Reed, John. *The War in Eastern Europe.* New York: Charles Scribner's Sons, 1916.

Roja, Bolesław. *Legendy i fakty.* Warsaw: nakładem księgarni F. Hoesicka, 1931.

Rossowski, Stanisław. *Lwów pod czas inwazji.* L'viv, Ukraine: H. Altenberg, G. Seyfarth, E. Wende i SKA, 1917.

"Russische Wählarbeit in Galizien und der Bukowina." *Ukrainische Rundschau* 8, no. 1 (1910): 15–27.

Der russischer Nachrichtendienst an der Front Ob. Ost: nach der Erfahrungen der Geheimen Feldpolizei. N.p.: Oberbefehlshaber Ost, 1917.

Rybalka, I. K., ed. *Grazhdanskaia voina na Ukraine, 1918–1920: sbornik dokumentov i materialov v trekh tomakh, chetyrekh knigakh.* 3 vols. Kiev: Naukova Dumka, 1967.

Sands, Bedwin. *The Russians in Galicia.* New York: "Ukrainian National Council," 1916.

Seefeldt, Fritz. *So war es in Galizien: persönliche Erzählungen.* 2 vols. Eutin, Germany: Gesamtherstellung Struve's Buchdruckerei und Verlag OHG, 1933.

Serhiichuk, Volodymyr, ed. *Pohromy v Ukraini, 1914–1920: vid shtuchnykh stereotypiv do hirkoi pravdy prykhovuvanoi v radians'kykh arkhivakh.* Kiev: vydavnytstvo imeni Oleny Telihy, 1998.

Shavel'skii, Georgii. *Vospominaniia poslednego protopresvitera russkoii armii i flota.* 2 vols. New York: izdatel'stvo imeni Chekhova, 1954.

Shchegolev, P. E., ed. *Padenie tsarskogo rezhima: stenographicheskie otchety doprosov i pokazanii, dannykh v 1917 g. v Chrezvychainoi Sledstvennoi Komissii Vremennogo Pravitel'stva.* 7 vols. Leningrad: Gosudarstvennoe izdatel'stvo, 1925.

Sokolnicki, Michał, ed. *Polska w pamiętnikach wielkiej wojny, 1914–1918.* Warsaw: Instytut Wydawniczy "Biblioteka Polska," 1925.

Spiridovich, A. I. *Velikaia voina i fevral'skaia revolutsiia, 1914–1917* gg. 3 vols. New York: vseslavianskoe izdatel'stvo, 1960–1962.

Sprawozdania stenograficzne Sejmu Ustawodawczego. Warsaw: Druk Bogusławskiego, 1919–1920.

Spund, Simon. *Die Schreckenherrschaft der Russen in Stanislau: selbsterlebte Schilderungen.* Budweis, Czech Republic: Selbverlag, 1915.

Stepankovsky, Vladimir. *The Russian Plot to Seize Galicia /Austrian Ruthenia/.* Jersey City, NJ: Ukrainian National Council, 1915.

Szczepanowski, Stanisław. *Nędza Galicyi w cyfrach: program energicznego rozwoju gospodarstwa krajowego.* L'viv, Ukraine: Gubrynowicz i Schmidt, 1888.

Tăslăuanu, Octavian C. *With the Austrian Army in Galicia.* London: Skeffington & Son, n.d.

Theilhaber, Felix A. *Die Juden im Weltkriege: mit besonderer Berüchsichtigung der Verhältnisse für Deutschland.* Berlin: Welt-Verlag, 1916.

Tomashivs'kyi, Stephan. *Die weltpolitische Bedeutung Galiziens.* Munich: F. Brückmann A. G., 1915.

Voennye prestupleniia Gabsburgskoi monarkhii: Galitskaia Golgofa. Trumbull, CT: Peter S. Hardy, 1964.

Voina i yevrei. St. Petersburg: n.p., 1912.

Wagner, Marian E. *Lwowski chłopaka na wojnach: strzępy wspomnień z walecznych lat 1918–1921.* N.p, n.d.

Waniorek, Jarosław, ed. *Obrona Lwowa, 1–22 listopada 1918.* 2 vols. Warsaw: oficyna wydawnicza Volumen, 1991–1993.

Wiszniewski, Stanisław. *Brzeżany i kresy w wojnie ukraińsko-polskiej, 1918–1919.* L'viv, Ukraine: wydawnictwo Biblioteki Kresowej, 1925.

Zavoevanie vostochnoi Galitsii. Moscow: izdatel'stvo Sytina, 1914.

Zhalibna knyha: poimennyi spys polehlykh chleniv UHA u vyzvol'nii viini. Zhovkva, Ukraine: N.p., n.d.

Newspapers

Armeiskii vestnik, Kiev, 1914–1917.

Borot'ba, Kiev, 1919.

Chwila, Lwów, 1919–1921.

Dzień, Krakow, 1919.

Dziennik Polski, Lwów, 1915.

Gazeta Poranna, Lwów, 1918.

Gazeta Żydowska, Krakow, 1919.

Głos Narodu, Krakow, 1914–1920.

Grzmot, Lwów-Krakow, 1892, 1896–1898.

Jednośċ (Organ Żydów Polskich), Warsaw, 1911.

Jüdische Rundschau: Allgemeine Jüdische Zeitung, Vienna, 1915–1917.

Kievskaia mysl', Kiev, 1918.

Kurjer Stanisławowski, Stanisławów, 1918.

L'vovskii vestnik, Lwów, 1915.

L'vovskoe voennoie slovo, Lwów, 1914–1915.

Neue Lemberger Zeitung, Lwów, 1918.

Nova Rada, Kiev, 1917–1918.

Novyi krai, Lwów-Tarnopol, 1915.

Nowy Dziennik, Krakow, 1918.

Pobudka: organ Komitetu Obywatelskiego VI-go okręgu m. Lwowa, Lwów, 1918.

Pravitel'stvennyi vestnik, St. Petersburg, 1914.

Prikarpatskaia Rus', Lwów, 1914–1915.

Russkoe znamia, St. Petersburg, 1915.
Słowo Polskie, Lwów, 1914.
Ukrainische Nachrichten: Mitteilungen des Bundes zur Befreiung der Ukraina, Vienna, 1914–1915.
Ukrainskaia zhyzn', Moscow, 1914–1915.
Ukrains'ke slovo, Tarnopol, 1918.
Vpered, Lwów, 1919.
Die Wahrheit: unabhängige Zeitschrift für jüdische Interessen, Vienna, 1915.
Zjednoczenie: pismo poświęcone idei zespolenia Żydów z narodem polskim, Lwów, 1918.
Żołnierz Polski, Warsaw, 1919.

Secondary Sources

Abramsky, Chimen. "Lucien Wolf's Efforts for the Jewish Communities in Central and Eastern Europe." *Jewish Historical Studies: Transactions of the Jewish Historical Society of England 29* (1982–1986): 281–295.
Abramson, Henry. *A Prayer for the Government: Jews and Ukrainians in Revolutionary Times, 1917–1920.* Cambridge, MA: Harvard University Press, 1999.
Achiezer, A. "Antisemitizm v Rossii: vzgliad kulturologa." *Vestnik yevreiskogo universiteta v Moskve* 1 (1992): 98–128.
Almanach i leksykon żydostwa polskiego. L'viv, Ukraine: nakładem Hermana Dikera, 1937.
Altshuler, M. "Russia and Her Jews: The Impact of the 1914 War." *Wiener Library Bulletin* 27:30–31 (1973–1974): 12–16.
Andlauer, Teresa. *Die jüdische Bevölkerung im Modernisierungsprozess Galiziens (1867–1914).* Frankfurt am Main: Peter Lang GmbH, 2001.
Arendt, Hannah. *On Violence.* New York: Harcourt Brace, 1970.
Arski, Stefan. "Działalność polskich organizacji w Galicji w świetle korespondencji dyplomatychnej z okresu 1906–1912." *Sprawy Międzynarodowe* 13, no. 10/103 (1960): 53–66.
——. "Rozmowy z wywiadem austriackim przed pierwszą wojną światową." *Sprawy Międzynarodowe* 12, no. 11–12/92–93 (1959): 68–77; 13, no. 3/96 (1960): 67–94.
Bachmann, Klaus. "Kriegsgrund Galizien: Der ostgalizische Nationalkonflikt und seine aussenpolitischen Auswirkungen vor dem Ersten Weltkrieg." *Österreichische Osthefte* 32 (1990): 40–68.
Bailly, Rosa. *A City Fights for Freedom: The Rising of Lwów in 1918–1919.* London: Publishing Committee Leopolis, 1956.
Bakhturina, A. Iu. *Politika Rossiiskoi imperii v vostochnoi Galitsii v gody pervoi mirovoi voiny.* Moscow: AIRO-XX, 2000.
Baren, Karen, and Mark von Hagen, eds. *After Empire. Multiethnic Societies and Nation-Building: The Soviet Union and the Russian, Ottoman, and Habsburg Empires.* Boulder, CO: Westview Press, 1997.
Barkan, Steven E., and Lynn L. Snowden. *Collective Violence.* Needham Heights, MA: Allyn & Bacon, 2001.
Baron, Salo W. *The Russian Jew under the Tsars and Soviets.* New York: Schocken Books, 1987.
Berkowitz, Leonard, and James A. Green. "The 'Stimulus Qualities' of the Scapegoat." *Journal of Abnormal and Social Psychology* 64, no. 4 (1962): 293–301.
Bestuzhev, I. V. *Bor'ba Rossii po voprosam vneshnei politiki, 1906–1910.* Moscow: izdatel'stvo Akademii Nauk SSSR, 1961.

Beyrau, Dietrich. *Militär und Gesellschaft im vorrevolutionären Russland.* Cologne: Böhlau Verlag, 1984.

Bieberstein, Johannes Rogala. *Die These von der Verschwörung, 1776–1945: Philosophen, Freimaurer, Juden, Liberale und Sozialisten als Verschwörer gegen die Sozialordnung.* Frankfurt am Main: Peter Lang GmbH, 1976.

Blicharski, Czesław. *Tarnopol w latach 1809–1945 /od periodu epopei napoleońskiej do wypędzenia.* Biskupice, Poland: N.p., 1993.

Breysach, B., et al., eds. *Ze sobą, obok siebie, przeciwko siebie: polacy, żydzi, austriacy, niemcy w XIX i na początku XX w.* Krakow: wydawnictwo "Znak," 1995.

Bronstejn, Szyja. *Ludność żydowska w Polsce w okresie międzywojennym: studium statystyczne.* Wrocław, Poland: Zakład Narodowy im. Ossolińskich, 1963.

Bross, Jacob. "The Beginning of the Jewish Labor Movement in Galicia." *YIVO Annual of Jewish Social Science* 5 (1950): 55–84.

Brown, Stephen. "Communists and the Red Cavalry: The Political Education of the Konarmiia in the Russian Civil War, 1918–1920." *Slavonic and East European Review* 73 (1995): 82–99.

Brubaker, Rogers. "Nationalizing States in the Old 'New Europe'—and the New." *Ethnic and Racial Studies* 19, no. 2 (1996): 411–437.

Burke, Eldon Ray. "Polish Policy of the Central Powers during the World War." PhD diss., University of Chicago, 1936.

Buszko, Józef. *Galicja 1859–1914: polski Piemont?* Warsaw: Krajowa Agencja Wydawnicza, 1989.

Chernavin, V. V. "Gibel' kadrovykh russkikh ofitserov." *Voenno-istoricheskii zhurnal* 5 (1999): 85–93.

Chłopecki, Jerzy, and Helena Madurowicz-Urbańska, eds. *Galicja i jej dziedzictwo.* 8 vols. Rzeszów, Poland: wydawnictwo Szkoły Pedagogicznej, 1995.

Ciołkosz, Adam. "Dzielnica żydowska obozu w Jabłonnie." *Zeszyty Historyczne* 20 (1971): 178–200.

Coetzee, Frantz, and Marylin Shevin-Coetzee, eds. *Authority, Identity, and the Social History of the Great War.* Providence, RI: Berg, 1995.

Cohen, Israel. "My Mission to Poland (1918–1919)." *Jewish Social Studies* 13 (1951): 149–172.

Cohn, Norman Rufus C. *Warrant for Genocide: The Myth of the Jewish World-Conspiracy and the "Protocols of the Elders of Zion."* New York: Harper & Row, 1967.

Dąbkowski, Tadeusz. *Ukraiński ruch narodowy w Galicji Wschodniej, 1912–1923.* Warsaw: Instytut Krajów Socyalistycznych PAN, 1985.

Dallin, Alexander, et al., eds. *Russian Diplomacy and Eastern Europe, 1914–1917.* New York: King's Crown Press, 1963.

Dashkevych, Ya. R. "Vzayemovidnosyny mizh ukrains'kym ta yevreis'kym naselenniam u Skhidnii Halychyni [kinets' XIX-pochatok XX st.]." *Ukrains'kyi istorychnyi zhurnal* 10 (1990): 63–72.

Davies, Norman. "Great Britain and the Polish Jews, 1918–1920." *Journal of Contemporary History* 8, no. 2 (1973): 119–142.

———. *White Eagle, Red Star: The Polish-Soviet War, 1919–1920.* New York: St. Martin's Press, 1972.

Debreczeny, Paul, ed. *American Contribution to the Ninth International Congress of Slavists, Kiev, September 1983.* 2 vols. Columbus, OH: Slavica Publishers, 1983.

Dubanowicz, Edward. *Stanowisko ludności żydowskiej w Galicji wobec wyborów do parlamentu wiedeńskiego w r. 1907.* L'viv, Ukraine: Drukarnia "Polonia," 1970.

Duker, Abraham G. "Jews in the World War: A Brief Historical Sketch." *Contemporary Jewish Record: A Review of Events and a Digest of Opinion* 2, no. 5 (1939): 6–21.

Eisenbach, Artur. "Emancypacja Żydów w dobie rewolucji 1846–49." *Biuletyn Żydowskiego Instytutu Historycznego* 1/141 (1987): 39–54.

Flockerzie, Lawrence J. "Poland's Louvain: Documents of the Destruction of Kalisz, August 1914." *Polish Review* 28, no. 4 (1983): 73–87.

Frankel, Jonathan. "The Paradoxical Politics of Marginality: Thoughts on the Jewish Situation during the Years 1914–1921." *Studies in Contemporary Jewry* 4 (1988): 3–21.

Franko, Ivan. *Opovidannia ta povisti.* Kiev: derzhavne vydavnytsvo khudozhnioi literatury, 1963.

Fuks, Marian. "Żydzi w zaraniu niepodległości Polski." *Biuletyn Żydowskiego Instytutu Historycznego* 2/150 (1989): 35–44.

Gatrell, Peter. *A Whole Empire Is Walking: Refugees in Russia during World War I.* Bloomington, IN: Indiana University Press, 1999.

Gelber, Michael Nahum. *History of Polish Jewry during the Revival of Poland.* New York: Shengold Publishers, 1990.

Gerrits, André. "Antisemitism and Anti-Communism: The Myth of 'Judeo-Communism' in Eastern Europe," *East European Jewish Affairs* 25, no. 1 (1995): 49–72.

Gliksman, William M. *In the Mirror of Literature: The Economic Life of the Jews in Poland as Reflected in Yiddish Literature, 1914–1939.* New York: Living Books, 1966.

Golczewski, Frank. *Polnisch-Jüdische Beziehungen, 1881–1922: eine Studie zur Geschichte des Antisemitismus in Osteuropa.* Wiesbaden, Germany: Franz Steiner Verlag GMBH, 1981.

Golovin, N. N. *The Russian Army in the World War.* New Haven: Yale University Press, 1981.

———. *Voennye usiliia Rossii v mirovoi voine.* 2 vols. Paris: Tovarishchestvo obyedinennykh izdatelei, 1939.

Gon, M. "Yevreis'ki politychni partii na Zakhidnii Ukraiini, 1918–1929." Candidate of Historical Sciences diss., Kiev State University, 1998.

G-r, Nachman. "Peredistoriia ta istoriia zhydivs'koho proboyovoho kurinia I korpusu UHA." *Ukrains'kyi skytalets'* (February 1921): 14–23.

Grabets, Myroslav. *K istorii Marmaroshskogo protsessa (delo 94-kh: 29/XII 1913–3/III 1914).* Uzhhorod, Ukraine: izdanie Karpatorusskoi Trudovoii Partii, 1934.

Graf, Daniel W. "Military Rule behind the Russian Front, 1914–1917: The Political Ramifications." *Jahrbücher für Geschichte Osteuropas* 22, no. 3 (1974): 396–411.

———. "The Rule of the Generals: Military Government in Western Russia, 1914–1915." PhD diss., University of Nebraska, Lincoln, 1972.

Greenspoon, Leonard, ed. *Yiddish Language and Culture: Then and Now.* Omaha, NE: Creighton University Press, 1997.

Gronsky, Paul P. *The War and the Russian Government.* New Haven, CT: Yale University Press, 1929.

Grossfeld, Leon. *Polityka państw centralnych wobec sprawy polskiej w latach pierwszej wojny światowej, 1914–1918.* Warsaw: Państwowe Wydawnictwo Naukowe, 1962.

———. *Polskie reakcyjne formacje wojskowe w Rosji, 1917–1919.* Warsaw: Państwowe Wydawnictwo Naukowe, 1956.

Haberer, Erich. *Jews and Revolution in the Nineteenth-Century Russia.* Cambridge: Cambridge University Press, 1995.

Halpern, Leopold. "Polityka żydowska w Sejmie i Senacie Rzeczypospolitej Polskiej, 1919–1933." *Sprawy Narodowościowe* 7, no. 1 (1933): 3–45.

Herwig, Holger H. *The First World War: Germany and Austria-Hungary, 1914–1918.* New York: St. Martin's Press, 1997.

Hirniak, Nykyfor. *Ostatnii akt trahedii Ukrains'koi Halyts'koi Armii.* Perth Amboy, NJ: vydannia Ukrains'koho Viis'kovo-Istorychnogo Instytutu v SShA, 1959.

Hödl, Klaus. *Als Bettler im Leopoldstadt: Galizische Juden auf dem Weg nach Wien.* Vienna: Bohlau Verlag, 1994.

Holzer, Jerzy, and Jan Molenda. *Polska w pierwszej wojnie światowej.* Warsaw: Wiedza Powszechna, 1963.

Horn, Elżbieta. "Posłowie żydowscy i problem żydowski w galicyjskim sejmie krajowym w 1861 r." *Biuletyn Żydowskiego Instytutu Historycznego* 1/149, part 1(1989): 25–42; 4/152, part 2 (1989): 33–58.

Horowitz, Donald L. *The Deadly Ethnic Riot.* Berkeley and Los Angeles: University of California Press, 2001.

Ingenhorst, Heinz. *Die Russlanddeutschen: Aussiedler zwischen Tradition und Moderne.* Frankfurt: Campus Verlag, 1997.

Isaevych, Yarosalv, Feodosii Steblii, and Mykola Lytvyn, eds. *L'viv: istorychni narysy.* L'viv, Ukraine: Instytut Ukrainoznavstva im I. Krypyakevycha NAN Ukrainy, 1996.

"Iz chernoii knigi rossiiskogo yevreistva: materialy dla istorii voiny 1914–1915." *Yevreiskaia starina* 10 (1918): 195–296.

Jeziorny, Dariusz. "Sprawa ochrony praw mniejszości żydowskiej w Polsce w dobie konferencji pokojowej w Paryżu w 1919 roku." In Pawel Samuś, ed., *Z dziejów Drugiej Rzeczypospolitej,* series *Acta Universitatis Lodziensis* 54 (1995): 37–61.

Johnpoll, B. K. *The Politics of Futility: The Central Jewish Workers Bund of Poland, 1917–1943.* Ithaca, NY: Cornell University Press, 1967.

Kalinka, Waleryan. *Galicya i Kraków pod panowaniem austriackiem.* Krakow: Spółka Wydawnicza Polska, 1898.

Kavtaradze, A. "Iiun'skoe nastuplenie russkoi armii v 1917." *Voenno-istoricheskii zhurnal* 5 (1967): 111–117.

Kenez, Peter. "A Profile of the Pre-revolutionary Officer Corps." *California Slavic Studies* 7 (1973): 121–158.

Kestler, Stefan. *Die deutsche Auslandsaufklärung und das Bild der Ententemächte im Spiegel zeitgenössischer Propagandaveröffentlichungen während des Ersten Weltkrieges.* Frankfurt am Main: Peter Lang, 1994.

Kiryk, Feliks, ed. *Żydzi w Małopolsce: studia z dziejów osadnictwa i życia społecznego.* Przemyśl, Poland: Południowo-Wschodni Instytut Naukowy w Przemyślu, 1991.

Kiselinovski, Stojan. *Grchkata kolonizatsija vo egeiska Makedonja,* 1913–1940. Skopje, Macedonia: Institut za natsionalna istoria, 1981.

Klembovskii, V. "Organizatsiia voennogo shpionstva v Avstrii vo vremia voiny 1914–1918." *Voenno-istoricheskii sbornik: trudy voenno-istoricheskoi komissii* 4 (1920): 85–97.

Klier, John D. *Imperial Russia's Jewish Question, 1855–1881.* Cambridge: Cambridge University Press, 1995.

———. *Russia Gathers Her Jews: The Origins of the "Jewish Question" in Russia, 1772–1825.* DeKalb: Northern Illinois University Press, 1986.

Klier, John D., and Shlomo Lambroza, eds. *Pogroms: Anti-Jewish Violence in Modern Russian History.* Cambridge: Cambridge University Press, 1992.

Kołodziejczyk, Ryszard, ed. *Społeczeństwo polskie w dobie I wojny światowej i wojny polsko-bolszewickiej 1920 roku.* Kielce, Poland: Kieleckie Towarzystwo Naukowe, 2001.

Konieczny, Zdzisław. *Walki polsko-ukraińskie w Przemyślu i okolicy: listopad-grudzień 1918.* Przemyśl, Poland: spółdzielnia inwalidów "Praca" w Przemyślu, 1993.

Kopstein, Jeffrey S., and Jason Wittenberg. "Who Voted Communist? Reconsidering the Social Bases of Radicalism in Interwar Poland." *Slavic Review* 62, no. 1 (2003): 87–107.

Korkis, Abraham. "Die wirtschaftliche Lage der Juden in Galizien." *Der Jude: Eine Monatschrift* 2 (1917–1918): 464–471.

Korotkii, E., B. Kun, and O. Piatnitskii. *Pervyi Kongress Kominterna: mart 1919 g.* Moscow: partiinoe izdatel'stvo, 1933.

Kozik, Jan. *The Ukrainian National Movement in Galicia: 1815–1847.* Edmonton: Canadian Institute of Ukrainian Studies of Alberta, 1986.

Kozłowski, Maciej. *Zapomniana wojna: walki o Lwów i Galicję Wshodnią, 1918–1919.* Bydgoszcz, Poland: Instytut Wydawniczy "Świadectwo," 1999.

Kramarz, Henryka. "Lwów i jego samorząd w chwili wybuchu wielkiej wojny." *Studia Historyczne* 35, 2/137 (1992): 189–203.

———. *Samorząd Lwowa w czasie pierwszej wojny światowej i jego rola w życiu miasta.* Krakow: Wydawnictwo Naukowe WSP, 1994.

Kreppel, J. *Juden und Judentum von Heute.* Zürich: Amalthea-Verlag, 1925.

Kryp'yakevych, Ivan. *Istorychni prokhody po L'vovi.* L'viv, Ukraine: nakladem Tovarystva "Prosvita" u L'vovi, 1932.

Kudela, Jiri. "Die Emigration galizischer und osteuropäischen Juden nach Böchmen und Prag zwischen 1914–1916/17." *Studia Rosenthaliana* 23, no. 2 (1989): 119–134.

Kutschabsky, W. *Die Westukraine im Kämpfe mit Polen und dem Bolschewismus in den Jahren 1918–1923.* Berlin: Junker und Dűnnhaupt Verlag, 1934.

Landau, Zbigniew, and Jerzy Tomaszewski. *W dobie inflacji.* Warsaw: Książka i Wiedza, 1967. Vol. 1 of *Gospodarka Polski międzywojennej, 1918–1939.* Warsaw: Zakład Najnowszej Historii Gospodarczej Polski.

Lechicki, Czesław. "Z dziejów prasy galicyjskiej na przełomie dwoch wieków /'Ruch Katolicki'-'Przedświt'/." *Studia Historyczne* 14, 2/53 (1971): 161–189.

Leinwand, Artur. "Obrona Lwowa w 1920 roku." *Rocznik Lwowski* (1991): 25–33.

Leszczyński, Jan. *Rządy rosyjskie w kraju tarnopolskim, 1809–1815.* Krakow: Druk W. L. Anczyca i Spółki, 1903.

Levene, Mark. "Britain, a British Jew, and Jewish Relations with the New Poland: The Making of the Polish Minorities Treaty of 1919." *Polin: Studies in Polish Jewry* 8 (1994): 14–41.

———. *Wars, Jews, and the New Europe: The Diplomacy of Lucien Wolf, 1914–1919.* Oxford: Oxford University Press, 1992.

Lewandowski, Jerzy. "History and Myth: Pinsk, April 1919." *Polin: Studies in Polish Jewry* 2 (1987): 50–72.

Liekis, Sarunas, Lidia Miliakova, and Antony Polonsky. "Three Documents on Anti-Jewish Violence in the Eastern Kresy during the Polish-Soviet Conflict." *Polin: Studies in Polish Jewry* 14 (2001): 116–149.

Lindemann, Albert S. *The Jew Accused: Three Anti-Semitic Affairs (Dreyfus, Beilis, Frank), 1894–1915.* New York: Cambridge University Press, 1991.

Liulevicius, Vejas. *War Land on the Eastern Front: Culture, National Identity and German Occupation in World War I.* Cambridge: Cambridge University Press, 2000.

Lohr, Eric. *Nationalizing the Russian Empire: The Campaign against Enemy Aliens during World War I.* Cambridge, MA: Harvard University Press, 2003.

———. "The Russian Army and the Jews: Mass Deportation, Hostages, and Violence during World War I." *Russian Review* 60 (2001): 404–419.

Löwe, Heinz-Dietrich. *Antisemitismus und reaktionäre Utopie: Russischer Konservatismus im Kampf gegen den Wandel von Staat und Geselschaft, 1890–1917.* Hamburg: Hoffman und Campe Verlag, 1978.

Lozyns'kyi, Mykhailo. *Halychyna v rr. 1918–1920.* New York: vydavnytstvo "Chervona Kalyna," 1970.

———. *Halyczyna w rr. 1918–1920.* Vienna: Drukarnia J. N. Vernau, 1922.

Łukomski, Grzegorz, Czesław Partacz, and Bogusław Polak. *Wojna polsko-ukraińska, 1918–1919: działania bojowe-aspekty polityczne-kalendarium.* Koszalin, Poland: Wydawnictwo Uczelniane Wyższej Szkoły Inżynierskiej w Koszalinie, 1994.

Łukomski, Grzegorz, Bogusław Polak, and Mieczysław Wrzosek. *Wojna polsko—bolszewicka, 1919–1920: działania bojowe-kalendarium.* 2 vols. Koszalin, Poland: Wyższa Szkoła Inżynierska w Koszalinie, 1990.

Lundgreen-Nielsen, K. *The Polish Problem at the Paris Peace Conference: A Study of Politics of the Great Powers and the Poles, 1918–1919.* Odense, Denmark: Odense University Press, 1979.

Lutman, Tadeusz. *Studja nad dziejami handlu Brodów w latach 1773–1880.* L'viv, Ukraine: Zakład Narodowy im. Ossolińskich, 1937.

Lysiak-Rudnyts'kyi, Ivan. *Istorychni ese.* 2 vols. Kiev: "Osnovy," 1994.

Lytvyn, M. R., and K. E. Naumenko. *Istoriia ZUNR.* L'viv, Ukraine: Instytut ukrainoznavstva HAH Ukrainy, 1995.

Lytvyn, M. R. "Nove pro diial'nis't' Halyts'kogo orhanizatsiinogo komitetu KP(b)U." *Ukrains'kyi istorychnyi zhurnal* 2, no. 347 (1990): 126–130.

Mack, Karl-Heinz, ed. *Galizien um die Jahrhundertwende: politische, soziale und kulturelle Verbindungen mit Österreich.* Munich: Verlag für Geschichte und Politik, 1990.

Magocsi, Paul Robert. *A History of Ukraine.* Toronto: University of Toronto Press, 1996.

———. *The Roots of Ukrainian Nationalism: Galicia as Ukraine's Piedmont.* Toronto: University of Toronto Press, 2002.

Mahler, Raphael. "The Economic Background of Jewish Emigration from Galicia to the United States." *YIVO Annual of Jewish Social Science* 7 (1952): 255–267.

Makarchuk, S. A. *Ukrains'ka Respublika Halychan: narysy pro ZUNR.* L'viv, Ukraine: Svit, 1997.

Mańkowski, Zygmunt, ed. *Niepodległść Polski w 1918 roku a procesy państwowotworcze w Europie środkowo-wshodniej.* Lublin, Poland: wydawnictwo Uniwersytetu Marii Curie-Skłodowskiej, 1996.

Markovits, Andrei S., and Frank S. Sysyn, eds. *Nationbuilding and the Politics of Nationalism: Essays on Austrian Galicia.* Cambridge, MA: Harvard University Press, 1982.

Martovych, Les'. *Za mezhu: opovidannia.* Kiev: vydavnytstvo khudozhnioi literatury "Dnipro," 1968.

Martyniuk, Ivan. *Moye ridne selo Tseniv v Berezhanshchini—Ceniv, My Native Village in the Country of Berezhany.* New York: Drukarnia Dzh. A. Press, 1976.

Matejko, Roman, and Bohdan Kravchuk. *Za ridnyi krai, za narid svii: Ukrains'ka Halyts'ka Armiia na Ternopil'shchyni.* Ternopil', Ukraine: N.p., 1993.

Mendelsohn, Ezra. "From Assimilation to Zionism in L'vov: The Case of Alfred Nossig." *Slavonic and East European Review* 49, no. 117 (1971): 521–534.

———. *Zionism in Poland: The Formative Years, 1915–1926.* New Haven, CT: Yale University Press, 1981.

Meyer, Michael A., ed. *German-Jewish History in Modern Times.* 4 vols. New York: Columbia University Press, 1997.

Mich, Włodzimierz. *Obcy w polskim domu: nacjonalistyczne koncepcje rozwiązania problemu mniejszości narodowych 1918–1939.* Lublin, Poland: Wydawnictwo Uniwersytetu Marii Curie-Skladowskiej, 1994.

Michlic-Coren, Joanna. "Anti-Jewish Violence in Poland, 1918–1939 and 1945–1947." *Polin: Studies in Polish Jewry* 13 (2000): 34–61.

Mick, Christoph. "Nationalisierung in einer multiethnischen Stadt: interethnische Konflikte in Lemberg, 1890–1920." *Archiv für Sozialgeschichte* 40 (2000): 113–146.

Moran, Daniel, and Arthur Waldron, eds. *The People in Arms: Military Myth and National Mobilization since the French Revolution.* Cambridge: Cambridge University Press, 2003.

Mroczka, Ludwik. *Galicji rozstanie z Austrią: zarys monograficzny.* Krakow: Wydawnictwo Naukowe WSP, 1990.

Müller, Armin. "Galizien-Krisenherd in den Beziehungen zwischen Österreich-Ungarn und Russland, 1910–1914." *Jahrbuch für Geschichte der sozialistischen Länder Europas* 28 (1984): 207–233.

Nahayevs'kyi, Isydor. *Istoriia ryms'kykh vselens'kykh arkhyyereiv.* 3 vols. Munich: vydannia Ukrains'koho Katolyts'koho Universytetu im. Sv. Klymenta Papy, 1964–1979.

Nahorna, L. *Feliks Kon.* Kiev: derzhavne vydavnytstvo politychnoi literatury, 1963.

Najdus, Walentyna. *Szkice z historii Galicji.* 2 vols. Warsaw: Książka i Wiedza, 1958.

Nash L'viv: yuvileinyi zbirnyk 1252–1952. New York: vydavnytstvo "Chervona Kalyna," 1953.

Nelipovich, S. G. "General ot Infanterii N. N. Yanushkevich: 'nemetskuiu pakost' uvolit' i bez nezhnostei." *Voenno-istoricheskii zhurnal* 1 (1997): 42–53.

——. "Repressii protiv poddanykh 'Tsentral'nykh Derzhav': deportatsii v Rossii, 1914–1918 gg." *Voenno-istoricheskii zhurnal* 6 (1996): 32–42.

Neuberger, Mary. "The Russo-Turkish War and the 'Eastern Jewish Question': Encounter between Victims and Victors in Ottoman Bulgaria, 1877–8." *East European Jewish Affairs* 26, no. 2 (1996): 51–66.

Ostap'iuk, Bohdan. *Davnii Ternopil': istorychni narysy, postati, kartyny khliborobs'koi pratsi, tradytsiini sviatkuvannia, spohady.* Miami: Zemliats'ke Ob'yednannia 'Ternopil'shchyna', 1984.

Österreich-Ungarn in der Weltpolitik, 1900 bis 1918. Berlin: Akademie-Verlag, 1965.

Pajewski, Janusz. *Budowa Drugiej Rzeczypospolitej, 1918–1926.* Krakow: nakładem Polskiej Akademii Umiejętności, 1995.

Panayi, Panikos, ed. *Minorities in Wartime: National and Racial Groupings in Europe, North America and Australia during the Two World Wars.* Oxford: Berg Publishers, 1993.

Petersen, Roger D. *Understanding Ethnic Violence: Fear, Hatred, and Resentment in Twentieth-Century Eastern Europe.* Cambridge: Cambridge University Press, 2002.

Pierce, Richard A. *Russian Central Asia, 1867–1917: A Study in Colonial Rule.* Berkeley and Los Angeles: University of California Press, 1960.

Pisarev, Ya. A. *Serbiia i Chernogoriia v pervoi mirovoi voine.* Moscow: izdatel'stvo "Nauka," 1968.

Plaschka, Richard Georg, Horst Haselsteiner, and Arnold Suppan. *Innere Front: Militärassistenz, Widerstand und Umsturz in der Donaumonarchie 1918.* 2 vols. Munich: R. Oldenbourg Verlag, 1974.

Podhorodecki, Leszek. *Dzieje Lwowa.* Warsaw: Oficyna Wydawnicza Volumen, 1993.

Pogrebyns'ka, Iryna, and Maksym Gon. *Yevrei v Zakhidnoukrains'kii Narodnii Respublitsi:*

do problemy ukrains'ko-yevreis'kykh vzayemyn. Kiev: Instytut natsional'nykh vidnosyn ta politologii NAN Ukrainy, 1997.

"Pogromen in Polen und Galizien." *Neue Jüdische Monatsheft* 3, no. 5 (December 1918): 51–56.

Polska-Polacy-Mniejszości Narodowe. Wrocław, Poland: Zakład Narodowy imienia Ossolińskich, 1992.

Porter, Brian. *When Nationalism Began to Hate: Imagining Modern Politics in Nineteenth-Century Poland.* New York: Oxford University Press, 2000.

Potichnyj, Peter J., and Howard Aster, eds. *Ukrainian-Jewish Relations in Historical Perspective.* Edmonton: Canadian Institute of Ukrainian Studies, 1988.

Pulzer, P. G. J. *The Rise of Political Anti-Semitism in Germany and Austria.* New York: John Wiley & Sons, 1964.

Rabinbach, Anton G. "The Migration of Galician Jews to Vienna, 1857–1880." *Austrian History Yearbook* 11 (1975): 44–54.

Rabinovich, Sarra. "Obrazovanie yevreev v Galitsii." *Vestnik yevreiiskogo prosveshcheniia* 23 (1913): 116–123.

Rempel, David G. "The Expropriation of the German Colonists in South Russia during the Great War." *Journal of Modern History* 4, no. 1 (1932): 49–67.

Riasanov, A. S. "Nemetskaia armiia mozhet konkurirovat' s voinami kannibalov." *Voenno-istoricheskii zhurnal* 4 (1998): 40–45.

Rink, Friedrich, and J. M. Richey. "Expulsion of the German Colonists from Wolhynia, 1915–1916." *Heritage Review* 25, no. 1, (1995): 19–22.

Rogger, Hans. *Jewish Policies and Right-Wing Politics in Imperial Russia.* London: Macmillan, 1986.

Rosenfeld, Max. "Die jüdischen Gemeinden in Österreich." *Der Jude* 2 (1917–1918): 152–162.

Roskies, David G., ed. *The Dybbuk and Other Writings: S. Ansky.* New York: Schocken Books, 1992.

Rossiiskie nemtsy: problemy istorii, iazyka i sovremennogo polozheniia: materialy mezhdunarodnoi konferentsii, Anapa, 20–25 sentiabria, 1995. Moscow: "Gotika," 1996.

Rostunov, I. I. *Russkii front pervoii mirovoii voiny.* Moscow: izdatel'stvo "Nauka," 1976.

Rubin, Barnett R., and Jack Snyder, eds. *Post-Soviet Political Order: Conflict and State Building.* London: Routledge, 1998.

Sanborn, Joshua A. "Drafting the Nation: Military Conscription and the Formation of a Modern Polity in Tsarist and Soviet Russia, 1905–1925." PhD diss., University of Chicago, 1998.

Savchenko, V. N. "Vostochnaia Galitsiia v 1914–1915 godakh (etnosotsial'nye osobennosti i problema prisoyedineniia k Rossii." *Voprosy istorii,* no. 11–12 (1996): 95–106.

Schall, Jacob. *Żydostwo galicyjskie w czasie inwazji rosyjskiej w latach 1914–1916.* L'viv, Ukraine: nakładem Księgarni I. Madfesa, 1936.

Schatz, Jaff. *The Generation: The Rise and Fall of the Jewish Communists of Poland.* Berkeley and Los Angeles: University of California Press, 1991.

Schipper, Ignacy. *Dzieje handlu żydowskiego na ziemiach polskich.* Warsaw: nakładem Centrali Związków Kupców, 1937.

Schipper, Ignacy, Arieh Tartakower, and Aleks Hafka. *Żydzi w Polsce odrodzonej: działalność społeczna, gospodarcza, oświatowa i kulturalna.* 2 vols. Warsaw: nakładem Wydawnictwa "Żydzi w Polsce Odrodzonej," 1930.

Schleuning, Johannes. *Im Kampf und Todesnot: Die Tragödie des Russlanddeutschen.* Berlin: Bernard & Graefe, 1930.

Schmidle, Erwin A. *Juden in der K.u.K Armee, 1788–1918[Jews in the Habsburg Armed Forces].* Eisenstadt, Austria: Österreichisches-Jüdisches Museum, 1989.

Schoenfeld, Joachim. *Jewish Life in Galicia under the Austro-Hungarian Empire and in the Reborn Poland, 1898–1939.* Hoboken, NJ: Ktav Publishing House, 1985.

S. E. "Galichina v tsyfrakh (statisticheski-demographicheskaia spravka)." *Ukrainskaia zhizn'* 3–4 (1915): 18–26.

Seefeldt, Fritz. *Der Deutsche in Galizien.* Berlin: Verlag von Julius Belz, 1937.

———. *So war es in Galizien: Personliche Erzählungen.* 2 vols. Eutin, Germany: Struve's Buchdruckerei und Verlag OHG, 1933.

Seniavskaia, E. S. "Obraz vraga v soznanii uchastnikov pervoi mirovoi voiny." *Voprosy istorii* 3 (1997): 140–145.

Shelukhin, A. Yu. "Razvedovatel'nye organy v strukture vysshego voennogo upravleniia Rossiiskoi Imperii nachala XX veka, 1906–1914." *Vestnik Moskovskogo universiteta.* Series 8 (History), 3 (1996): 24–31.

Skaradziński, Bohdan. *Polskie lata, 1919–1920.* 2 vols. Warsaw: Oficyna Wydawnicza Volumen, 1993.

Skrzypek, Jozef. "Lwów w listopadzie 1918 r. w oświetleniu uczestników walk." *Niepodległość* 14, 2/37 (1936): 304–318.

Slepcov, Igor. "K problematike 1. svetovoi vojny na východnom Slovensku v rokoch 1914–1915." *Historie a vojenstvi* 42, no. 3 (1993): 55–78.

Smal'-Stotskyi, Roman. "Graf Bobrinskii und die österreichischen Ruthenen." *Ukrainische Rundschau* 10, 2–3 (1912): 38–48.

Sobczak, Mieczysław. *Stosunek Narodowej Demokracji do kwestii żydowskiej w Polsce w latach 1918–1939.* Wrocław, Poland: Wydawnictwo Akademii Ekonomicznej im. Oskara Langego, 1998.

Stankiewicz, Witold. *Konflikty społeczne na wsi polskiej, 1918–1920.* Warsaw: Państwowe Wydawnictwo Naukowe, 1963.

Stein, Hans-Peter. "Der Offizer des russischen Heeres im Zeitabschnitt zwischen Reform und Revolution, 1861–1905." *Forschungen zur osteuropäischen Geschichte* 13 (1967): 346–507.

Stillschweig, Kurt. "Nationalism and Autonomy among Eastern European Jewry: Origins and Historical Development up to 1939." *Historica Judaica: A Journal of Studies in Jewish History, Especially in the Legal and Economic History of the Jews* 6 (1944): 27–68.

Stone, Norman. *The Eastern Front, 1914–1917.* London: Hodder and Stoughton, 1975.

Stopnevich, B. "Naselenie Galitsii." *Ukrainskaia zhizn'* 11–12 (1914): 43–54.

Strauss, Herbert A., ed. *Hostages of Modernization: Studies on Modern Antisemitism, 1870–1933/39.* Berlin: Walter de Gruyter, 1993.

Stricker, Gerd von, ed. *Deutsche Geschichte im Osten Europas: Russland.* Berlin: Siedler, 1997.

Szczepański, Janusz. *Społeczeństwo Polski w walce z najazdem bolszewickim 1920 roku.* Warsaw: Naczelna Dyrekcja Archiwów Państwowych, 2000.

Tartakower, Arieh, and Kurt R. Grossman. *The Jewish Refugee.* New York: Institute of Jewish Affairs of the American Jewish Congress and World Jewish Congress, 1944.

Tomaszewski, Jerzy. "Lwów, 22 listopada 1918 roku." *Przegląd Historyczny* 75, no. 2 (1984): 279–285.

———. "Pinsk, 5 April 1919." *Polin: Studies in Polish Jewry* 1 (1986): 227–251.

———. *Rzeczpospolita wielu narodów.* Warsaw: Czytelnik, 1985.

———, ed. *Najnowsze dzieje Żydów w Polsce: w zarysie (do 1950 roku).* Warsaw: Wydawnictwo Naukowe PWN, 1993.

——, ed. *Żydzi w obronie Rzeczypospolitej: materiały konferencji w Warszawie 17 i 18 października 1993 r.* Warsaw: Wydawnictwo Cykady, 1996.

Tomaszewski, Leszek. "Lwów—listopad 1918—niezwykłe losy pewnego dokumentu." *Dzieje Najnowsze* 25, no. 4 (1993): 163–173.

Vital, David. *A People Apart: The Jews in Europe, 1789–1939.* Oxford: Oxford University Press, 1999.

Vorobets', Viktor. "Pershi dni ukrains'koi derzhavnosti v Kolomyi." *Ukrains'kyi skytalets'* (February 1921): 7–14.

Walicki, Jacek. "Położenie Żydów polskich podczas kampanii 1920 r." *Acta Universitatis Lodziensis* 52 (1995): 113–125.

Wasiutyński, Bohdan. *Ludność żydowska w Polsce w wiekach XIX i XX: studium statystyczne.* Warsaw: wydawnictwo Kasy im. Mianowskiego, 1930.

Weeks, Theodore R. *Nation and State in Late Imperial Russia: Nationalism and Russification on the Western Frontier, 1863–1914.* DeKalb: Northern Illinois University Press, 1996.

Weinerman, Eli. "Racism, Racial Prejudice, and the Jews in Late Imperial Russia." *Ethnic and Racial Studies* 17, no. 3 (1994): 442–495.

Weisl, Wolfgang. "Juden in der Österreichischen und Österreichisch-Ungarischen Armee." *Zeitschrift für die Geschichte der Juden* 8, no. 1–2 (1971): 1–22.

Wendland, Anna Veronika. *Die Russophilen in Galizien: Ukrainische Konservative zwischen Österreich und Russland, 1848–1915.* Vienna: Verlag der Österreichischen Akademie der Wissenschaften, 2001.

Wildman, Allan K. *The End of the Russian Imperial Army: The Old Army and the Soldiers' Revolt (March–April 1917).* Princeton, NJ: Princeton University Press, 1980.

Wistrich, Robert S. "Austrian Social Democracy and the Problem of Galician Jewry, 1890–1914." *Leo Baeck Institute Year Book* 26 (1981): 89–124.

Wolf, G. "Zur Lage der Juden in Galizien." *Monatschrift für Geschichte und Wissenschaft des Judentums* 16 (1867): 196–207.

Wróbel, Piotr. "Barucha Milcha galicyjskie wspomnienia wojenne, 1914–1920." *Biuletyn Żydowskiego Instytutu Historycznego* 2/158 (1991): 87–98.

——. "The Jews of Galicia under Austrian-Polish Rule, 1869–1918." *Austrian History Yearbook* 25 (1994): 97–138.

——. "The Seeds of Violence: The Brutalization of an East European Region, 1917–1921." *Journal of Modern European History* 1 (2002): 125–149.

——. "Żydzi polscy w czasie I wojny światowej." *Przegląd Historyczny* 83, no. 4 (1992): 633–655.

Yakupov, N. M. *Revolutsiia i mir: soldatskie massy protiv imperialisticheskoi voiny, 1917-mart 1918 gg.* Moscow: "Mysl'," 1980.

Yefremov, P. N. *Vneshniaia politika Rossii, 1907–1914.* Moscow: izdatel'stvo Instituta Mezhdunarodnykh Otnoshenii, 1961.

Yeroshkin, N. P. *Istoriia gosudarstvennykh uchrezhdenii dorevolutsionnoi Rossii.* Moscow: "Vysshaia shkola," 1983.

Zechlin, Egmont. *Die Deutsche Politik und die Juden im Ersten Weltkrieg.* Gottingen, Germany: Vandenhoeck & Ruprecht, 1969.

Zhylin, A. P. *Posledneie nastuplenie (iyun' 1917).* Moscow: izdatel'stvo "Nauka," 1983.

Żurawski vel Grajewski, Przemysław Piotr. *Sprawa ukraińska na konferencji pokojowej w Paryżu w roku 1919.* Warsaw: Wydawnictwo Naukowe Semper, 1995.

Index